Up and Down Merton's Mountain

Up and Down Merton's Mountain

by Gerald Groves

CBP Press
St. Louis, Missouri

photos courtesy International Thomas Merton Society and Gerald Groves.

Library of Congress Cataloging-in-Publication Data

Groves, Gerald.
Up and Down Merton's Mountain.

1. Groves, Gerald. 2. Ex-monks—United States—Biography. 3. Merton, Thomas, 1915-1968. I. Title.
BX4668.3.G76A3 1988 271'.125'024 [B] 88-9544
ISBN 0-8272-3801-0

Printed in the United States of America

Contents

Preface

Several years ago I wrote a biography—not a critical biography, but a "life"—of Thomas Merton, the Trappist monk and author. I thought that having already written two articles on him and having lived at Gethsemani Abbey with him for fourteen years qualified me for that endeavor. At least I knew that I had more insight into Merton's personality and into the monastic order of which he was a member for over twenty-seven years than the half dozen or more of his biographers who had not even met him. However, as I got into the work I realized that neither my observations of him nor conversations with him gave me much access to his inner being. Since I had confined my study to his monastic career, for the most part, I had few events to shape into a pattern that would reveal his character. Consequently, I could not comment on Merton's feelings about or attitudes toward those events but had to offer my own. I presumed that they would be close to Merton's, since we shared not only many of the same experiences but even the same tastes and temperament. But in so doing I got into the way of my subject in the same manner Henry Miller gets into the way of his—Rimbaud—in *The Time of the Assassins*. It occurred to me that, had Miller been writing his autobiography and had he gracefully worked in analogies between his life and that of Rimbaud, the direction might be clearer. Therefore, I decided to present my own story, which, as a spiritual autobiography, could not have been written honestly without including Merton, since he was a major influence on my spiritual formation.

But it's one thing for a famous person to write an autobiography and quite another for an unknown to do the same. In this matter the influence of Merton also guided me. After all, who was he when he wrote *The Seven Storey Mountain*? He had published a few articles and poems, none of which brought him fame and fortune. Yet he knew that, as a young man who had renounced the possibility of fame and fortune to enter the Trappist order, one of the most austere in the Catholic Church, he and his story could attract readers. Consequently, I figured that, as a former Trappist, my account might have the same appeal. Perhaps even more. For I had not only gone up Merton's spiritual mountain but had come down again. In other words, Merton's autobiography showed the public what it's like to enter a Trappist abbey or monastery; mine lets the public know what it's like to leave one. And if my own story is less edifying than Merton's, those who read it can enjoy, at least—as James Thurber said in regards to reading memoirs—"the comforting feeling that one has had after all, a pretty sensible and peaceful life, by comparison."

Another reason why I, an unknown, dared to write about my own experiences was the fact that many unknown authors write autobiographical novels and have them published. After all, many modern novels take the form of autobiographies, and many autobiographies feature elements of the novel, such as fictional names of persons, places, and events. I could not understand why I should feel uncomfortable writing in the one genre and not in the other. In both instances I had to draw the plots, events, attitudes, motives, and characters from the past and place them in the present. In both cases memory and imagination seemed to work so closely together to meet the expectancies of the reader—illumination and entertainment—that sometimes I found it difficult to know where one left off and the other began. Of course a strict allegiance to historical facts becomes the autobiographer; but facts without judgments or impressions—which might be subjective and false—beget boredom. A character truly epitomizing the "paragon of virtue" may well exist, yet not excite much interest unless he at least suggests his vulnerability to temptation. In writing my own account, I could not help feeling less than honest in making the subject more human and interesting, whereas in a novel I would have suffered no inhibitions in so doing. Consequently, whether it be appropriate or not, I feel compelled to apologize to the readers for talking about myself so much and yet to hope that they enjoy the story.

1

A Born Catholic

Ever since the famine in Ireland in 1847, members of my family have been migrating to America. Unlike many of their countrymen who stayed in New York, Boston, and other port cities of the Northeast, my ancestors pushed on to St. Louis, Missouri, once a predominately French town on the banks of the Mississippi River. Eventually the French element migrated to Ste. Genevieve, Germans settled in South St. Louis, and the Irish established a ghetto in the West End. Because of their virility and taboos connected with birth control, the Irish bred like mice. By 1924, the year I was born to a pair of them, the Irish had formed one of the largest religious groups in the city. Catholicism in West End St. Louis united the Irish in respect to politics, labor, education, and just about everything else.

But my background is not totally Catholic. My maternal grandmother, née Annie Stack, was born in Cork. As a girl she left for Belfast to look for work in the linen factories there. But the only job she could find was that of a maid in the home of John Wadsworth Carson, a professor of foreign languages at Queen's University. John's only son, Jay Wroy, fell in love with Annie and, to the chagrin of his parents, staunch Presbyterians of the middle class, married her.

Jay Wroy must have loved his wife dearly because he agreed to leave Belfast after listening to Annie's continual complaining that her in-laws snubbed her. However, he absolutely refused to settle down with her in Cork among the papists. As a compromise and an adventurous fling, he consented to accompany her to St. Louis, Missouri, aware that her uncle and aunt lived in that American city, but ignorant of the vast Irish-Catholic concentration around them. Not that Jay Wroy had anything in particular against Catholics; he was equally contemptuous of all religions that attempted to control the beliefs and attitudes of their members. Jay Wroy proclaimed himself a freethinker and, from what I am told, spent most of his life studying the implications of his manifesto.

Jay Wroy and his bride took a flat on Evans Avenue in St. Ann's parish and furnished it with the best furniture that credit could buy from the Union-May-Stern store on Twelfth and Olive streets. Then he went out and got a job at the Mallinckrodt Chemical Company as a two-fingered typist. A few years later, my mother was born, either in St. Louis or in Ireland during one of my grandparents' visits there. Incredible as it may seem, I never knew if her real name was Zella or Ann. Some people called her this; others called her that. But I do know that Grandfather called her Katie. And I'm positive that was not her real name.

One story that I think rather credible is that Grandfather, at Mother's baptism, gave her name as Zella, but the pastor, Father McGee, refused to perform the ceremony on the grounds that no saint—Irish or otherwise—with such an appellation existed. (Uncle Dinny told me that the pastor went so far as to say *Zella* was a nigger name and directed Grandfather to the holy rollers on Delmar Boulevard.) Grandfather told the pastor to name the child any damn thing he wanted to but to get on with it. The pastor called her Ann after her mother or the parish church or the grandmother of Jesus Christ, but Jay Wroy recognized her only as Katie.

Katie was reared a Catholic. Like her Irish-American cousins, she went to St. Ann's Parochial School, made her first holy communion at eight and, at ten, prepared to receive the sacrament of confirmation. For weeks Father McGee announced the coming events whose splendor would be enhanced by the presence of the archbishop, Cardinal Glennon. Annie begged her husband to attend, hoping that the ritual might inspire him to embrace the Catholic faith. Jay Wroy was easily bored at church services, and would have declined had Annie not challenged him to prove his "freethinking" by exposing himself to religion.

On the day of the ceremony the weather was very hot; in fact, it was the hottest Sunday in May recorded in the past seventy-two years. Consequently, Father McGee had set up an electric fan to the side of the altar to keep the cardinal and his assisting ministers from suffocating in their many layers of sacerdotal robes. Everything was going well until the cardinal and his ministers sat down in the presbytery and Father McGee came to the altar rail to give the sermon. Behind him the electric fan oscillated from a point where it could not blow out the candles on the altar to the exact spot where the preacher stood. And each time the gale struck McGee's back, it lifted his toupee like an asbestos shingle off a roof. Uncle Din told me that Skeets and Gallagher, the comedians, could not have invented a funnier scene. The congregation seemed to find the spectacle more a cause for anxiety than for laughter. Everyone appeared concerned about the possibility of the wind ripping the hairpiece right off the pastor's skull and flipping it at one of the confirmees sitting in the first pews. But Jay Wroy guffawed like someone at a music hall. That afternoon, at home, he sat in the parlor, drinking beer, looking out the window, and chuckling like an Olympian god contemplating the foibles of men.

Everyone presumed that Katie would go to high school at Rosati-Kain, a Catholic girls' school. But Katie enrolled in Brown's Business College on Grand Avenue and, after graduation, went to work as a secretary at Fleischman's Yeast Company. Katie was a girl with modest ambitions and proximate goals. As soon as she saved enough money, she quit her job and took another trip to her grandparents' home in Belfast. She returned to St. Louis six months later with her future husband, Gayle Groves, an engineer.

Katie's fiancé was the talk of the parish. He was well over six feet tall, slender, blond, blue-eyed, with teeth as white as chalk. Everyone said he looked like Charles Farrell, the American movie star. Although he wasn't Catholic, he promised to become one before the marriage. He began taking instructions in the faith from Father Todd, the pastor's assistant. Despite his qualification as an engineer, he took a job as maintenance man at Laclede Gas and Light Company without even knowing what the salary was. When Annie suggested that he and Katie move into her home until they found their own place, Gayle shrugged his shoulders and said, "Fine." As much as Jay Wroy liked his prospective son-in-law, he felt uneasy about his seemingly nonchalant attitude toward where he would live, what he would do for a living, and how he would worship; he appeared to lack roots and even the desire to strike them.

Gayle and Katie were married and lived with my grandparents in relative harmony. In June of 1924, while Gayle was at a company picnic, Mother was rushed to St. John's Hospital on Kingshighway Boulevard. I refused to be born and, like Macduff, was "from my mother's womb untimely ripped." Three years later we were in West End, Grand Bahamas, where Gayle had found a job as an engineer that paid him extremely well. He worked on the motor cars, "lorries," boats, and airplanes used by American and British bootleggers who were running liquor to the East Coast of the United States. It was a terrible place: shootings, hijackings, gambling, and other forms of underworld activity must have given it an atmosphere similar to that of Tombstone, Arizona, in the nineteenth century. Outside of town, several English, American, and Bahamian families led quiet and respectable lives. After 1933, the year prohibition ended in the United States, the debased elements at West End either left the island or turned to lawful occupations, such as fishing or sponge-gathering.

While the bootlegging lasted, my father made plenty of money, enough to build us a white stucco bungalow near the ocean in a place called Boodle Bay. In about 1930, he and an aviator friend flew to America as they often did, to shop and have a good time. But they never came back. Mother told me that she thought they had crashed into the sea over the Bermuda Triangle.

Later, after Grandmother died from cancer in St. Louis, Grandfather came to live with us in West End. He and I spent most of our days in a large aluminum rowboat bought from Sears-Roebuck in Miami. We fished for grouper, seined for conch, and gigged lobster. Almost everything one bought on the island was expensive because it was imported from England or America. But no one who liked fish and could catch them would starve. The very poor—and most of the native, black Bahamians were very poor—ate fish every day with the traditional staples, peas and rice.

Not only the food but life on the island in general, was monotonous while I was growing up. Yet the clear water of the ocean and the pink sandy beach were—and still are—the most beautiful on earth. I spent delightful days swimming out to the reefs and sailing along the coasts. In the spring, my companions and I followed the great "marches" of lobsters (really crawfish) along the coral bottom of the sea. In shallow waters we watched them through glass-bottom wooden buckets and gigged as many as fifty apiece every day. We sold them to a hotel keeper from

Nassau for a shilling each.

In the evenings we fished for shark. About five o'clock in the afternoon, we went a few hundred yards from shore and chummed the water to lure our prey from beyond the reefs into the shallows. Then we set our lines—two-hundred weight, with steel leaders—buoyed up by cork floats or inflated balloons, or "bladders" as the natives call them. As soon as night fell, we lighted big bonfires on the beaches to help attract the shark, or to aid in seeing them, or just for the fun of it. We wore gloves or wrapped our hands in rags so that, when a hammerhead struck, we let him run with the bait and hook in his gills. Pulling him in was always exciting. It usually took two or three of us to drag him, twisting and turning, onto the sand while another cracked his head with an ax.

The experiences most relevant to this story are the Sunday morning religious services. Mother and I were two of the twelve Roman Catholics in West End. There probably weren't many more on the rest of the island during that period. We had no proper church and depended upon missionaries from Miami and Nassau to say mass for us. We were lucky to have one service a month. It usually took place in the Blue Dolphin Club on Queen's Highway. The club belonged to Francis Hepburn, a Baptist. He let us use his place since we all patronized it during the week. All the Roman Catholics were white and mostly of English origin. We were the "American family," and one couple came from Cuba.

The services were quite dull, but none lasted longer than forty-five minutes, even when we sang hymns. Two of the Catholic boys, Richard and Roger Boswell, both near my age, often took the father fishing after mass and, in the late afternoon, the entire congregation gathered in the Blue Dolphin for dinner. Then we ran our priest out to the airstrip, which my own father had helped build for the bootleggers back in the twenties. Fred Jenkins, one of the pilots in West End, usually took the missionary to Miami or West Palm Beach, just about sixty miles to the northwest.

Until I was eight or nine years old, there was no school at West End. The older white children were either educated by their parents, as I was by my grandfather, or sent to the United States or Nassau. Mother had no objection to Grandfather's tutoring me; although he had neglected his own education in Belfast, he had a good mind and skill in teaching. However, Grandfather had neither the knowledge nor the inclination to instruct me in the Catholic religion. Also, after several years of premature retirement, he took a job at a new West End manufactory that bought and processed shark skins to be sold to several shoe companies in Canada and the United States. Consequently, he had less time to give me lessons. He liked his job in the company office and, especially, the pretty Bahamian girls who worked with him.

Mother took advantage of the situation to make a trip back to St. Louis. She planned to stay there an entire year, to determine at what level I was academically, and especially to expose me to religious instruction. We stayed with Uncle Din and Aunt Margaret, and I enrolled at St. Ann's parochial school directed by the nuns of the Precious Blood. When I wrote Grandfather about the name of their congregation, he wrote back commenting that the nuns' group sounded more like a hospital corps than an order of teachers. Grandfather's letters always had some satire on Catholic nuns. It seemed he delighted in making up religious names for them, such as Sister Francis Xavier of the Old Rugged Cross, Sister Mary Jeanine of the Sacred Spleen, or Sister Insomnia of the Holy Vigil Light Burning Night and Day.

After I spent two weeks in the second grade, the sister superior advanced me to the third. Even that was easy after Grandfather's drilling on grammar and arithmetic. I learned the Baltimore Catechism by rote—Grandfather depended heavily on rote learning of grammar—and was ready, academically, for holy communion. I could answer many questions about God, the Catholic Church, and the liturgy; but I understood very little. However, at St. Ann's I got plenty of practical experience. The nuns made us attend the eight o'clock mass every morning except Saturdays. Most of these masses were "requiems," services for the souls of the dead. I was even one of those chosen for the choir, and I remember all the times we sang the dirge *Dies Irae, Dies Illa* while Father McGee walked around the black catafalque in his black robes, waving a smoking thurible at a crucifix, helped by an acolyte. I can still smell the incense carried in that smoke and see it form a filmy cloud in the presbytery. I can still feel the cold wood of the choir pew under my chin as I looked down from the chancel onto the congregation below.

On Sundays I sat half listening to the pastor's homilies, during which he often described hell as a place full of spiritual fire that burnt disembodied souls without ever consuming them; and heaven, the joyful alternative, as a great chorus singing "Holy, Holy, Holy" to an unimaginable deity who, though invisible, was the object of eternal contemplation. On Sunday afternoons at one-thirty, we were again obliged to gather into the church for benediction, a service involving the recitation of the rosary and litany of the saints, hymn singing, and adoration of the Blessed Sacrament. The latter was in the form of a wafer of bread. It tasted like bread. It looked like bread. Yet we were instructed to give up our lives rather than say it was bread. But none of us children thought too much about that mystery. We were preoccupied with the anticipation of going to the movies afterward.

I was content, the following June, to return to West End. Grandfather had visited us over the Christmas holidays, but after another six months I was eager to see him again. However, something had happened to me. Before, I could laugh at his stories about his flirtation with the two Bahamian girls in his office. The vision of the old rascal pinching their bottoms and hugging them amused me. Perhaps it was because I was a year older then that I sensed the impropriety of such conduct. Yet I am sure the indoctrination of the nuns had the most to do with it. Not that the nuns explicitly instructed us in sex. But they continually praised the purity of Jesus, Our Lady, and St. Joseph. Moreover, Father Todd told one of the boys that after our bodies are resurrected from the dead, they will have no genitals. It seemed that both the priests and nuns esteemed purity or chastity more than all the other virtues and, in turn, regarded sexual lust as the principal vice. Moreover, their teaching had definitely influenced my own set of values. Although I never criticized Grandfather for his flirtations—which I had often witnessed while with him at his office—I felt embarrassed and a bit ashamed of him.

About a year after Mother and I returned to the island, she got a job as a secretary at the West End office of the Nassau Sponge Exchange. Her boss was a good-looking white Bahamian named Jack Russell. They started dating and doing all the things that lovers do, I guess. I saw them hold hands and kiss, at least. Often they went out to sea in Jack's twenty-four-foot cabin cruiser to fish or paint. Jack had a style very much like that of Winslow Homer, who also painted melodramatic scenes connected with the Bahamian waters. Grandfather was very happy that Mother had found such a boyfriend—especially in an area where white people of culture were so few. I did not approve of the situation at all and told her so. Nevertheless, I didn't go too far. I'm sure that had it not been for her friendship with Jack, she would have returned to St. Louis, with or without Grandfather and me.

Mother and Jack went together for about five years before they were married. I think the delay was due to Mother's uncertainty that my father was dead (not that she was hoping he would turn up). Either the British or American government (maybe both) will declare a person legally dead only if he or she has not been heard of for seven years. Without waiting for this, Mother got a divorce, which permitted her to marry again, but not in the Catholic Church. She was excommunicated. It seemed ironic to me that she should be so careful to rear me in the Catholic faith and to foster in me the supreme Catholic virtue of chastity, while she herself (to my way of thinking then) abandoned them.

Perhaps as a consequence of my occasional sarcastic remarks to her and Jack in regard to the situation, Mother arranged for me to spend a year in Nassau with a friend of mine, Phil Howard, who with his family, had moved there from West End. I had just turned fourteen and was assured by my new teachers in West End, Barry and Jean Sommers (he a former headmaster at Dulwich in England and the main reason why I passed the "eleven plus" examination two years before), that I could make the grammar school in Nassau.

My schooling at Nassau was far less remarkable than the experience I received at the home of the Howards. Phil, my old companion at West End, had a younger sister named Marcy. She was only my age but built like a Varga girl. At first she regarded me as an interloper and seemed to resent even my existence. I wasn't at all sorry when she left that October for school in England. But when she returned for the Christmas holidays, she began to show interest in me. In fact, she sought me out for swimming or horseback riding. While on her black Arabian, "Ebony," Marcy acted as if no one else were alive. But at the beach, she rubbed my back with suntan oil, held my hand as we walked barefoot over coral, and even threw her arms around my neck when we encountered a barracuda or sand shark. And when we returned home, we showered in the beach house, not together but in cubicles separated only by a plywood partition. At night I could hear her moving about in the room next to mine, especially when I went to the window that looked out upon the beach house and the ocean. The section of the house containing her room jutted out beyond the rest of the structure about five feet and contained a window at a right angle to my own. It offered a clear view of one interior corner, in which stood a large armoire. One evening I knelt in front of my own window, looked across into Marcy's room, and noticed that she had rearranged the furniture. In place of the armoire was a dressing table upon which rested a mirror with three panels, so set up that I could see the entire interior. Suddenly, Marcy came out of her bathroom wrapped in a towel. Then she slowly unwound it and let it drop to the floor. She laughed, waved, and said, "So, Gerald, do you like our show?"

As the weeks went by, Marcy and I were inseparable. At the dinner table we couldn't look at each other without blushing. By the time for dessert, she had slipped out of her shoes and was rubbing her bare feet on my ankles. I felt rather ashamed of letting her seduce me; however, our affection for each other seemed to lessen the guilt. Several times I insisted that we stop seeing each other, but she merely laughed as if I were a child who had expressed his concern about a ghost in the attic. She was the first truly natural, amoral person I had ever met.

When I returned to West End that year, I had a broader outlook on life and the intention of reconciling myself to Mother and Jack. However, that marriage had broken up. Jack had left the island, and the sponge company no longer existed. Mother decided to return to St. Louis. In fact she left only a few days after my arrival. She planned to stay with Uncle Din and Aunt Margaret until she got a job and a house ready for us. Grandfather had agreed. With me gone during the past school year, he had gotten bored.

That summer we had a good time together and, when autumn came around, I studied with Barry and Jean Sommers, who had opened up a school in their house. The following spring, I returned to Nassau to sit for the General Education Certificate. The Howards weren't home but vacationing in Canada. But my return made no difference as far as Marcy was concerned. She hadn't written since Easter.

I passed the exam at the "0" level and returned to West End.

My mother kept in close touch; however, she had trouble finding a job. But West End became a more interesting place to live. More and more tourists, mostly fishermen, were coming to the new hotel. Also, a cruise ship started to run from Miami to West End and on to Nassau. But just as Grandfather reconciled himself to staying on for another year, he became ill. We sold the white stucco bungalow and the Sears-Roebuck boat and took the cruise ship to Miami, and from there, a train to St. Louis.

2

Among the Jesuits

The following year, Grandfather died and was buried beside Grandmother. He left me enough money, about two thousand dollars, to pay my tuition through four years at St. Louis University. I would have preferred enrolling in Washington University in the suburbs, but my aunts and uncles persuaded my mother to put me under the Jesuits at SLU, who would, they said, "keep me on the right track." So I entered that institution in the autumn of 1943. I even went to Sunday mass at St. Francis Xavier Church, "the college church" as most people called it. Not that I had begun to like the Jesuits or churchgoing, but I preferred St. Francis Xavier's to St. Ann's for several reasons. My relatives didn't go there; also, the Jesuit church had a noon mass, which allowed me to sleep late on Sunday mornings. Even though the noon mass was solemn and long and disgraced by the most cacophonic singing of Schubert's and Palestrina's polyphonies, Father O'Neill always preached the sermon. No matter what his proposed topic—Christmas, hell, or brotherly love—he inevitably introduced a story about some adventure he had as a young missionary. I always thought he might end his homilies with something like: "And now we must say good-bye to the Dayak headhunters of Malay Archipelago as the golden sun sets below the summit of Mount Kinabalu."

I not only appreciated listening to a good sermon but liked to drop into the college church between classes just to sit in the quiet, dark pews for a while. It was a good place to get my thoughts together. And sometimes the organist was soloing in the chancel. There were times when I believed that, remove the ceremonies, sacraments, restrictions, and threats from the Catholic religion, and I could come to like it. The Jesuits—especially Father Finn—did their best, it seemed, to stress the unattractive features. Finn was strong on devotions, such as the recitation of the rosary and the wearing of holy medals. He saw everything, as he admitted, *sub specie aeternitatis*, and regarded even education as less important than piety. Many of us thought Finn concentrated on religious practices because he wasn't bright enough to teach. Certainly he was the antithesis of Father Wade, our professor of philosophy, who scorned the mixing of the spiritual with the academic. He advised us, using the words of the Jesuit founder, St. Ignatius of Loyola, to pray as if everything depended on God but to work as if everything depended on us.

Finn's main job was chaplain of the men's sodality—a kind of religious club—to which every Catholic male student belonged in virtue of his being a Catholic. It met at 11:40 a.m. every Wednesday for the recitation of the Angelus. Immediately afterward, Finn ushered us into the chapel and sent out some conscientious seniors to round up the forgetful or reluctant. Escape was possible unless Finn's wranglers caught you coming out of class, or in the gym, or standing in line at the cafeteria. Before what Finn considered very important meetings, his agents checked out the Regal Cafe, across the street from the college church, where my instructor in freshman English, Professor Marshall McLuhan, dined surrounded by a dozen or more male and female admirers. Even Walgreen's drugstore, on one corner of Olive and Grand avenues, and Garavelli's Italian Restaurant, on the other, offered no safe refuge from Finn's men.

But most of us attended the sodality meetings regularly. There were few rebels during those years of World War II. None of us complained about the mawkish hymns we had to sing, or the sodality president, who led us in a rapid-fire recitation of the rosary (he had a lisp and would say, "Thimon of Thyrene helpth Jesuth carry Hith croth"), or even the half-hour meditation performed while kneeling on hardwood floors. The latter started with a reading, by Finn himself, from *The Spiritual Exercises of St. Ignatius*. We were given a scene in the Gospel, such as Jesus in the Garden of Olives, or the prodigal son coming home, or St. Paul riding on the road to Damascus. There was one describing Job sitting upon a dunghill. Its lesson was, of course, humility and acceptance of God's will; but it became an occasion for adolescent attempts at humor manifested by audible sniffing and grimacing.

After the reading, Finn ordered us to place ourselves in the presence of God. I would have done so gladly but hadn't the faintest idea how. Frankly, the injunction seemed to me rather arrogant. Nevertheless, despite my negative attitude toward the Ignatius-Jesuit method of meditation, I did learn from it how to entertain myself while sitting in the dark, quiet church between classes—at least until I arrived at a point when I no longer felt the need for entertainment. I didn't realize it at the time, but while still a reluctant churchgoer and an enthusiastic pursuer of women, I enjoyed contemplation. Much later, I read about the nature of my experience. It seemed to fit Lagrange's description of the Prayer of Quiet or what Hubert Von Zeller called the "Prayer of the Blank." Like the rather impious Corinthians in the days of St. Paul, who nevertheless possessed charismatic gifts, I—by all standards a tepid Catholic—seemed to have received mystical favors.

Finn was also chaplain of the student nurses at Firmin Desloge Hospital on Grand Avenue, just south of the medical school. Many were from out of town and consequently lonely. He arranged dances for them on Saturday nights in a large conference room of the hospital, and made it mandatory that every member of our sodality show up, except for the two married students and three others who had declared a serious interest in entering the Jesuit seminary at Florence, Missouri. Finn considered attendance at these outings as a "corporal work of mercy." However, the slow dances of the 1940s permitted the closeness of two bodies in a vertical position, which in a horizontal position would have caused a scandal. After the first two or three dances, the hall was filled to capacity on Saturday nights. By ten o'clock most of Finn's charges had paired off and left for other kinds of entertainment.

I had been a regular at Finn's dances until I met Maggie, a senior at Clayton High. She was dancing with a friend of mine at the Candlelight House one evening. I looked at her when I waved hello to him and she smiled, aware that I had appraised her favorably. I cut in, introducing myself as her most ardent admirer. She stood ramrod straight, which gave her a certain dignity and made her appear taller than her five-feet-two. The softness of her light-blue cashmere sweater contrasted with the tenseness of her back as I encircled it with my arm. Her mouth was red and round and full like a plum. I thought I had never seen any mouth as sensuous in my life. To this day, I am not able to describe the color of her eyes, except that they were dark and flecked with gold in certain lights. I know those eyes were a trifle too close together and framed in naturally arched brows, but their color, even as I see them now in my imagination, I cannot determine. Her hair, a glossy dark brown, parted in the middle, hung straight down her back like that of a maiden in some medieval painting. With her small, slightly aquiline nose, she looked like Rebecca as illustrated in an old copy of *Ivanhoe* I had once read. But she wasn't Jewish. She was Catholic and therefore acceptable to the family, had we ever intended to marry.

I saw her the next day, and almost every school day for months afterward, at a drugstore soda fountain between Clayton High and her home in Ladue. Instead of Saturday nights at Finn's dances at Firmin Desloge, Maggie and I went to the Candlelight House, providing I had enough money; and if not, to Rammelkamp's, a popular "juke joint" in Clayton. For about two dollars, Maggie and I could eat "pedigree hot dogs" (a wiener garnished with bacon and cheddar cheese on a bun), drink several Stag beers, and feed the jukebox until time to go home.

One night I was without Maggie at a private party at the Chase Hotel. Everyone there seemed to talk like Clifton Webb and with the authority of Walter Lippmann. Around midnight someone suggested that we visit a fellow downtown named William Inge. We piled into a Chrysler Airflow and a Packard and wound up in front of a newly built, Bastille-like apartment house of gray concrete and tarnished steel, surrounded by weather-smoothed, smoke-stained brick factories. Directly across the street a confectionary, covered with Coca-Cola and Clabber Girl signs, was snuggled between two warehouses. Three black kids, bowed under a steel lamp, were lagging nickels.

We hauled ourselves up the stairway until we reached the landing of the third floor. Someone kicked on the steel door and, immediately, a speakeasy-type slot emitted a square beam of yellow light and then closed. The man who let us in had the long upper lip and Grecian nose of John Barrymore and wore a suit of mechanic's white overalls, with hoops that jutted on the sides and fastened from neck to crotch with brass buttons. We entered an L-shaped room partitioned by a bamboo curtain. A Toulouse-Lautrec print covered almost one entire wall, a bookcase another, and a phonograph and record case the third.

After introductions we began to discuss, among other things, the opening of the Russian Ballet at Kiel Auditorium. Suddenly the talk stopped and Inge ran into his kitchen and closed the door. He emerged doing an *entrechat*, clad in tee shirt and jockey shorts, and brandishing a pair of butcher knives. Of course, we laughed. But when Inge got into his Java dance, we watched with jaw-dropped admiration. He moved as gracefully as Nijinsky.

That summer of 1943, I went to several parties at Inge's. During one, he got out his sketch pads and charcoal pencils and demanded that the artists compete in a contest and the rest of us act as models. (I still have one of his sketches of me. It hangs on the wall of my study.) Through Inge I got to know many artists and to appreciate art in general. One of Inge's artist-friends was Ralph, a self-confessed agoraphobiac, who could not even stick his head out of a window without trepidation. Another was Norman, an alcoholic who, during any party, simply sat in a corner sweating and sipping a whiskey sour, agreeing with everyone, unmindful or unconcerned about holding contradictory opinions on an issue. And there was Nana, the so-called Russian countess, who did Aphen Bran beer posters for an advertising company downtown. In the winter her feet were always cold; whenever she sat down, she would take off her shoes and stick her feet into her thick, woolen knitting bag. Eventually I got the idea that gifted people were somewhat crazy. And when these same artists told me I was neurotic, I felt a touch of complacency. I belonged.

But it was Inge himself who gave me a taste for art. At the time, he held an eighty-dollar-a-week job as fine arts critic with the *St. Louis Star-Times*. Publishers sent him free books and recordings. He received complimentary tickets to all the concerts, films, ballets, and plays. It was with Inge that I first heard Lily Pons sing and Isaac Stern play the violin. With Inge, I attended an exhibition of "Ashcan" artists at the Forest Park Museum and fell in love with a Birchfield picture entitled *Tief*. Also with Inge, I saw my first professional play at the old American Theatre: *The Corn Is Green*, with Ethel Barrymore. Inge had introduced me to a part of life that I had never experienced before. He had provided me with the opportunity to cultivate a taste for things that did not naturally attract me. I never think of Inge without calling to mind the saying of Horace: "We grow tall by walking with giants."

But I learned something from Inge far more important than the appreciation of art. I learned that a man who attains success, even in the profession of an artist, may still be unhappy. When I knew Inge back in 1943, I thought he had already accomplished much in life. He had earned a master of arts degree at Peabody College, had taught English and drama at Stephen's College in Columbia, Missouri, and had held a prestigious post on a leading newspaper. He had respect, freedom, and interesting work. What gnawed away at his peace of mind was his ambition to become a great playwright—another Ibsen. This much he told me while we suffered through a dead musical called *The Emperor's Waltz* or something like that. Afterward I went with him to his apartment where he read the play he had just finished. He called it *Farther off from Heaven*, the story of an ordinary family in Oklahoma. He admitted that the story was autobiographical and that he was the kid with the album of movie-star photos. I pointed out things that I liked about the play, but I considered it, taken as a whole, rather boring. I think Inge did too, really, for I never heard him talk about it again until he began to rewrite it following his meeting with Tennessee Williams three years later. Whether Williams read Inge's play and advised him on it, I don't know. However, I know he got the play in good enough shape to persuade Margo Jones to produce it in a theater in Dallas. He had changed the title to *The Dark at the Top of the Stairs*.

At last, I thought, Inge had reached his goal. He was no Ibsen, but his plays certainly had gained him fame and fortune. I had to admit that, as an aspiring writer myself, I felt a pang of envy. But later, after I had left the abbey, I made a point to read all Inge's works and, in the foreword to *Four Plays by William Inge*, he lamented the inability of becoming a celebrity to fill the void in his soul: "Where were the gloating satisfactions I had always anticipated? I looked everywhere for them. None were there." As a playwright, an artist-philosopher, Inge could not have imagined that his observation was extraordinary. That goals, once attained, lose their value is a well-known truism. He should have been mature enough to cope with frustration. But during the 1970s, while still at the zenith of the wheel of fortune, he committed suicide.

In the summer of 1943, I took Maggie and her mother to Union Station. They were going to Chicago, where a member of their family, Commander Raymond Stanton of the United States Navy, was stationed. A few days later, after an afternoon of swimming in the Meramec River, I returned home with a fever and went to bed. That evening my knees swelled up to twice their size and something gripped my heart so that I could hardly breathe. I woke up the next morning at St. Anthony's Hospital with a case of rheumatic fever.

According to St. Teresa of Avila, suffering either inclines a person to seek consolation in God or to rebel against him. I lay for about two weeks mentally raging at the figure upon the cross that hung on the wall in front of my bed. I could receive no visitors except my mother, the doctor, the nurses, and a priest. I refused to see a priest. The doctor came in every morning, looked at my chart and my fingernails, and begged me to eat. My mother showed up every night at seven o'clock. Since I was too weak to talk, she just sat near me saying the rosary.

My nurse was a small nun with soft, gray eyes and small, even, white teeth that looked like kernels of sweet corn. Whenever she came into the room, she dipped the fingers of her right hand into the holy water stoop fixed to the jamb and then made the sign of the cross. It was not a perfunctory action. I saw her lips form the words "Father," "Son," and "Holy Ghost" as she touched her forehead, chest, and shoulders. After she had given me my medicine or taken my temperature, she stood at the foot of my bed smiling. I figured she was sympathetic. Unless the penicillin started to work, she knew, I would die. I was too ill to speak, so I used to close my eyes, but not entirely. I used to lie there, appearing to be asleep, watching her observe me. Her face, from forehead to chin, was framed in a white, starched wimple that extended like a knight's breastplate almost to her waist. A white cotton veil covered her head and fell over her shoulders. Her white robe reached her ankles and was girded with a simple piece of rope having three knots in it. On her feet she wore black lisle stockings and kid-leather shoes. I found determining her age difficult, since I could not see her hair or the exact proportions of her body. I supposed that she was about thirty-five.

About three weeks after I entered the hospital, the penicillin began to work. No more swellings or fever. And I began to eat. I ate my regular meals, the sandwiches Mother brought me each evening, and all the snacks my nurse, Sister Veronica, brought in.

I not only began to enjoy eating, but listening to the radio and reading books as well. However, the highlight of the day was the bath. When Veronica rubbed my back with alcohol and talcum powder or placed her hand upon my behind as she injected it with penicillin, I seemed to feel a tenderness in her touch that transcended mere sympathy. Veronica had been praying for me. She had even used the sacramental gimmicks associated with prayer: She doused me with Lourdes' water and St. André's oil; and she had pinned to my pajama jacket so many scapulars and sacred medals that I looked like a German field marshal. For someone with her faith the argument *post hoc, ergo propter hoc* is not a fallacy. Nor was she silenced when I remarked that the same God who had made me well also nearly killed me. She maintained that "whom God loveth he chastiseth."

The illness did give my life a redirection. I had been in premedical school with aspirations of becoming a surgeon. But after seven weeks in a hospital—even under the best of conditions—I wanted nothing to do with medicine. I was about to be drafted into military service, but with the scars on my aorta valve I was a 4-F. I started going to mass again and signed up to be shriven the next time the chaplain visited the hospital to hear confessions.

That July Fourth, I was in my room awaiting the arrival of Father Barnabas. Since I had been confined for many weeks, I had to think pretty far back to come up with any important material. The priest entered my room wearing his brown Franciscan robe and rope girdle, scapular with hood attached, black sandals and socks, and upon his head a yellow panama hat with a plaid band and the brim turned up, baseball-fan style. It would have taken more courage than I had just to walk down the hospital corridor in that costume. But Father Barnabas had come from his priory on Virginia Avenue, about three miles away, on a trolley car. As dedicated to tradition as Barnabas seemed to be, I thought he would be severe with lapsed Catholics such as I. However, he was both efficient and benign. He listened to my confession and straightway absolved me from my sins. I have since thought of him as a kind of instant spot remover.

Had Barnabas been a sensible, conventional priest, he might have made no impression upon me. However, his gruff manner and outlandish dress appealed to my imagination. He belonged to the Middle Ages, among dusty old manuscripts, or in a dense forest talking to the birds. I swore that if I were he, no one, not even the Pope, would get me out of my monastery. I thought I would wear a hairshirt, eat nothing but black bread and yellow cheese, and spend the nights praying with my arms extended in the shape of a cross. In fact, for several days after meeting Barnabas, I thought it would be very mysterious of me to disappear into some monastery away from war news, girlfriends, and relatives. Also one evening my mother, knowing that Somerset Maugham was my favorite writer, brought me his latest novel, *The Razor's Edge*. The hero was a young man living in Chicago who, despite his good looks and money, could not find contentment. In his quest of self-knowledge, he wandered into a Benedictine monastery. The kind and wise abbot put him up in a private room. He studied, meditated, and worked but never actually became a monk. He never went to mass or to choir; to pray he just sat in a quiet, dark church as I liked to do. Eventually, he left the Benedictines and traveled around the world, and at last found peace with the Dali Lama in Tibet.

With both Franciscans and Benedictines on my mind, I visited the hospital library one day to get more information on monks. I told the librarian what I wanted, and she introduced me to a novel by, I think, Robert Hichens, called *The Garden of Allah*. The hero of this story is a monk of the Trappist monastery in El Authroum (Africa). He sees a beautiful woman visitor and falls in love with her. He leaves the monastery and searches for her in Algiers. Having broken at least a dozen of his vows, it seemed, he nearly went mad with remorse and returned to the monastery to do penance.

I told Veronica about *The Garden of Allah* and my fascination with the Trappists. She shook her head tolerantly, as if I had just proposed to swim the English Channel. One night I had a dream about my becoming a Trappist. I was dressed in a long white robe and hood and was digging potatoes with several other monks in a garden just in front of a monastery. A bell rang and we all dropped our shovels and slowly marched into the monastery wherein each of us retired to our individual cells. The next day Veronica brought me a book, *Three Religious Rebels*, written by a Trappist monk of Gethsemani Abbey, Father Raymond Flanagan. By noon that day, I had finished it, but only to discover that the monks in my dream were quite different from Trappists.

The latter wear black scapulars, not white. Moreover, they sleep in common dormitories, not private cells.

But it was not the costumes, or their manual labor, or their silence, or their abstinence from meat and fish, as described by Father Raymond, that cooled my ardor concerning the Trappists. It was their intense community life. I wanted a private room, with bath if possible. Consequently, I never brought up the Trappists again to Veronica.

At home in St. Louis, I continued to recuperate. However, I was still too weak to attend the university and to engage in much social life. I visited Sister Veronica now and then until she was sent to another hospital in Chicago and I lost contact with her. I got several invitations from the Howards in Nassau to come for a visit; from the Sommerses at West End too. But at the time I did not want to travel, even to the nearby Bahamas. I stayed in my third-story room of the house Mother had bought. In the evenings, I often went to a neighborhood movie or played records, mostly pieces by Debussy, Ravel, and Stravinsky. Also, I began to write a novel about a young man who had joined a Trappist monastery after the girl he loved married someone else. After a few years, she realized that she really loved the monk and, dressing up as a boy, joined the same monastery. Since, in the story, the monks never take off their hoods, even in church, the Trappist and his beloved live together under the same roof for thirty years without his knowing the situation. Seeing that he is happy in his vocation, she never reveals her identity to him. She eventually dies. Only then, while her body is being treated for burial, do the monks find out she is a woman. Of course, her former lover prays for her soul until he dies and joins her in heaven.

I thought the story was dramatic and original. It was neither. When I later became a monk, I read in the abbey library *Les Mémoires du Comte de Comminge* by Madame de Tencin. The plot was almost identical to that of my novel. By that time, my taste in literature had improved, so I did not regard the similarity of the stories as a convergence of genius.

What was significant about my novel was the fact that it became a distillation of my fears and desires concerning monasticism. It reflected a kind of death wish, a wish for death to the chaotic unstable life I had been living so far. And after I started back to school and resumed a social life, everything I did seemed ephemeral, as though studies, work, and pleasures existed in a vacuum, unrelated to anything in my present state. But, just as many people fail many times in their attempts to commit suicide, so I failed to take even the first steps toward becoming a monk. There was one thing I felt sure about at the time: I wanted to live in a monastery as a civilian, not as a monk, and to live there only as long as I liked, not forever. I certainly did not want a life dedicated to liturgy that I found barely tolerable one hour a week. And I didn't want to castrate myself with a vow of celibacy. I remained in this limbo of indecision for about two more years.

3

A Retreat at Gethsemani

I never finished that novel but I did finish school—and with honors. After the graduation exercise, Father Finn congratulated me. "You've become a real Renaissance man," he said. I tried to look humble. "Not only because of your grades," he added, "but because I don't know anyone more geared to material things."

I was rather glad he said that. I didn't want to leave the university thinking that I had disliked him unfairly. But his remark did trouble me. I remembered how detached from this world I had been last summer, when I thought I was dying. Since then I had been going to mass on Sundays, but reluctantly. So I reread *Three Religious Rebels* and began thinking about Trappist monasteries again.

One day the *St. Louis Globe-Democrat* ran a story about Trappists coming through St. Louis enroute to Utah. They were establishing a new monastery near Ogden. I had nothing to do that afternoon, so I went down to Union Station, hoping to see the caravan. About noon the train rolled in. From a coach with all its windowshades drawn stepped an old man as thin and fragile looking as a Haviland teacup. He wore a gold cross that hung from a purple cord encircling his neck. Blasts of hot air coming off the tracks tossed his black hood from one shoulder to the other like a windsock. His black scapular, attached to the hood, was a kind of poncho and partially covered the white muslin robe worn beneath it. Around his waist he had on a tan leather belt. It must have been six feet long and, after joining at the buckle, it split into two strips, from which hung several rings of keys. When he walked toward a group of priests and nuns, I noticed that, instead of socks, he wore white duckcloth buskins. They were stuffed into a pair of black oxfords so crudely made that I imagined each could be worn on the opposite foot with equal discomfort. The treaded heels, obviously cut out of automobile tires, destroyed a momentary illusion that I was looking at some-one from the medieval age. Just for an excuse to meet him, I sauntered up to the group and, before he boarded the train, introduced myself. I asked if he received visitors at Gethsemani. He smiled and invited me to make a weekend retreat there.

A few weeks later I got off a train at New Haven, Kentucky. There were no taxis, so I walked up a tarmac road, almost liquid under the late afternoon sun, past a distillery veneered with corrugated tin panels, toward a single Gothic spire looming above a copse of sweet-gum trees. I turned into a road that ran for about a hundred yards between a field of corn and another of grass and rose to a summit upon which stood a stone statue of St. Joseph holding the Infant Jesus. I veered left and followed the road, flanked on either side by cinder-block walls high enough to obstruct my view of the abbey compound. The silence seemed studied, positive, arranged—like the duration between two movements of a symphony. The road ended at a row of squat buildings made of cinder blocks and painted white, bisected by a wooden double door. Above it, in a niche, stood a nearly life-size statue of Our Lady, balancing the Infant Jesus upon a hip. Beneath, along the base of a Roman arch, were inscribed the words: *Pax Intrantibus* (Peace to those who enter).

I pulled the rope hanging from a bell mounted above the double door and, almost immediately, the window of a room to my right shot up. A lay brother appeared, his skull shaven and his face covered with red whiskers. Behind the steel-rimmed glasses, his eyes seemed fixed upon my left shoulder and I instinctively gave it a brush. I later observed that the brother never looked anyone in the eyes.

Also Brother Alexander—that was the porter's name—was not only porter of the abbey, but also postmaster for the little community settled in the surrounding hills. In fact, I had not disturbed him from contemplation but from sorting the mail. After I volunteered my purpose in being there, he closed the window without assuring me that I was welcome or that he would let me in. However, in a few seconds, one panel of the double doors opened. I followed him into a garden and toward a large ginkgo tree beneath which was a park bench. "Wait here," he said, and actually trotted, Indian fashion, up a yellow concrete walk, around a statue hidden under crawlers laden with pink roses, and on again until he reached the white stone steps that led into the main door of the guest house.

Except for the long, narrow, green louvred windows, there was nothing to break the monotony of the rectangular structure of four stories with a facade of stone-patterned yellow concrete, in places revealing its base of red brick. Two men, also retreatants, strolled along the yellow concrete walk that encircled the garden, their faces turned toward another wall beyond which the sun seemed to teeter upon the treetops of the wooden knolls (called "knobs" by the natives) that enclosed the entire abbey and its several hundred acres like the fluted edges of an enormous pie-crust. (Today that view is cut off by the *new* guest house built in the sixties.) As they continued, they rounded that part of the gate house—as the squat, white building was called—where both men and women were permitted to shop for books and religious articles and even visit their monk-relatives. As the men approached the double door, one turned down the same path taken by the porter and stopped before a pool containing goldfish the size of mature trout. The other carried on in the same direction, past the post office, the ginkgo tree, the wall leading into the compound and, finally, up the white stone steps and into the guest house.

Actually, the guest house included only the top three floors of one wing of the abbey. The first floor was used as a kitchen at one end, and as offices at the other. In one of them, a staff of clerks and typists took care of the abbey's internal affairs. In another, two monks read and censored all incoming mail. And in the one at the very end of the corridor, the abbot received both visitors and monks. But the room adjoining the abbot's office was, by far, the most distinguished. It was entered through two doors of heavy steel and, for that reason, was called the "vault." It contained shelf upon shelf of rare books bound in wood, leather, and even vellum. With its doors and windows closed, the vault was as quiet as a tomb; yet it overlooked the garden and the gatehouse where, in the years to come, hordes of visitors would walk, converse, laugh, and smoke throughout the day. Ironically, from 1949 to 1965, a monk wrote and studied there in silence like a person caught in the tranquil eye of a tornado. He even slept there during his bouts of illness and insomnia.

The brother returned with a monk whom he introduced as Father Francis, the guest master. I knew he was a monk because he was dressed in black and white, whereas the brother's habit was entirely brown. He grabbed my valise and led me into the vestibule of the guest house where, on a wall, were painted the words "God Alone." The monk lifted his skirt and started up a flight of stairs, taking two at a time. When we reached the fourth floor, his head, bald but for a horseshoe-shaped ring of gray hair reaching from temple to temple, was scarlet. Panting through an incomplete set of teeth, he said, "This is how I get my exercise." He must have been sixty years old.

He left me in a large room, dark because of the closed shutters. I flicked open several louvres, and sunshine sprawled upon the brown planks of the sagging floor. The walls, painted a vile aquamarine, were further disgraced by large framed paintings, so blackened by age and dirt that the figures were hardly discernible. There was no bath. Against one wall stood a washstand burdened with a mirror, metal basin, galvanized pitcher, several bars of Lifebuoy, and a stack of white towels. Against the opposite wall stood three single iron beds, suggesting multiple occupancy, each hiding, it seemed, under the folds of one coverlet, a ceramic pot bedecked with figures of blue jays. I had never seen one before, but I imagined it served a basic need.

That evening the retreat master, Father Odilo, came into my room to see if I wanted confession. He said it was standard procedure during retreats, so I said yes. Afterward he gave me absolution and settled back in his chair. Then he remarked, "You have very long fingers. Do you play the organ?" "No," I said. He shook his head. "Too bad. We could use another organist." It was soft sell, but a definite pitch for recruitment. Then he began to tell me about one of the monks there—Frater (Brother) Louis, known later to the world as Thomas Merton. He said Merton had made a retreat at Gethsemani without intending to enter. In fact, Odilo went on, Merton really wanted to join a Carthusian monastery in France, but the war prevented him from traveling overseas.

Odilo seemed to imply that God had arranged World War II to happen at the exact time Merton decided he would become a monk. And I certainly got the impression that Odilo believed that I too was being "called" to Trappist life. I should never have told him I had read the *Three Religious Rebels* while in the hospital or had met Abbot Dunne in St. Louis. He insisted that those incidents were providential. He even argued that my repugnance toward Trappist life might indicate that God wanted me to sacrifice all—even my preference concerning religious orders. After he left, I actually felt that I would sadden the angels by not becoming a monk.

As the retreat continued, my distaste for Gethsemani Abbey grew. I thought about the helter-skelter layout of the buildings, the aesthetic poverty of the paintings and statues, the dreadfully long ceremonies in church. Even the Salve Regina service in the evenings—so popular with the other retreatants—annoyed me. The hymn itself is beautiful, but the theatrics that accompanied it were corny. The service began after the lights in the church were turned off. Then a statue of the Blessed Virgin, perched upon a high pedestal behind the main altar, was illuminated by an oval network of 100-watt bulbs, much like that bordering the dressing-room mirrors of actors. (A few years later, the apparatus was replaced by a powerful spotlight set up outside the rear of the sanctuary and behind an art-glass window depicting the Blessed Virgin being crowned in heaven by a company of marveling saints and cherubim. The spotlight illumined the figures gradually, simulating those epiphanies described in medieval stories of holy men and women. Some improvement, but not much.)

The next day, Father Odilo dropped in to give me a tour of the novitiate, that is, the section of the monastery where young men are tested and trained for two years before really joining the order. He led me through the cloister, past the refectory or monks' dining room. We entered the novitiate from a wing of the cloister and through a door that opened to a vestibule. Dust filled the cracks between the floor planks, and the stuccoed walls were covered with whitewash that chipped off if you rubbed against them. To the right, a stairway led up to the dormitory and chapel. Next to the doorway of the vestibule hung a bulletin board stuck over with thumb-tacked sheets of paper advertising the horarium, schedule of conferences, and acolytes for the week. Here and there hung pictures, probably lost and unclaimed, of the Little Flower, St. Bernard, St. Benedict, and other notables, many of which had been printed at the monastery of St. Sulpice in France that specialized in holy cards edged in lace! They were yellowed, curled, and stiff with age, and must have been there even before Merton arrived seven years before.

To the left of the vestibule ran a narrow passageway that led into the Latin classroom, well lighted by a large window, and then veered to the left, past the music room and the master of novices' office and, finally, into the scriptorium. There the novices spent most of the time not dedicated to choir service or manual labor. Only on the darkest days were the overhead lamps turned on because six or eight lancet windows, each larger than an ordinary door, let in plenty of light from three directions. In the mornings, about five o'clock, the novices sat reading on benches fixed to the walls or at the six long tables, writing with pencil stubs or scratchy steel pens and ink into notebooks made from the backs of used envelopes. (The monk secretaries actually saved their discarded envelopes and worn-down pencils for the novices. This was an immemorial custom among Trappists, designed to teach the novices a sense of poverty and humility.) They kept their materials in "common boxes" built into the wall benches, each properly identified by a slip of paper with the novice's name on it.

Besides a statue of the Little Flower and another of Our Lady, a large crucifix decorated with dried-out fronds of palm, and several bookcases, the scriptorium also had two or three steel radiators, which, on cold mornings, would begin to clank and sizzle about seven-thirty. They threw out heat only about a foot and, to keep warm, the novice practically had to hug them. Of course, to stand before or sit near one was a sign of self-indulgence, and only the most uninhibited novice did so. Besides, being near the radiators, the novice could not record his thoughts with a pen because the inkwells were fixed into the tables. Consequently, in the winter, many fingers were numb and blue until the rays of the sun filtered through the dirty panes of those lancet windows. By the time the scriptorium warmed up, the novices were down the steep hill, upon which the novitiate had been built, and in the woodshed, a pavilion about the size of a tennis court, sawing and splitting logs to feed the boiler that repaid them poorly for their efforts to keep it fueled.

The novices' scriptorium was also the lecture room. Every night Dom Vital, the master of novices, gave instructions on monastic rules. He had been, about thirty years before, the abbot of Achel, the Trappist monastery in Luxembourg. For some reason he resigned his post and asked to go to another house of the order. He chose Gethsemani in America, where, he believed, the streets were paved with gold. The abbot of Gethsemani, Edmund Obrecht, himself a German-speaking Alsatian, received him kindly and even made him master of novices. But Dom Vital soon fell into disgrace. He ordered one of his novices to do something the abbot disapproved of, and the abbot said to the novice, "Go tell your father master he's a fool." To add injury to insult, the abbot fired Dom Vital and made him a cement mixer for the work gang in charge of veneering the ugly red-brick buildings with yellow, stone-patterned concrete and erecting cinder-block walls around the compound. When Obrecht died and Father Frederick Dunne became abbot, Dom Vital regained his old job and with it, a vestige of dignity.

I learned Dom Vital's history many years later. But that very day I discovered that his main route to heaven, for himself as well as for his novices, would be through the valley of humility. On the evening Father Odilo took me to the novitiate and introduced me to the novice master, the latter eyed my Brooks Brothers topcoat and Threadneedle Street shoes and must have decided I was a dude. Before the lecture started, he called the novices' attention to the fact they had a visitor—"Anudder Pig Shot" were his words. His accent was as thick as knockwurst and undermined the vocal irony he tried to project. The novices laughed. He paid them no mind but shook his head up and down a few times, as if affirming by gesture the words he had spoken. He sat back in his chair, his short legs hardly touching the floor, and rolled from side to side on his buttocks, waiting for his venom to take effect.

"I was only fifteen when I came to the monastery. I was a good kid," he said. He hunched his shoulders and looked up, I suppose, at the mental image of himself as a good kid. Those jutting eyebrows; long, pointy nose; and unshaven, square jaw would have looked perfect under a Prussian spiked helmet. Yet there was something about his eyes that suggested compassion, even sentimentality. They were fixed upon me when he said, "If you have come here to love God, you have come to get shitted on!" He actually used the vulgar term.

He held up his pectoral cross. "You see this? This means I'm abbot. But a good-for-nothing abbot since I'm retired. I take orders like everybody else, and you will take orders from me. You think the fasting and vigils are tough? They are nothing. It's those *verdammt* humiliations that will kill you. Not the humiliations you make yourself, kneeling before a superior, accusing yourself in the chapter of faults, writing with pencil stubs. Kid stuff. Real humiliations come from obedience, but especially from sin. Yes, my children, from sin. You think because you are Trappists you have no sins? I tell you, you got them. I got them. Trappists go to purgatory because they are proud."

Several novices glanced at each other and winked as though they knew what was coming. "Sins are rotten stuff—manure. But is the farmer sorry he's got manure? It don't look good. It don't smell good neither. But the farmer knows it will make his plants grow. He spreads his manure on his plants and, after a few months—if it rains too, of course—what comes out of the ground? More manure? No—beautiful vegetables. Your sins are spiritual manure that can make you humble like Jesus. Don't be a *dummkopf* and try to sin. But if you do, thank Jesus for the humiliation. Be manure saints."

On the last day of the retreat, I had many reasons for my aversion to Trappist life, and Dom Vital's "manure spirituality" was not the least of them. So at lunchtime in the guests' dining room, I figured I would never see this place again.

I watched the old brothers in their starched, white aprons over their brown robes carrying plates of steaming food. Father Odilo gave the blessing and then waved to a young monk sitting, unmonastically, on a windowsill with a book in his hands. The toes of his shoes were unpolished and the heels sloped to nothing on the outer edges.

He strolled to the center of the dining room, stopped, pulled at his flat nose, and began turning the pages of his book roughly, like a man defoliating a cabbage. He looked around and smiled, displaying the gray metal of a dental bridge that lacked several porcelain facings. He had a common face except for his eyes—large, blue, and alert.

He announced the title, which I have forgotten, and the name of the author, Fulton Sheen. His accent was American, without any regional peculiarity. I would never have guessed he had been born in France and educated mostly in England.

The book had something to do with the Mystical Body of Christ and rambled on in long, classical periods laced with scholastic axioms. It was serious. But the monk's smiles and explosive guffaws undermined the book's pious tone. I didn't understand the humor in it but sided with the monk and joined in the merriment.

Later, Father Odilo told me the reader had been the young monk he had mentioned on the first night of the retreat—Frater Louis a.k.a. Thomas Merton. But the name didn't mean anything to me, for Merton had not yet become famous. I liked him, nevertheless, especially after Father Odilo told me a few stories about him. One involved Merton's superstition. It seems that after making a retreat at Gethsemani, he returned to St. Bonaventure's College in New York, where he was teaching at the time. He was ambivalent about returning. Then one night he said a prayer for enlightenment, opened his Bible at random, and placed his finger upon a text: "Behold thou shalt be silent." He took "silent" to be synonymous with "Trappist." Though he might have read the passage so often that the book fell open at that particular page, he regarded the incident not as a coincidence but as an omen. And one evening, while strolling on the campus, he imagined hearing bells ring from the belfry of Gethsemani's church. Merton made Gethsemani look better.

Just before I left that afternoon, Father Francis set me loose in the monks' library. I went straight to a shelf marked "Religious Orders" and pulled out a copy of the *Cistercian Usages*. It was the same book studied by every Trappist since the days of Abbot Armand de Rancé, the seventeenth-century French reformer of the Cistercians from whose own abbey, La Grande Trappe, the name "Trappist" derives. The book contained prescriptions for nearly every move the monk makes. While in the cloister he must put his arms inside the sleeves of his cowl, but upon entering the church his arms must hang at his sides. When meeting another monk he should bow his head, but the abbot should be greeted with a bow from the waist. And a novice may not be saluted at all. Before reading a book, the monk was to kneel and say a prayer for enlightenment. He was obliged to put on his hood while using the latrine. And so on. I imagined that Thomas Merton regarded these usages a little more than curiosities.

I recalled that Merton had once been attracted to the Carthusians. I found an old tome bound in white vellum and written in French on La Grande Chartreuse. It contained several pictures—daguerreotypes protected by sheets of transparent paper—featuring monks dressed in white cowls, walking and kneeling in various attitudes of piety. The anonymous author described the Carthusians' daily agenda. They spend most of the day in their small apartments, praying, doing carpentry work, and eating their two scant meals. At times they meet in choir, visit the community library, and take walks together in the forest. Their motto is not some pious slogan but a kind of boast: *Numquam reformata quoniam numquan deformata* ("Never reformed because never deformed"). However, I also read that the monks make a liqueur, drink wine, and eat fish. After the passage containing this information, someone had written an exclamation mark.

On the way home that evening, I thought of the Trappists and the Carthusians. La Grand Chartreuse seemed like a country club in comparison with Gethsemani. The latter appealed to me as a kind of training ground for death. Moreover, I liked the simple Trappist funeral—no mourners, no flowers, not even a coffin. I imagined an iron cross bearing the inscription *Hic jacit Frater Geraldus* and the date. The place was as romantic as a passage from one of Chateaubriand's novels. I was hooked on the place.

Gerald Groves, just before entering Gethsemani in 1948.

4

The Dread Decision

A fellow retreatant took me as far as Louisville. From there I could have bought a bus ticket all the way to St. Louis, but it seemed wanton to be in a strange city and waste the opportunity to check it out. Moreover, I believed that I was one of those chosen people to whom things happen, and I expected to find adventure wherever I went. So I had a fantastic dinner of roast duck at the Brown Hotel, then took a room for the night, quite aware that I had nearly spent all of my money and would have to trust to providence the next day. Actually, I said the same to myself and felt rather pious for it.

In my elegant room, I took a shower, changed into fresh pajamas, and read the *Louisville Courier* in bed. After I had turned out the table lamp and covered myself with the top sheet, I heard someone a few doors down the hall. I let myself anticipate a gentle, even discreet, knock on the door. Then I imagined the door swinging open and Betty Grable standing on the threshold in a black nightgown and desperately wanting company—my company. It then occurred to me that I had just made a retreat. It was embarrassing to realize that, despite my spiritual renewal, I still had the same old urges. Only now, I had to admit, I felt guilty about them.

I woke up at about nine o'clock rather let down at the prospect of leaving the opulence of my hotel room for the austerity of the open road. But before hitchhiking, I had a cup of coffee and an enormous cinnamon bun at a nearby Toddle House. Then I was entirely broke. But, at a stoplight on Broadway—which leads to an interstate highway—I got a ride in a new Lincoln Continental convertible, my favorite car in all the world. The driver wasn't Betty Grable, of course, but an amiable young man, heavy set, and good looking. We bolted away from a green light and tore down the road. At each sharp turn I made an act of contrition, despite laughing at the driver's bawdy jokes. I really wanted to say something consoling or edifying to him because he was on his way to the Veterans' Hospital in St. Louis to have his left leg amputated below the knee. At least, that's what he told me.

As we passed over the Eads Bridge into downtown St. Louis, he asked me to direct him to a good hotel. I took him to the Mayfair on Seventh and Olive avenues. There he was within walking distance of Wohl's Piano Bar, the Loew's Theatre, and even the Garrick Burlesque. I could have, and should have, taken him to the old French cathedral down on the levee, but I figured that would not be appropriate for his night on the town.

With the dime I borrowed from the young man, I took a Washington Avenue bus heading toward the West End. As usual for five o'clock on a weekday evening, it was packed with late shoppers and people just off from work. There were no empty seats. I stood next to a girl almost six feet tall, and when the bus picked up more passengers at Twelfth Street, both she and I twisted and turned to allow them to pass. As a result, we ended up facing each other. She looked straight into my eyes. "Care to dance?" she asked. She was charming. "Under the circumstances, I guess we should at least pretend to," I said. She laughed and rested her chin on my shoulder. For a few moments, we didn't say anything, swaying in unison with the movements of the bus, aware—at least I was—of the other's severe proximity. I tried to distract myself by reading the advertisements lining the walls of the bus just above the windows: Jantzen Swimwear, Falstaff Beer, Famous-Barr Dollar Day, and so on. "A penny for your thoughts," she said. I couldn't see her face, but I knew she was smiling. Just before I got off the bus, we promised to meet the following Sunday afternoon at the Shaw Park swimming pool in Clayton.

Sometimes I found it hard to banter, especially with a person I wanted to impress. As Perry Como used to sing, "Words wouldn't come in an easy way." But with Gloria—that was the girl's name—I had been on a roll. She was that kind of individual whose own honesty demanded honesty. Moreover, she drew more ideas and quips out of me than I ever dreamed I could muster up. Ordinarily, I would have delighted in speculating on our date at the pool. Yet I knew I wasn't going to see her again. In the light of my future plans, she had no place in my life. Like cigarettes, liquor, movies, novels, good food—Gloria would become another luxury I would soon have to give up. I got off the bus and walked home.

I would also have to give up our old, red-brick, three-story house on Evans Avenue. Like the other houses on the block, it was surrounded on all sides with elm trees. I had to climb exactly thirteen concrete steps to get from the sidewalk to the front porch. This made coming home a kind of mystical experience, especially since my mother, who had grown uncommonly pious during her forties, had named the four pillars supporting the roof Matthew, Mark, Luke, and John. That same slate-covered roof, topped by an aluminum weathercock that actually spun during wind storms, lay just beyond the bay window that drew the morning light into my mother's room.

For a moment, I stood before the artificially grained wooden panels and door that made up the entrance. Their panes of beveled glass were partly covered with gold-tinted lace curtains. Behind them was a white Venetian blind, that epoch's mark of modernity. In the mailbox was a pink sheet of paper advertising Nussbaum's Kosher Meat Market on Page Boulevard. I had been to a New Year's party with Ruthy Nussbaum a year before and kissed her at midnight with considerable pleasure.

I swung open the door and stepped onto the blond, hardwood floor that gleamed from Mother's frequent rubbing with Johnson's wax. Very few people entered our foyer without remarking on the beautiful floors. Few also failed to notice the picture that hung on the wall next to the closet under the stairway. It was of Christ sadly pointing to his exposed heart that flamed up like a Bunsen burner. Suddenly the kitchen door opened and Smokey, Mother's neurotic cocker spaniel, charged in to greet me. In her excitement, she peed on the floor, slipped on the wet wax, and slammed into my legs. Then Mother called, "Glad you're home, Lovey. Mary and Frank are here." I yelled hello and started up the stairway. On the first landing was a red-and-gold art-glass window, which, at dusk, reflected the light of the setting sun throughout the foyer and adjoining parlor. On the second floor I stopped to admire the wallpaper I had hung a few weeks previously. The gray and red vertical stripes made the ceiling look twelve feet high. When I reached my room on the third floor, I dropped my valise and fell upon the bed. Near my pillow lay a copy of Ayn Rand's *Fountainhead*, opened at the scene of Roark's breaking into Dominique's boudoir.

I would have fallen asleep but for my hunger and eagerness to see Mary, Mother's cousin, and her husband, Frank. I put on a clean shirt, washed my hands, and went down the back stairs that led into the kitchen. Everyone was sitting around the table eating pot roast. As usual, Frank had buttered three slices of bread and stacked them next to his plate. Unlike Mother and Mary, who ate in the European manner, Frank used bread to push food onto his fork. Mary had tried to teach him to eat left-handed, but Frank maintained that eating southpaw would make him stutter.

As I sat down, Frank waved his fork in salutation and gave me a mischievous wink. "Frank, will you please finish your story," asked Mary. She was impatient, not because she enjoyed her husband's conversation, but because he habitually led up to what promised to be the climax of a story only to light a cigar or take a long drink of beer, studying his audience all the while, as deadpan as a poker player.

"Well, it took fifteen firemen and three fire engines to put out the blaze. Not a stone was left upon a stone, as the good book says. That was the end of Silver's Saddle," he said. "Now, there's a pity," remarked my mother, serving me a slice of pot roast. It was one of her automatic responses to a sad event.

But Mary had been listening intently and sympathetically. "Heavens, what a shame!" she said. With that, Frank settled back in his chair, looking as confident as a Philadelphia lawyer. Mary put a piece of potato into her mouth and chewed pensively for a few seconds. Frank studied her from the corner of his eye and probably knew the bait had been taken. Mary looked over at him.

"Frank, where is this Silver's Saddle?" she asked. At first, Frank feigned to have just snapped back to attention. Then he smiled. Then he chuckled. Then he laughed—so hard that his heavy shoulders pumped up and down. Finally, he composed himself just enough to reply, "Under the Lone Ranger's ass." With that, he doubled over in his chair, and I nearly choked trying to laugh and swallow at the same time. Even Mother smiled, but Mary looked at her husband with contempt.

"Another one of your vulgar shop jokes and Gerald here just back from his retreat," said Mary.

Later that evening our conversation centered on Gethsemani. Mother seemed astounded to hear about Dom Vital's manure spirituality and Frater Louis' antics while reading in the guests' dining room. I guess they expected Trappists to be on a loftier plane. Nevertheless, they seemed very impressed when I told them I intended to join the abbey. That was the first time I actually put the resolution into words.

I really had no reason for remaining at home that autumn. I didn't procrastinate hoping to win back Maggie. I thought of her, of course, but she had married a soldier during my stay at St. Anthony's Hospital. And it wasn't that I wanted to contact old friends before my departure. Several of my former classmates at St. Louis University had telephoned during July and August, but I never accepted their invitations to go out. Sister Veronica had been transferred from St. Anthony's to another Catholic hospital in Chicago. So *she* didn't keep me in town.

In September I took a job at the Scullin Steel Company on Manchester Avenue. I had studied just a little chemistry in high school and college, but the work involved only quantitative analysis. The laboratory was a comparatively modern and clean brick building. I had to leave it about three times a day and enter the immense steel shed that housed the blast furnaces. The inside was filled with floating dirt, sounds of whistles and clanging metal, and the giant shadows of half-naked men shoveling coal into flaming furnaces. It reminded me of the boiler-room scene on O'Neill's *The Hairy Ape,* which itself suggested popular images of hell.

Whenever I left the furnace floor with my samples of the batch of steel about to be tapped, I thanked God for the comfort of the clean lab and for the lovely Mary McCormack, another chemist who worked there. The third employee on our three-to-eleven shift was a student of pharmacy at Washington University—a wimp called Jonesy. He liked to tell me ribald stories, knowing that Mary couldn't help overhearing them, especially if she were standing before the burettes, titrating a solution of manganese.

On weekends, one of us took off on Saturday and another on Sunday. Consequently, Mary and I often worked the shift alone. I knew that she liked me, for she frequently grabbed me by the arm and said something like, "That's my sweet boy." But she was four years older than I, so I interpreted her signs of affection as sisterly. Now and then she asked me about girls and seemed to be reaching for an invitation. However, I didn't want to spoil our relationship by coming on to her, so I never asked her out. But, one Saturday afternoon in December, Mary parked her car outside the lab and sort of wobbled through the door on her spiked-heel pumps. She wore a purple dress that clung to her thin-hipped, heavily bosomed body like the skin on a grape.

"I've been to a tea dance," she said, "and I'm a little drunk." I smiled and put my arm around her waist to help her into the control room where we did most of our work. I was about to seat her on a long, wooden bench when she suddenly put her arms around me. My response was spontaneous. Without thinking where I was or what I was doing, I kissed her. But I quickly gained composure and smiled at her, benignly, as if I had merely patted her head: "There. That's for being such a pretty girl." She released me and flopped down onto the bench. Then she looked up angrily. "Bull!" she said. "You meant it. You know you did."

The following week I decided to quit my job at Scullin Steel, partly because my relationship with Mary had become strained, but mainly because I had intended to stop working before Christmas anyway. I couldn't leave without telling Mary goodbye, but I felt reluctant to say where I was going. However, when the time came, she demanded to know. So I told her. Instead of laughing, as I expected, tears swelled up in her eyes. "So that's why you never came on to me!" she said. It wasn't exactly true, but I let her think so. Then she kissed me again and said, "That's for being so nice."

For Christmas, Sister Veronica sent me a book entitled *The Monks of Mount Athos* or something like that. The pictures of the monastery and hermitages were fascinating, but what interested me most was the monks' method of contemplation. It involves reducing the heartbeat and, consequently, the flow of blood to the brain. The monk sits in his cell fingering a rosary and reciting a mantra, such as "Jesus Christ, Son of David, have mercy on me." The slower the fingering of the rosary and the slower the recitation of the mantra, the slower the blood circulates. Eventually, all images stop flowing through the mind and the monk sort of passes out, maybe for five or ten seconds. When he comes around, he discovers details of ordinary things that he never noticed and enjoyed before. He sees clearly the grain in a wooden board, the graduated colors on a flower petal, the particular movements of a bird.

In my room, I practiced this "Prayer of Jesus," as it is called by the Hesychist monks of Mount Athos. Also, I made a study of Helen Waddell's *The Desert Fathers*, which is a translation of recorded axioms and stories of the first hermits. About the only times I left my room were for meals and morning mass at St. Mark's Church and an evening chat with Mother.

Late in January of 1948, I received a response to the letter I had written to Abbot Dunne just before Christmas. He invited me to come to Gethsemani as a prospective novice. He suggested a date: January 1, the Feast of Circumcision. Leaving home, like dying, doesn't scare you until you know when. I would not have been disappointed had he refused me. But the die was cast. On the morning of my departure, Mother gave me a porterhouse steak for breakfast, and we sat drinking tea and smoking cigarettes until the taxi sounded its horn in front of the house. "I'll keep your room ready," she said. I gave her a hug and opened the door.

5

My New Old Kentucky Home

On the way to Union Station, the taxi passed St. Ann's Church where, twenty-three years before, I had been baptized. That's when my life in the Catholic Church began. Mother often said I was a "born Catholic," but I liked to remind her that from my birth to my baptism—two weeks—I was a child of Satan. At least the Catholic ritual of baptism implies as much, since it directs the officiating priest to ask the prospective Christian if he renounces Satan and all his works. Of course, I didn't know what was going on. So my godfather, Uncle Dinny, did all the renouncing for me, and with no little uneasiness, since he wasn't entirely sure of his destiny. Nevertheless, his was the obligation to see that I learn Catholic doctrine and fulfill my obligations contracted at baptism.

I guess that, for most of my life, I disliked being a Catholic. There were so many things I could go to hell for doing or not doing: missing mass on Sunday, eating meat on Friday, drinking—even water—before going to Holy Communion. Yet I never considered becoming a Protestant. So many different kinds claimed to teach the truth that I concluded none of them did. I loved Jewish music—the "Kol Nidre" and "Eli, Eli"—but I felt uneasy with Jews who wore beards and yarmulkes. So I never even thought about joining a synagogue. What really appealed to me, as far as religion goes, was Mohammadanism. I liked the idea of wearing turbans, praying on a rug, dying in a holy war, and going straight to a sensational paradise!

As the taxi pulled into the station, I reflected that, in a certain way, I was about to reach the zenith of Catholicism. I had no admiration for parish priests, or bishops, or even for the Pope. Somehow, to my mind, they lead rather easy lives and gain a respect based on their offices rather than on personal accomplishments or sacrifices. I regarded cloistered monks and nuns as the true religious heroes of the Catholic Church.

I could not remember exactly when I had decided to become a monk myself, although I had thought about it during my stay at St. Anthony's Hospital. I recalled deciding to join the Trappists during a walk through the graveyard at Gethsemani. I didn't really know why. Perhaps because with a defective heart I would soon die, or because I believed dying as a Trappist and being buried without a coffin was about the most romantic way to go. What caused my conversion, I still am not sure, but I know that it had little to do with logic. As Havelock Ellis wrote: ". . . we know at all events [conversion] is not intellectual, not even necessarily moral transformation, though it may react in either direction, but primarily an emotional phenomenon."[1]

Although the train that morning took me closer and closer to Gethsemani, I could not help wondering if my choice of monastic orders was the best. After all, I had once thought about becoming a Carthusian. As such, I would have a private room, a place where I could take off my social face and take an honest look in the mirror. However, I realized that in entering the novitiate I hadn't bound myself to the Trappists. I could try them out and, if they didn't suit me, I could always leave and join the Carthusians. For some reason, I never considered other options.

That evening I stepped off the train onto the snow-covered ground of New Haven, Kentucky. Immediately, the engine gathered steam and pulled out of the small station as if eager to get to balmy Atlanta. Near the tracks, a red-haired old man slung a sack of mail onto the bed of his blue pickup truck. Its doors were inscribed: *Gethsemani Farms.* He agreed to take me to the abbey and said he was always on the lookout for retreatants and postulants (potential novices) when he came to collect the mail. When I told him I hoped to become a monk, he said, "You'll like it. The abbot's a fine feller." He refused the two dollars I offered him as we drove up to the abbey.

In the gate house, Brother Alexander looked up from sorting the mail as I entered. He had his hood on, but I could identify him by the rimless glasses and auburn beard. "Have you come to stay this time?" he asked in a tone devoid of encouragement. He turned me off, and I answered with a curtness that drew from him a long stare: "I want to see Father Odilo." He picked up a phone, dialed two numbers, and mumbled something unintelligible. Then he returned to his mail.

From a window, I saw Father Odilo, as round as he was tall in his heavy, white, woolen cowl, coming down the path from the guest house through the snow. He looked like a mobile igloo. Just as he opened the door, the church bells began to ring in that ridiculous Gothic steeple made of wood swathed in strips of tin and painted aluminum. "Just in time for vespers," said Odilo in a French accent more pronounced, it seemed, than it was the previous summer. Apparently he was not only happy to see me, but triumphant. On the way to the guest house, he said as much: "I'm glad you decided to enter. Misery loves company."

We climbed the dark stairway of the guest house to the even darker corridor on the third floor. Odilo shoved my valise into one of the rooms, led me to the door to the chancel, and told me to stay until he returned. Below, in the church, as long as a football field, the monks in their long, white cowls began entering the choir stalls. They held their enormous sleeves close to their sides and looked rather like so many ducks.

I felt as if I had just walked off the street into a theater featuring some medieval epic drama. I imagined Henry Wilcoxon, in glistening armor, riding into the church on a caparisoned horse and demanding from the abbot recruits for a holy crusade. I had no idea, in those days, of "aesthetic distance" but immersed myself in any well-directed theatrical production or even in a heroic scene conjured up in my vivid imagination. As I knelt there, I was ready to "swell the progress" by joining the abbot and the monks against Henry. Moreover, as I reflected, being there in the abbey, I was indeed about to become a character in the play. I was ready to accept the responsibility of "putting on" a new personality, and I refused to worry about not being "genuine." The Catholic Church had taught me that I could resolve all doubts about whether or not I could fulfill my destiny by simply acting as if I believed I could.

After breakfast the next morning, Odilo had me help the brothers clean the guests' dining room. As much as I hated taking orders, coming from him they gave me a sense of belonging. A Trappist couldn't tell me what to do if I weren't a Trappist as well. And when I returned to my room, I found two large Hershey bars on my bed—a kind of a Mardi Gras celebration or the condemned man's last indulgence before extinction. However, before I had the tinfoil off one bar, old Brother Matthias walked in with a bucket and mop, and proposed—in a nearly unintelligible Italian accent—that I clean the corridor. When I agreed, he smiled and said, as if one saint to another, "You prayuh for me, and I prayuh for you."

After lunch, while eating the second chocolate bar, I heard a sharp knock on the door. My first reaction was annoyance: "What the hell do they want now," I said to myself. My second was to stash the candy bar. When I opened the door, Dom Vital, old "spiritual manure" himself, strode in, looked around, and flopped into an arm chair. "Ach, so, Mister Pig Shot again," he said. "Did you miss our beautiful novitiate? Maybe the police are after you."

"Good to see you again, Father," I said, dissimulating like a diplomat.

"Take a good look, maybe I kick you out," Vital said. Again I could sense the drama—specifically the comedy—of the monastic theater. He was acting out a prescribed method for testing my humility. *Golly*, I thought, *even old Grandma Carson would have been able to see through this farce*. "Do you know Latin?" he asked. I declined *ipse, ipsa, ipsum* as fast as I could. "A parrot knows as much," he remarked contemptuously and continued to belittle me in his factitious manner. Then, he noticed my chocolate bar half-hidden behind a washbasin. He got up, walked over to it, broke off a square, and popped it into his mouth. "Come," he said. "We see if Reverend Father [Abbot Dunne] still wants you here."

In front of the abbot's door we waited in semidarkness for one of the two signs—"Please Wait" and "Come In"—to light up. Nothing. So we walked down the corridor to another room. Inside, a young monk sat before what was possibly the first typewriter ever made. He looked up, smiled, waved, and took a slip of paper from Dom Vital. The latter told me to hand over to the monk my valuables, and I did—wallet, Parker fountain pen, and Elgin wristwatch. Then he typed two pieces of paper: One was a receipt for my things, and the other was a waiver of claims for compensation regarding the work I might do at the abbey. I signed the latter and followed Dom Vital to the tailor shop, where an old brother measured me for my novice robe. He simply glanced at me, wrote down a few figures, and waved us out. And I never even bought suits off the rack, I recalled!

In the novitiate that evening, Dom Vital lectured on Trappist life as one of the highest vocations in the Catholic Church. I was already convinced of that, or else I would not have come to Gethsemani. I agreed with Odilo that young men and women are led to Trappist abbeys only by a special providence. What I could not understand was why God would bring them to the cloister and then dump on them so many miseries. Take, for instance, my "guardian angel," the novice assigned to help me as a newcomer. I liked Frater Henry as soon as Dom Vital introduced him to me. When Henry wasn't teaching me the Trappist sign language or the usages, he was kneeling in the novitiate chapel, reciting the Psalms. I marveled at such a pastime since, in those days, Trappists recited the Divine Office, Office of the Blessed Virgin, and Office of the Dead—all composed principally of psalms. Then, one day, the good-natured fellow went out of his mind. The entire morning of the day he was sent home, he sat in a corner of the scriptorium, smiling at his shoes.

Whereas Henry was "spaced out" in a rather benign way, another fine novice, recently admitted to the novitiate despite having undergone a nervous breakdown a year before, went crazy one night in the dormitory. He threw clothes, mattresses, blankets, pillow, even a holy water font out the window. Later, Dom Vital told us the boy had tried too hard. He had been frightened by St. Bernard's saying, "He who does not go forward in the religious life, goes backward."

And there was another amiable novice—from Australia. He began complaining of stomach pains. The infirmarian tried everything—special diet, paregoric, baking soda—but could not relieve the symptoms. So, the abbot put the novice in St. Joseph's Infirmary in Louisville. After several weeks of treatment, the physicians had not helped him a bit. So a psychiatrist was called in. Analysis revealed that the boy hated monastic life but was too ashamed to admit it. As soon as the abbot told him his place was in the world outside the cloister, he got well.

The most pleasant novice I knew toppled over one day in the woodshed while pounding a steel wedge into a log with a heavy maul. Our local physician, Dr. Green, checked him over and found nothing wrong. So the novice tried splitting logs again and fell over, unconscious. For some reason, the infirmarian had the novice examined by a visiting dentist. For another reason I never understood, the dentist pulled out every tooth in the novice's head. After a few days' rest and a pep talk from the infirmarian, the novice returned to the woodshed, split one log, and fainted. Alarmed, the abbot sent him to St. Joseph's Infirmary, where x-rays showed a slipped disk. Without waiting for the false teeth promised by the dentist or the blessing of the abbot, the novice packed his bags and fled.

There were so many other novices who left Gethsemani. Our only Negro novice quit after a few weeks because, as he told one of his superiors, "Man, I have to talk to somebody, and I can't go to confession every day." A Jesuit priest got leave to attend his father's funeral, but never came back. One easygoing fellow turned in his garb without any excuses, except that he got bored. Two little fellows from New England developed a "special friendship" and were asked to go. One novice, so preoccupied with contemplation that he took a hour to hoe a single bean plant, was dismissed, having been judged—ironically—unfit for the contemplative life. Others, caught wearing colored argyle socks, listening to contraband radios, or making excursions outside the enclosure, also got sacked.

Each morning as I arose from my straw mattress, I wondered if I too would get sick—or worse, bored—with Trappist life. But as the days went by, I never felt more robust; learning the rules and following the religious exercises kept away boredom. I experienced no pangs of homesickness and, what was truly remarkable, I never once craved a cigarette. I really felt that the Lord had me in mind when he said, "Many are called but few are chosen."

---

[1] Havelock Ellis, in introduction to J. K. Huysmans, *Against the Grain*. Dover Publications, 1969, p. xxvi.

6

Merton the Jester

I met Thomas Merton one evening in February 1948, in the refectory, the monks' dining room. I had been in the novitiate only a few weeks and therefore was still in my secular clothes. I had just eaten a frugal supper—"collation" is the monastic term—of barley brew, bread, and honey. I washed my knife and ceramic mug, then headed for the rear of the refectory with my dishes. As I poured the bread crumbs from my saucer into a large oil drum, almost brim-full of dirty water, it slipped from my hand, floated upon the surface for a moment, then plunged like a torpedoed boat to the bottom. St. Benedict, whose rule Trappists follow, had regarded the tools of the monastery on a par with the sacred vessels used at mass, so I had to recover that saucer. Before I could take off my Brooks Brothers coat, a young monk came from behind me, rolled up the sleeve of his cowl, and shoved his bare arm into the water. He fished around for the saucer, frowning terribly, while I just stood there, too astonished even to cheer him on. Eventually he pulled the saucer out of the water, bits of food clinging to the hairs of his arm, and smiled at me. The gallant retriever was Merton.

From that day onward, Merton and I exchanged smiles whenever we met, although we never saluted each other with a bow of the head, since novices and monks were forbidden by the usages to communicate formally. Also, I watched him every day in the refectory; until he began to take his meals with the infirmed monks in an adjoining room, he sat just opposite me. He was a dependable source of entertainment which, considering his reputation for being a mystic, seemed strange.

During the noon meals, while most of the monks at his table bent over their bowls of soup, their heads buried in their hoods, Merton sat upright on the end of his long spine with his hood pushed back behind his ears. As the weekly *lector mensae* (reader at table) stumbled over some passage, failed to stop at a period, or

Merton in work clothes.

used the wrong inflection, Merton, grinning broadly, engaged another monk, sitting a few places down from me, in Trappist dactylology. Many of his signs, made with hands moving as fast as fan blades, were digital portmanteaux, not found in the manual and therefore forbidden. One I recall was a combination of "soup," "fish," and "all." It meant *superficial.* He also frequently made a legitimate sign that, from the circumstances, could be interpreted as a *double entendre*, and must have shocked the new postulants who were still unfamiliar with it. The sign consists of showing the fist with palm turned upward and with only the middle finger extended. In Trappestese it means "president of the work" or "boss." Most Americans recognize it as an obscenity.

One morning during Lent, Merton entered the refectory, filled a tin cup with steaming barley brew from an aluminum kettle at the rear of the room and carried it to his place, taking sips from it on the way. Merton placed his cup on the table, turned toward the crucifix hanging in the middle of the far wall above the abbot's place, and said a prayer. Then he sat down and opened his napkin that lay folded partly upon the table and partly over his ceramic mug. There should have been two slices of bread under the napkin, but that morning the baker must have skipped Merton. That frequently happened whenever the former ran out of bread and had to go to the bakery for more. He would return and resume his distribution at the wrong place, not taking the trouble to check under all the napkins.

The monk next to Merton was also eating that morning but, with his hood over his eyes and his nose well into his mug, he failed to notice Merton's distress. According to the usages, he should have checked to see if his neighbor had bread and, if not, told the baker about it. On the other hand, the usages also prescribed that should a monk lack anything at table, he had no right to help himself. Dom Vital, in explaining this item, said that should a monk be really sick, he would eat in the refectory of the infirmed. Therefore, the monk deprived of regular fare should be healthy enough to endure hunger and should thank Jesus for the opportunity to offer up the inconvenience for the conversion of Russia.

But Merton was not in a magnanimous mood that morning, it seemed. When he unfolded his napkin, he gave it a loud snap. Yet, under the scrutiny of the novices sitting opposite him, he did not elbow his neighbor or go to the bakery himself. He just sat there, sipping his hot brew very slowly. I thought he was merely savoring the stuff. But really, from what followed, he must have been working on a plan. When the monk finished, he arranged his napkin and slipped a half piece of bread under it, a customary act of temperance. After the monk had left, Merton put down his cup and, feigning to straighten out his neighbor's napkin, surreptitiously extracted the bread and ate it.

When it came to doing without food, Merton was not up to it, even if this meant a delay in the conversion of Russia. But he seemed to delight in doing public penances. The usages prescribed that, should a monk spill more than a spoonful of liquid at dinner, his partner was to summon the *servitor mensae* (servant of the table) by rapping upon the table with the handle of a knife. This procedure created such a din that it attracted the attention of everyone in the refectory. As soon as the servant had mopped up, the klutz who spilled soup had to go before the abbot's place and prostrate himself.

That section of the floor was well trafficked, especially by brothers coming to dinner from the barns and pastures. On the day Merton spilled his soup it had been snowing, and the floor in front of the abbot's table was a pool of tracked-in slush. After the rapping and cleaning up, Merton blew the servant a kiss (the Trappist sign for thanks) and happily made his way to the place of prostration. The abbot, seeing the condition of the floor, smiled at Merton and waved him away. But too late. Merton belly flopped into the ooze with all the eagerness of a pig diving into a mud hole. That evening he appeared in the refectory for collation, looking very smug, and wearing a spanking-clean white cowl. The rest of the monks had worn theirs for months without a washing, and Merton stood out from them like a newly bandaged "sore thumb."

In choir, Merton usually behaved himself. However, once during vespers, as we were chanting an antiphone from the Canticle of Canticles that goes, "Comedi favum cum melle meo ("I ate the honeycomb with my honey"), Merton looked over at me and signed, "Me too." I almost laughed aloud, thinking of Merton the mystic having dinner with his "honey." But one morning he broke up the choir without any intention of being funny. During the hymn for matins, he leaned against the back of his choir stall, half asleep it appeared, reciting by heart. Once he came to and touched the floor with his knuckles. He must have garbled a few words and, in conformity to the usages, made a "little satisfaction." That caused him no embarrassment since, at 2:30 a.m., many monks made such mistakes.

However, on that particular occasion, Merton was the invitator, the monk whose duty, among others, is to lead the choir in the recitation of the *Venite, Adoremus Domino*. He was to recite one verse of that psalm, stop until the choir had repeated it, and then go on to the next. It is not a long prayer, and most of the monks recited it by heart while the church remained in total darkness. Merton had a fine memory and liked to show it off. That morning he decided to give it a try. He was doing well until the monk in front of him attempted to make a little satisfaction in the dark and hit his head against a choir seat on the way to the floor. There ensued a loud clunk and a moan: "Oh-h-h." Merton broke off his recitation and began to giggle. He quickly resumed it but gave out a verse that the choir absolutely refused to repeat. Merton knew he was in trouble. He switched on a light, grabbed his breviary (which contained the text of the prayer), and began to page it frantically. Holy cards flew out of it like flushed quail. Then Father Edward, the chief cantor, took up where Merton left off and finished the prayer. Merton was obliged to make a "big satisfaction," which the usages demand for a notable disturbance during a religious service. He left his stall, walked down the aisle and, arriving at the foot of the presbytery, prostrated himself upon the floor. For about thirty seconds he remained "under the lamp," a spot so called because, sixty years before, a sanctuary lamp had hung above it. After the abbot had recalled him by slamming a gavel against a choir desk, Merton returned to his stall, passing by his fellow monks, some scowling, some smiling, some winking.

Doing public penance for spilling soup in the refectory, Merton enjoyed. But failure of his mental powers in front of the entire community caused him real embarrassment. Most of his blunders in church, it seemed, resulted from a lack of preparation. Merton did not like to be bothered with rubrics while he was praying, and what he did not like he paid little attention to. Consequently, Merton subjected himself to many humiliations as assistant master of ceremonies, an office that required a thorough knowledge of the mechanics involved in a solemn pontifical mass (which the abbot, though not a bishop, had the privilege of offering on certain occasions). Merton's first job as leader of men in ritual, delineated in a manual of about two hundred pages of tricky Latin, was to direct a dozen or more ministers on Candlemas Day, the feast of the Presentation. On that morning, all the ministers lined up in the sacristy with Merton in the lead. As the procession moved toward the center of the church, there was Merton in a starched alb that flounced out like a hoop skirt, reaching only to his ankles. As he mounted the presbytery step, he tripped over the ends of his cincture, which should have been tucked in at his waist. This distraction must have caused him to forget that he was to pause there until all the ministers had exited the sacristy. Instead he forged ahead, went up the steps of the altar, and turned to find himself quite alone. The brothers who bore the candles and the processional cross knew their functions and did not budge until Merton, obviously annoyed, waved them on like a cop directing traffic. When at last most of the ministers had found their places in the presbytery, the abbot bowed his head toward Merton who, instead of removing the mitre, politely bowed back. At that, Father John, the master of ceremonies, a tall, ascetic, and irascible monk, grabbed the mitre from the abbot's head and slapped it into Merton's hands.

As the mass progressed, Merton frequently disappeared behind one of the massive pillars that surrounds the presbytery. From where I stood in choir I could see his arms and hands paging through a book, presumably the manual on rubrics. Every now and then he darted out of his cover to assert his authority on one of the ministers. Once he gave directions to the subdeacon who, it seemed, disagreed and waved him back. Merton responded with a few of his prestidigital signs, hunched his shoulders, and retreated behind the pillar, not to appear again until the mass ended. On the way back to the sacristy, he walked beside the crossbearer so as not to lose him. Halfway there, however, Father John came up from the rear and, looking at Merton, pointed to the choir. Merton returned to his stall like a baseball pitcher going off the field after walking six batters in a row.

During the flu epidemic of March 1949, I lost sight of Merton for three days. He was among the 75 percent of the community that lay semidelerious in the infirmary and even in the cold dormitories. But on the eighteenth, the weather turned warm, whippoorwills sang in the gardens, frogs croaked in the duck pond, and our bull serenaded his bovine harem during the moonlit night. The next morning, on the feast of St. Joseph, Merton showed up in chapter room.

After Father Odilo, by then the prior, invested another postulant and me with the novice's garb (in lieu of Abbot Dunne who was sick), Father Alphonsus (called "Apollinarius" in *The Sign of Jonas*) gave the sermon. Merton sat with his eyes closed, chewing the penicillin gum issued to all the monks by the infirmarian. Except for an occasional heroic sneeze, he remained as aloof from the mortals about him as the Olympian Zeus, not even wincing at the grammatical errors or platitudes of the preacher. I suspected that the infirmarian, Father Gerard, had pronounced him well enough to attend chapter that morning and Merton resented being there. However, when Alphonsus began to compute the year of Abraham's birth, starting with the creation of the world as 1 B.C., Merton's face and bald head lost their pallor. In fact, they turned crimson. He bounced up and down in his seat counting his fingers in mockery of the preacher's calculations. After chapter was over, I saw Merton in the cloister, joking with another monk, in sign language, about the sermon. But that evening in chapter, during the reading before compline, Merton was absent. Otherwise he would have witnessed Father Berchmans—old in years but puerile in mind—enter a few minutes after the reading had begun, his face covered with the grayish-white paste Trappists use to embalm their dead.

It was several days before I saw Merton again. In the meantime both of us had unfortunate experiences with motor vehicles. Mine occurred while working with another novice, Frater Bartholemew, a fat little fellow ever ready for mischief. Dom Vital had assigned us the task of building rose trellises. The first thing we had to do was get a load of two-by-fours from the monastic lumberyard. We went to the garage for the loan of a tractor and cart. There, Bartholemew ingratiated himself with the brother in charge by complimenting him (in sign language, of course) on his well-ordered tool bench, shiny hydraulic lift, and even on his new haircut. We were supposed to have a note from the cellarer (monastic foreman), permitting us to borrow a vehicle. But because getting such permission was unlikely since neither one of us was a designated driver, Bartholemew decided to trust in providence.

When the brother backed an immense John Deere out of the garage, Bartholemew signed to me, "Up-drive." I replied, "I-doubtful." Seeing my diffidence, the brother interrupted to demonstrate how the many gears and pedals worked. Meanwhile, Bartholemew hitched a flatbed trailer to the drawbar and got in. In a spirit of abandonment, I aimed the tractor at the lumberyard, where we collected the two-by-fours. From there we drove to the carpenter shop, where we made the trellises.

With Bartholemew and the trellises loaded onto the trailer, I directed the tractor down the road and turned into the steep and narrow path that ran up to the novitiate garden. Halfway to the top, I encountered another tractor driven by Father Joseph. He also was pulling a loaded trailer. He signed, "Go-down." Backing up would have been difficult for me even on a plane surface. But I shifted into reverse and slowly retreated, hoping the trailer would not swerve. However, it did. Just before it reached the bottom of the hill, one of its wheels found a rut and veered sharply to the left. Bartholemew yelled "*Oremus*" ("Let us pray") and jumped clear as a wheel of the John Deere ran over its own drawbar. Miraculously, it did not fall over. The next morning, during the chapter of faults, the monk who had been on the other tractor accused me of reckless driving. As a penance, the abbot had me kneel in the cloister near the church door.

As I approached the designated spot, Merton was already kneeling there and winking at everyone who passed him by. Although he shouldn't have, he pointed at me, squeezed his nose, mimicked turning a steering wheel. That meant, "You're a bad driver." Then he pointed to himself and raised two fingers: "Me-too." I later discovered that he had almost wrecked a Jeep. Later, in *The Sign of Jonas* he described his misadventure:

> Yesterday I took the Jeep and started off gaily all by myself in the woods. It had been raining heavily. All the roads were deep in mud. It took me some time to discover the front-wheel drive. I skidded into ditches and got out again. I got stuck in the mud, I bumped into trees and once, when I was on the main road, I stalled trying to get out of the front-wheel drive and ended up sideways in the middle of the road with a car coming down the hill straight at me.[2]

From that day on, I felt that a special bond of comradeship existed between us.

I witnessed many more incidents involving the playful Merton during my novitiate days. I'm sure he never intended to bungle things as invitator or master of ceremonies, to disedify the novices by stealing bread, wrecking Jeeps, or gaining weight during Lent. But he often played the clown deliberately, just to give pleasure. I regarded him and his antics kind of "external graces," that is, divine favors—not holy or even proper in themselves—granted to help me get through that trying period.

---

[2]Thomas Merton, *The Sign of Jonas*, Harcourt, Brace and Company 1953, p. 258.

7

The Death of an Abbot

Most religious orders keep their candidates in the novitiate for one year. But the Trappist order, consistently extreme, trains their novices twice as long. This custom was begun and retained by wise administrators, for during their second year, novices usually encounter the most problems. I certainly did. The excitement of having been time-warped back to the Middle Ages waned. I reflected, that I, a modern young man, was living in an anachronism, and I asked myself a dangerous question: What the hell am I doing here?

Moreover, I began to find many of the new novices rather disagreeable. In fact, I thought of them in terms of the hairshirt, that penitential garb worn next to the body that is a constant source of irritation.

One novice, Frater Wilbur, had the table manners of a Polyphemus. He used to encircle a bowl with one arm while spooning from it with the other. I imagined his thinking: *This is my soup; you don't get any.* My other companion at meals was Frater Gervaise. He was very fat when he entered the novitiate, but soon slimmed down from what I thought was fasting. I admired him until the infirmarian started serving him "relief," that is, food such as eggs, butter, even cake, which was not the regular fare. But I thought he was sick and did not begrudge him those extras. However, one day in Lent I was so hungry from fasting almost twenty-four hours and splitting logs that morning that I ate my soup, my portion of vegetables, and an entire loaf of bread. When I finished, he turned to me and signed, "Pig!" I was furious.

When Dom Vital fired Frater Bartholemew from his gardener's job, he appointed Frater Andrew, a former secular priest and pastor as his replacement. I was made Andrew's assistant, and my main job was to water the peonies. One morning, when it started to rain, I dropped my bucket and took shelter in the doorway leading to the novitiate grand parlor. Andrew, carrying my bucket, followed me in and demanded that I take it and get back to work. I felt like a pledge of a fraternity, ordered by a member to scrub the sidewalk with a toothbrush. I pointed to the rain and shook my head "no." He stomped back to the garden despite the downpour and, thereafter, treated me as though I were dead. The next morning, Dom Vital sent me with the regular work gang to the woodshed.

Frater Vincent never tried to antagonize me. However, his physical appearance and mannerisms made him as hateful as a swarm of sandflies. He loved to wear his hood and gaze at his reflection in the windows (we had no mirrors in those days). He reminded me of a child in a Christmas cowboy suit, enchanted with the vision of his ideal self. So enraptured was he in his role of Trappist—symbolized by the hood—that he often entered the church with it on. He would dip his hand into the holy water font, make a sign of the cross with sweeping movements of his arm, propel his tall willowy frame to the center of the main aisle, bow low toward the tabernacle for a full thirty seconds, straighten up, stand motionless for a while, pivot on his left heel, and march into the choir with heavy, slapping steps. When he arrived at the stall beside mine, his small head was still buried in his hood, revealing only those dull, gray eyes behind steel-rimmed glasses, fuzz-covered fat cheeks, tiny pug nose, and large lips.

But I suppose the worst hairshirt was Frater Felix, the ex-music teacher. He had been charged with training some of his fellow novices to sing a Palestrina mass for the Abbey's centennial celebration the coming summer. Ever since those Sunday masses at the college church of St. Louis University, I hated polyphony. However, all the novices had to audition, and I was one of those selected. Every morning work period that spring, I followed Felix's direction of *Ecce Sacerdos Magnus* and other Renaissance numbers. I could not completely hide my aversion to the enterprise, and Felix got angry. He had permission to speak during the practice sessions, and he threw at me such remarks as, "Hey, Buster! Keep the pitch."

Another significant change occurred during my second year in the novitiate: Abbot Dunne died. On a train bound for Conyers, Georgia, he suffered a fatal coronary. It was not his first heart attack. He had fainted from cardiac arrest one morning in the chapter room during a theological debate. Two monks had gotten into a verbal row over the interpretation of a dogma. One said that the Catholic Church was right in defining the doctrine of the Immaculate Conception; the other said that the Catholic Church should have let it alone, since it further estranges the Protestants.

The next day, the abbot's body lay upon the same black, wooden bier brought to America from France by pioneer Trappist monks of Mellarary Abbey a century before. During the night the novices had the duty of keeping vigil. Frater Wilbur and I took our turns at about eleven that night. While we recited the penitential psalms, a storm arose. A heavy draft blew out three of the six burning candles surrounding the bier, and lightning flashed through the art-glass windows, mottled the abbot's face—smeared over with white embalming paste—with purple, yellow, and green. As I recited the prayers, I thought about my first meeting with him in St. Louis, a year before. That initial good impression never changed; after my grandfather, I guess that I had liked no other man better than I did Abbot Dunne.

On the day of the funeral, Abbot Sortais, superior of Bellefontaine Abbey in France, arrived at Gethsemani. He had been at another Trappist abbey in Quebec and, upon hearing of Abbot Dunne's death, swung down south before returning to Europe. The next day, many more Trappist abbots arrived, as well as a considerable number of monks, priests, and laymen. After the funeral mass, the body of Abbot Dunne was carried by four brothers from the church to the graveyard just outside the chapter room. At a grave, dug early that morning, the procession stopped. Abbot Sortais, the celebrant, blessed the body and laid a cloth over the dead man's face. Then, two brothers lifted the abbot's body from the black bier and lowered it (without casket) to the bottom of the grave. As the body gradually disappeared beneath the bright-red clay shoveled in by the monks, I felt both sad and . . . excited.

And if I, a novice, was excited over the prospect of having a new abbot, the veteran monks must have been beside themselves. For all his seeming goodness, Abbot Dunne liked some monks more than others. And, from what I had been told, he was not above favoring his friends and ignoring his adversaries. I could imagine what it would be for talented, sensitive monks to be relegated to oblivion for decades, just because they didn't see eye-to-eye with him. With a new abbot, the underdogs would have an opportunity to compete with their companions for the few privileges obtainable in a Trappist abbey, such as being sent to Rome for advanced studies, or working at an interesting job, or holding an office of authority.

But the death of any monk involves something agreeable to his survivors. Just attending a funeral is a welcome break in the daily routine. It usually takes place during working hours and therefore has the effect of a holiday. Moreover, the death of a monk naturally creates vacancies. As one monk takes over the vacant job, vacant choir stall, or vacant seat in the refectory, other monks fill the vacancies the first monk has left—and so on. Some monks may find themselves in duller jobs and next to companions more irritating than before. However, as Washington Irving wrote, "Any change is a pleasure, even if it is for the worse."

After the funeral, the first vacant post to be filled was that of abbot. Even though we novices had no vote, we enjoyed speculating among ourselves about who the new abbot would be. He could be any monk from any Trappist house in the world, so long as he had made solemn profession. However, customarily, only priests are chosen as abbots.

Some of the novices favored Father Raymond, a former Jesuit priest, professor of rhetoric, and star halfback at Boston College. As a monk, he wrote books, sang beautifully, preached interesting sermons, and observed the usages. I had seen him run down a row of corn swinging a machete, the muscles of his short, powerful arms bulging like melons and his handsome face as red as fire.

Old Father George was also popular. For many years he had been subprior (third in command) of the abbey. One of his jobs was to awaken monks who slept during services. I had seen him shuffle down the aisles of the choir in his clumsy, homemade shoes, nudge a nodding monk with his fist, and flash under his nose a sign that read, "God sees you." He had brought with him from France, about forty years before, the old-world attitude toward Trappist life: devotional, austere, funereal. To George, loving God meant setting a suicide pace at work, chanting the loudest in choir, and fasting like a desert father. He held the record for over a quarter of a century of regular attendance at monastic services. But at the time, George was very old and living in the infirmary.

Some novices wanted none of Raymond or George; they preferred a mild-mannered monk for an abbot. Their choice was Father Gerard, the infirmarian. He was about fifty, diabetic, paternal, and undistinguished except for his catlike gait, continuous smile, and inevitable response—"Splendid, my dear"—to any news short of calamitous. Those of us who had spent some time in the infirmary under Gerard's care learned his brand of religiosity. He was a fan of St. Teresa of Lisieux, otherwise known as "The Little Flower." Although the saint's teachings seemed orthodox, Gerard's interpretation of them suggested a kind of spiritual passivity. At least, I thought so. His idea of penance was a joyful acceptance of physical weakness, a dull mind, and abulia. He was a good monk, but I wanted someone more dynamic as an abbot.

Another champion of several novices was Father Urban. He reminded me of a recently hatched bird: bald, round shouldered, pale, and cadaverously thin. From behind his steel-rimmed glasses, he looked down his long, aquiline nose through slits of light-gray eyes as if searching for something smaller than himself to devour. However, he was the confessor of many novices, and they appreciated his counsel.

As a joke, I campaigned for Father Peter as our next abbot. Actually, before his mind began to wander and his lungs to disintegrate from tuberculosis, he had been a fine theologian. He stood next to Raymond in choir, eyes closed and jaws moving up and down, from side to side, as if chewing a piece of tough meat. Whenever he failed to turn the pages of his psalter (shared with the monks on either side of him) or to intone a hymn, Raymond would jab him in the ribs. Afterward, Peter would bow in gratitude like a Chinese merchant. But usually he didn't come to choir and, during the conventual masses, he sat in the benches reserved for the sick, bewhiskered and spitting from time to time into a cold-cream jar. His regular job was tending the turkeys, and he would lead them from one pecking ground to another while reading a red, leather-bound copy of *The Ascent to Mt. Carmel*, the most mystical of mystical works by St. John of the Cross. One day two brothers in a jeep sneaked up behind Peter and his flock and gave a blast on the horn. The turkeys went berserk. Three crashed into Peter, several flew over the enclosure wall, and the rest scattered in all directions. I never saw them again, and Peter opened a repair shop for typewriters and watches. He never became abbot.

The monks elected James Fox, the current abbot of Holy Ghost Abbey in Conyers, Georgia. That abbey had been founded only four or five years earlier by monks from Gethsemani with Fox at their head. According to Dom Vital, Fox was not a "manure saint" but an ascetic who habitually skipped frustulum (breakfast) and despised flowers. He certainly looked ascetic: thin body, hollow cheeks, and teeth yellow with decay. I had been reading *The Sayings of the Fathers*, those maxims on the penitential life as practiced in the deserts of Scete and Nitria during the fourth century *anno Domini*. Those old Catholic hermits had become my heroes, and I wanted a spiritual guide to help me emulate them. Abbot Fox promised to fulfill my need. So, while Dom Vital and others prepared themselves for the worst, I expected the best.

8

The Ascetical Ideal

A few months after the installation of its new superior, Gethsemani began to experience some important changes. The monks at that time bellowed a cacaphony comparable to that heard in a schoolyard at recess. While in Paris on business, Abbot Fox engaged a music teacher. Monsieur Lefevre was a man of great vitality, testified to by his eleven children and the frenetic manner in which he conducted his classes. On the evening of his debut, he struck a tuning fork on his knee, held it upright on a table for reverberation, and tra-la-laed his tongue against his only two front teeth: "Do-ray-me-fa-so-la-ti-do. Repeat!"

Amused by the professor's manner, the monks just smiled and shook their heads. He went through his routine again and, at the sweep of his arm, about twenty of them mumbled, "Do-ray." He bounced around the chapter room on his crepe-soled shoes, striking the tuning fork, sometimes on the table, sometimes on the floor, smiling painfully. Eventually, the monks got through one complete solfeggio, and the professor said, "You have lost zee peech."

The next morning, in the chapter room, Abbot Fox announced that there would be two chant sessions each day until the monks showed progress. However, people can't be forced to sing well, and the community, as a whole, didn't. After a month, the professor held only one session a day, and he began working with those monks whose voices he had tested and approved. Five scholas, composed of six monks each, were formed and placed at strategic positions in the choir, thereby violating the traditional placement according to seniority. This was resented by the older monks. Moreover, they were told to keep quiet!

Merton was chosen to lead one of the scholas during the conventual mass, and for a week he competed with the other leaders to become the new cantor. Eventually, the honor was given to Father Anastasius, the abbey's chief welder, who, despite his own gravelly voice, managed to keep the choir on key. From then onward, Merton joined the older monks both in ignoring the directions of the cantor and his schola and in drowning them out with loud singing. His motto seemed to be: If you can't join 'em, beat 'em.

Lefevre returned to France in defeat. But Abbot Fox went to France again and returned with another singing master, a Benedictine, called Dom Barron. Barron, like Lefevre, had no patience with the older monks. He too left without transforming the choir. So, Fox went to France again. This time he brought back Dom Desrochettes, another Benedictine, a tactful man who knew how to ingratiate himself with the community. He seemed to hit upon the quintessence of choral singing: good diction. He selected a few monks and shaped their voices into the mellowest instruments of Gregorian chant anywhere. Without forming scholas, or annoying the community by insisting on practice sessions, or bothering to change the cantors, he relied upon a few good singers to influence the choir unobtrusively by simply pronouncing every Latin syllable in the Italian manner. Although Merton was not among those monks individually coached by Desrochettes, he was delighted with the effects they produced.

Merton on railroad car. The note says, "The old man is turned loose and can travel. He's out to see the world. What progress in the last thirty years! But his mode of travel is still the same."

After Desrochettes left Gethsemani, the regular cantors tried to carry on his instructions but lacked both his pleasant demeanor and the talent of his protégés. Merton must have resented receiving chant lessons from those whose voices, and certainly whose pronunciation of Italian, were inferior to his. Every time the community met in the chapter room for a singing lesson, Merton closed his eyes and sat motionless as a bronze Buddha. But one morning the cantor had us practice singing an antiphone that contained the word *Gaudeamus*. He had been especially concerned with the pronunciation of the endings of Latin verbs in the first person plural. We sang, trilling the *r*'s and broadening the *a*'s down to *Gaudeamus*. Then he broke in, saying, "Watch out for the *mus* (sounded as "moose"). Suddenly Merton snapped out of his doze, rolled back in his seat, lifted an imaginary big-game rifle, and blasted away, onomatopoetically, at the spectre quadruped. The roar of laughter that followed—one brother told me afterward—could be heard as far as the guest house. Abbot Fox, who really had a sense of humor, was so far bent over in his throne trying to control a paroxysm of giggling, that he nearly fell out of it. The cantors never brought up diction in their chant sessions again, and even during mass, whenever the celebrant sang a *mus*, monks would smile.

However, the singing at Gethsemani did improve and, with it, my attitude toward Trappist life. And that same year, 1949, Abbot Fox produced another change that directly affected us novices. He made Frater Louis (Merton) lecturer of spiritual orientation. Several events occasioned this appointment. First of all, he had become famous as a mystic and writer of mysticism.

It all started even before Merton entered Gethsemani. He had been attracted to the supernatural while still a child. Like his favorite poet, William Blake, he claimed to have had a mystical experience at the age of four. At least he adored the gaslight fixture in his mother's kitchen. Also, while a tourist in Rome, young Merton sensed the presence of his dead father while in a hotel room. His account of it came to my mind years later when I read of a similar phenomenon in Agee's *A Death in the Family*. Again in his Manhattan apartment on a Sunday morning—before he actually became a Catholic—he felt an urge to go to mass. That led directly to his conversion to the Catholic Church.

He entered Gethsemani attracted to Catholic mysticism. He

believed the abbey would give him the silence and solitude conducive to contemplative prayer. However, he soon discovered that even though Trappists rarely verbalize, they "talk" plenty with their hands and—at least during the forties—have very little solitude. Nevertheless, he never lost the image of himself as secluded on some rugged crag or pathless peak, "absorbed" in contemplation. In fact, he spent most of his monastic career trying to become a hermit.

But being a mystic wasn't enough for him. He wanted people to know about it. A Trappist friend told me that, on the very day Merton entered the novitiate, he dumped a pile of manuscripts on the desk of Father Robert, the master of novices before Dom Vital got the job. "When you have time," he said, "look these over, will you, Father?" The old monk must have been shocked since, in those days, young men and women did not enter the Trappist order to pursue literary careers.

Nevertheless, Merton, while still a novice, began translating books from French into English and even writing his own. Most of his early works, however, were hagiographical pap, such as *Exile Ends in Glory* and *What Are These Wounds? Cistercian Contemplatives* and *The Waters of Siloe* (histories of Cistercian-Trappists) were better, but not momentous. But in 1944, three years after entering Gethsemani, he completed an enormous manuscript, entitled *The Seven Storey Mountain*. It included most of the material later published in *The Secular Journal of Thomas Merton*, a rather stout volume in itself. Although opposed by the Trappist censors because of the book's frank "confessions" and bad grammar, it was accepted in 1947 by Harcourt Brace.

After a slow start, sales of the book picked up. Catholics and non-Catholics viewed *The Seven Storey Mountain* as a statement about their disenchantment with the post-World War II civilization. They were still horrified by the Nazi atrocities, disillusioned in their hopes for a permanent peace, and afraid of annihilation by the H-bomb. They were looking for a metaphysical solution for their imbroglio, and Merton seemed to have one. He depicted himself as a fun-loving, hard-drinking, world-traveling, keen-witted young man who sympathized with the underprivileged, hated violence, and aspired to sanctity behind the grim walls of a Trappist abbey.

Of course, even a famous mystic might not have gotten the job as lecturer in spiritual orientation without becoming a priest. And he almost forfeited his right to that honor. He told Abbot Fox that he wanted to leave Gethsemani and join the Carthusians. He thought that he could become ordained and then hop a boat for France. He didn't realize that a religious superior can propose his subject for ordination only if the candidate intends to serve, in some way, in the diocese of the ordaining bishop. Abbot Fox made Merton swear to stay put before admitting him to holy orders. I always thought it ironical for Abbot Fox to appoint someone to guide novices in the Trappist religious life who wanted desperately to leave the Trappist order. However, Merton was ordained in 1949 and began his lectures.

At the time Abbot Dunne died, my old friend Father Odilo was the prior (first in commands after the abbot). But with the new administration he got fired, and Father Anthony, the professor of theology, took his place. Also Dom Vital quit his post as novice master, and the infirmarian, Father Gerard, took over. But before we got used to that arrangement, Abbot Fox sent Father Anthony and thirty other monks and novices to found a new Trappist house in Moncks Corner, South Carolina, on a 3000-acre tract donated by Clare Boothe Luce. With Anthony gone, Gerard became prior and Father Urban moved into the novitiate as master.

Consequently, we novices had to make several adjustments in spiritual practices. I was just getting used to Dom Vital's manure spirituality. It involved, mainly, obeying superiors without question and accepting the annoyances concomittant with community life. As for prayers, those recited or sung in choir were considered simply a matter of duty. For personal consolation, Dom Vital and the old Trappists made the stations of the cross and said the rosary. One favorite devotion at Gethsemani among the lay brothers was visiting the different altars in the church, such as Our Lady of Victory's, St. Joseph's, St. Bernard's, and others.

With Father Gerard, obedience and suffering were likened, not to manure, but to the thorns on rosebushes. In the teaching of his patron, St. Teresa, sanctity could be reached by those who walked in her "way of spiritual childhood." According to Gerard, St. Teresa advocated trying to enjoy the good things of this life and thanking God for them. But she also accepted disagreeable things with equal gratitude. For example, she would not deny herself an orange, which she loved, yet she would eat the rhubarb, which she loathed. I had to admit that St. Teresa's spirituality was admirable, but it seemed too passive—even sissified—for many of us.

I could never quite define Father Urban's spiritual formula. It was neither manure nor rose petals, but more like the desert fathers' doctrine of penance. Urban praised the fathers' vigils, fastings, self-scourgings, and arduous labor. He also exalted the practices of the first monks of La Grande Trappe, who, following the example of their abbot, Armand de Rancé, kept human skulls in their cells, meditated in their cemetery over an empty grave, and inscribed on their cloister walls such axioms as *Memento mori; Frère, il faut morir*; and *Cette nuit, peut-être*. But Urban's pitch for aceticism was not effective. He was so puny that he had to eat better food than the rest of us, rarely went out to work in very cold or hot weather, and slept until three o'clock in the morning instead of rolling out at two.

Nevertheless, many of us novices liked the examples of the desert fathers and monks of La Grande Trappe and began to emulate them. The most difficult practice for me was fasting. I began in earnest during Lent that spring and, for weeks, all I could think of was food. During matins and lauds, I dreamed of breakfast: pork sausages wrapped in slices of French toast, and fresh strawberries in cream. In the evening, after a day of hard work and no supper, I lay upon my straw couch ravished by hunger. I believe that if Jane Russell had appeared with a twinkle in her eye, I would have sent her down to New Haven for a hamburger.

Although I doubt that either the desert fathers or De Rancé's monks took cold baths for penance, I decided to take up that practice. Of course, I had no choice if I wanted to bathe anytime other than Saturday afternoon, from four o'clock to six. That's when the hot water heater for the single shower in the novitiate was turned on. Moreover, unless I got off early from afternoon work, I never found the shower open. So I regularly filled a two-gallon pail with cold water and took it to my cubicle in the dormitory. I sat upon my couch and pulled down my robe and undershirt down to my waist. Then I washed my face, arms, and chest. Then I dried those parts, rinsed them in the same water and, on cold days, put my robe and shirt on again. That done, I removed my shoes, socks, underpants, and hiked up the skirt of my robe. There were days in winter when I said a prayer before I stepped into that bucket of almost freezing water. I was afraid my heart would stop beating. With my skin turning blue and my teeth clacking like a maraca, I washed from hips to toes, rinsed, dried myself, put on my clothes, and dived under a blanket until I stopped shivering. Afterward, I took the bucket back to the grand parlor, where I washed my face with fresh water. I never let the water filled with suds from our homemade soap touch my eyes, for it would burn them out of their sockets.

But those cold baths had little effect on my libido. Just after taking one, I often went into the church to pray. As soon as I looked at the stained-glass window depicting Our Lady squirting milk from her breast into the mouth of St. Bernard kneeling below her, I felt like Paolo in the presence of Francesca. That disappointed me, since I wanted to reach a level of chastity that excludes even a desire for sex, such as some of the desert fathers had described.

In his orientation lectures, Merton usually began with a note on Cistercian spirituality, that is, the doctrines of medieval Cistercians, such as St. Bernard of Clairvaux. The stress was on manual labor, a simple liturgy, and mysticism. He disparaged the penitential spirit of the Trappists-Cistercians of the seventeenth century. He absolved us all from reading spiritual books from that era, such as *Holy Abandonment, The Sinner's Guide*, and the works of Father Faber and Alphonso Roderigues. They were the favorites of Dom Vital. But Merton said that these authors knew little about mysticism and thought that Transforming Union was an organization of electricians.

Although Merton scoffed at the old Trappist ideals, he often spoke enthusiastically about their spiritual progenitors, the desert fathers. He described them as simple, devout men, disappointed that the Roman persecutions had ended and, with them, their chances of martyrdom. But he never praised their asceticism. Rather, he criticized some for being perversely comfortable in their outrageous practices, such as fasting the entire period of Lent or living perched upon stone pillars or reciting the Book of Deuteronomy while sitting on a sand dune under the hot sun. He said they did not, as St. Paul advised, render to God a "reasonable service." He was right, of course. However, we soon learned that the very word *penance* affected him the way garlic does a vampire. His predilection for the desert fathers was based on their eccentric behavior and their love of solitude.

Merton's spiritual orientation lectures were gratefully attended by us novices. However, after a few months, a rivalry arose between Urban and Merton and the lectures stopped. I didn't care, since my two years were up and I would make my simple profession; that is, I would vow to stay for three years.

9

Abbot Fox's Business

Despite Abbot Fox's reputation as an ascetic, after a year as superior at Gethsemani, he introduced some changes that suggested a mellowing, even a softening, on his part. One of the first I can recall was his expensive dental work. He had his decaying yellow teeth ground down to thin slivers and then capped. It was a professional job and must have cost a great deal of money. The rest of us had our teeth worked on by Trappist brothers whom visiting dentists had trained to be dental technicians. I remember Brother Claude, the carpenter, polishing a chip on one of my teeth and, inadvertantly, grinding it down to half of its original thickness. After noting his error, he grinned and told me to "offer it up."

With his Hollywood dental work, Fox introduced the cult of smiling in the abbey. Not that we hadn't smiled until he came. But he promulgated smiling with a kind of obsession. After speaking to us, either individually or publically, he ended with the phrase "All for Jesus, through Mary, with a smile." He even had that motto made into a rubber stamp that he used in his correspondence. He seemed to think the saying was as artful as Hamlet's soliloquy. It didn't even make sense to me—at least, the "through Mary" part. But it caught on. Both those monks who sincerely liked the abbot and those who merely tried to cultivate him frequently used that salutation. Moreover, there arose a kind of obligation to smile whenever encountering another monk; otherwise, he would consider himself snubbed. Soon the abbey was divided into two factions—the smilers and the non-smilers. I never used the abbot's motto, but I felt obliged to smile at my companions. However, after several weeks of forcing grins, I became embarrassed. For a while, I tried to avoid meeting anyone in circumstances that required an exchange of greetings.

Abbot Fox began a publicity campaign, using Gethsemani's centenary to put the abbey in the limelight. He recruited Merton—then famous for his *Seven Storey Mountain*—to help. Merton was an especially good choice since he had just been ordained a priest and had fallen into a kind of "blue funk." He didn't enjoy praying anymore and wanted a lot of activity to keep his mind off the problem. With the abbot's blessing, Merton began working on a picture book about the founding of Gethsemani in 1848 and its evolution to the present. Merton called it the *Magnificat*, a word that means—in Latin—"he magnifies" and comes from the prayer "The Lord magnifies my soul." And on the day of the celebration, Merton was everywhere in St. Mary's Field—just outside the enclosure walls—chatting with reporters, posing for photographs, and directing the technicians from Fox Movietone.

Soon after, postulants began coming to the abbey in greater numbers than before. Since many potential lay brothers were as young as sixteen, Fox wisely did not require them to grow beards as the Trappist usages prescribed. Soon, many of the older brothers asked for the same privilege and, the day after they got it, many strange faces—uncommonly pale from the upper lip to the throat, where the sun never reached—appeared in the cloister. However, some of those who shaved rediscovered the scars and weak chins long concealed by their whiskers and, as a result, grew another crop.

The abbot also replaced the old, rusting, handmade tin cups with professionally manufactured aluminum mugs. In addition, he bought new aluminum bowls to match. The old ones must have been around for thirty years or more and were half stripped of their enamel. One olive-green bowl was about half the size of the others. I don't know how or why it was added to the collection, but it became an object of dread. I had seen monks sneak into the refectory just before dinner to check their places for that bowl. If one of them got it he would exchange it for his neighbor's. I found the small bowl at my place once, but the soup was in it, not the regular portion.

We also received some modern clothes: factory-made shoes with arch supports, socks that actually clung to the ankles, and, for work, denim blue jeans and shirts. The abbot decreed that each monk shave his own whiskers instead of having it done for him by designated monk barbers. Such an innovation revolutionized monastic grooming. It required that each monk have his own mirror and razor. Glass cabinets were set up in the grand parlors for dispensing razor blades, shaving brushes, and lathering soap. Monks could receive, as presents from their relatives, talcum powder, styptic pencils, and even cologne.

What is more, the abbot provided that the monthly haircuts be given by novices and monks with aptitude for the job. However, no skill was needed by the barbers of the novitiate; they had merely to run the electric clippers over the heads of their clients. The worst they could do was remove the eyebrows and eyelashes as well as the hair. But the monks required an expert barber, capable of trimming the monastic crown evenly. All but one inept barber was deposed, and that one was old Father William, who refused to be retired despite his palsied hands. In fact, he was still cutting hair when I became a monk, a year later. Even the least vainglorious tried to avoid Father William, who more often than not cut the crown so that it resembled a horseshoe leaning against a peg. Whenever he finished one victim, the monks sitting around the grand parlor waiting their turns would disappear until one of their companions would walk in, inadvertantly, and be nabbed by old William. Eventually, the abbot got rid of him, and the monks could look forward to hair cutting rather than dread it.

Abbot Fox had gastritis—maybe even an ulcer—and therefore gave much consideration to our food. After taking office and tasting our entrees, he removed Brother Fabian from the kitchen. The latter's dishes produced enough gas in monastic colons to lift a balloon. In winter, when only one meal a day was served, Fabian filled those old enameled bowls with potatoes and some other vegetable. Everybody could eat his food in the winter. But in summer, knowing that the monks would have a supper, he often experimented with the noon meals. His most remarkable failure, as far as I am concerned, was his celery, tomato, and macaroni casserole. The skins boiled off the tomatoes and rolled up into rubbery, red cylinders. And the boiled celery seemed to gather at the top of my chest and refuse to be swallowed or thrown up. As for Fabian's soup—it was abominable both winter and summer. It consisted of the leftovers from the monks' dinner the day before, and even bits of eggs, pancakes, French toast, and what have you from the guests' dining room. Desserts, except on special occasions, were either stewed plums or rhubarb. And we couldn't fill up on bread. Fabian was also the baker and, though his loaves tasted all right, they caused the stomach to sour.

Fox demoted Fabian to pot washer and appointed, as cook, Brother Adam, a former steward in the U. S. Navy. Adam gave us Irish potatoes every day—roasted, mashed, fried, even scalloped. He must have liked canned fruit, for we had canned fruit cocktail, pineapple chunks, and peaches-in-syrup even during growing seasons. In summer, for the evening meal, he served several kinds of cheese—including the Port du Salut that we manufactured—with plenty of mustard and ketchup. During the afternoon meals, Adam had his helpers go around with big aluminum buckets dishing out "seconds" to those wanted them. That was a scandal to the old-timers.

The postulants continued to enter the abbey and, as early as 1950, nearly three hundred bustled through the cloisters. They were former technicians, businessmen, engineers, and physicians who wanted nothing more for their services than sanctifying grace. Fox, a practical Yankee with a business degree from Harvard, capitalized on the situation. He set his monks to growing more crops and producing such items as ham, sausage, bacon, cheese, bread, fruitcake, and honey. From the sales of these goods, the royalties on Merton's books, and the many donations to the most famous abbey in America—even in the world, perhaps—the abbot could state (and actually did once) with pride that Gethsemani was worth about fifteen million dollars.

There is an adage I learned somewhere—perhaps at the abbey—that goes, "If you can make money, you must make money." Certainly the abbot did. He began to advertise Gethsemani's products in national magazines, such as *Gourmet* and *The Saturday Evening Post*. Orders poured in like water over the Hoover Dam. Soon more monks were needed to process the orders, manufacture more products, and ship them out. Eventually our monastic entrepreneurs developed a line of Christmas gift packages, enclosed in nifty wooden boxes and forwarded to any address in the world. The bigger the operation became, the more monks were needed. During the Christmas "rush" period, we had to work overtime and often missed vespers. And despite our large numbers, the abbot, at times, had to hire people living nearby.

Those of us who had been at Gethsemani before its industrial revolution began missed working outdoors, especially in the autumn when we harvested corn, pumpkins, and sweet potatoes. I enjoyed, most of all, those winter afternoons when we put on our hoods and, with an ax in one hand and a rosary in the other, marched single file from the novitiate through the tin gate near the mill and out to the fields and woods. Often, while we walked in silence, the snow drifted down and landed upon our eyes and cheeks. When we stopped at our work site, we would wipe our faces with an end of our scapulars, make the sign of the cross, and then choose a tree to fell or trim. Soon all the monks and novices would be working, and the entire hillside would echo the dull sounds of one ax after another slamming against tree trunks.

Even the frenetic log-splitting in and around the woodshed delighted me. We held undeclared contests to see what team of novices could split the most logs and pile the kindling the highest. I could work up a sweat wielding a maul, even on a cold day which, later, as I knelt in church before dinner, produced a glow of well-being and an enormous appetite.

But such work was not efficient, especially that involving long excursions into the woods. Besides, we stopped burning wood in the great boiler that heated—always ineffectively on very cold days—the church and scriptoriums. (I shall never forget the day when a huge dump truck unloaded a mound of shiny black coal just outside the boiler room near the refectory. To me, it seemed an appropriate monument to Gethsemani's industrialization.) Most of us were sent to the cheese factory or smoke house or shipping room where, the abbot often declared, "We would earn our bread and (ha ha) margarine."

As our business increased, so did our need to expand the facilities that housed our business. A new cow "palace" was built outside the enclosure near St. Stephen's Field where grazed the finest Guernseys our ever-augmenting coffer of tax-free money could buy. Each day those cows were milked by stainless-steel machines to Guy Lombardo's recordings of "the sweetest music this side of heaven." In the adjoining fields, blue-ribboned sows and boars fed on corn gathered, shucked, and stripped by an International Harvester as big as a silo.

One day in August, the old cow barn within the enclosure—recently converted into a loft—caught on fire. The roof and the old timbered beams went up like paper. But the rock-and-concrete foundation remained intact. The next day, we cleaned up the debris and, within a month, turned it into a slaughterhouse and office complex.

Several other buildings arose that year—all dedicated to industry. We worked hard to finish them, hoping soon to re-establish the old monastic atmosphere we once knew and to re-affirm the promise inscribed above the entrance of the gate house: *Pax Intrantibus*. But that peace never came—at least for all the years I was to spend at Gethsemani. Even the woods were noisy. Instead of chopping down trees for lumber, the monks were using chain saws. And instead of using horses and wagons to haul the logs back to the mill, they used trucks and tractors. Moreover, the D-4 Traxcavator, bought to dig out the foundation of the cheese lockers, dominated the compound. It rolled out to the ancient stable or "horse barn," where Merton played hermit during the free intervals, and knocked it down. Then it tore tons of red clay out of a bean patch to make a foundation for a *new* stable, which almost immediately became an extension of the garage, since we had sold the horses. One day I heard it rumbling through the woods, vying with the roar of the chain saws for dominance, on its way to a site destined to be dug out for a lake.

While the hills trembled from the noise of machinery, the brothers went to work on the dormitories with sledge hammers. Their objective was to tear out all the wooden floors and cubicles or cells and replace them with others made of, respectively, concrete and steel. Although I deplored the noise involved, I was not altogether opposed to that particular project. Those dormitories were chambers of torture. In the winter, since they were not heated, the holy water actually froze in the little fonts hanging on the wall of each monk's cell. And in the summer, hordes of mosquitoes swarmed through the screenless windows. From June to August, we awoke at 2:00 a.m. feeling as if we had lain all night on a bed of nails. The sweat had soaked our cotton undershirts and robes (we retired fully clothed except for shoes and belt) and caused our backs to break out in prickly heat. During any season the dormitory was noisy. The cells, open at the tops and bottoms like voting booths, were no buffers against sound. When I became a monk and was given a cell in the main dormitory, I had Father Stephen as a neighbor. He was old and simple-minded and brought food to snack on before retiring. I could hear him, every night, crinkling what I guessed were cellophane candy wrappers, or munching apples or pears. Also many nights, I lay awake listening to Father Joseph's prodigious snoring. It would start slowly and softly, mount to a crescendo, and end with a nasal explosion that sounded like the bark of a seal. Then I would get up and go to the "convenience," across from which Father Alphonsus lay in his couch groaning, "Jesus, oh Jesus." On the way back, I would reach into Father Joseph's cell, give his mattress a good shaking, and then run lest he awaken suddenly and catch me.

Four years later, the new dormitory was finished. Screens, ceiling fans, terrazzo floors—comparative luxury. But by that time, the abbey had acquired many more noisy vehicles, such as a ten-ton truck used to cart the steel girders and a genuine crane to hoist them and the concrete ladles up to the second and third floors. Moreover, the inconvenience to the community had been remarkable. Many of us had slept in the guest house, three or four to a room. And about fifty lay brothers had slept out of doors, in the *prieuré* separating the four cloisters. During the winter, these "Eskimos" suffered considerably, although one of them in his report—read by the abbot during chapter one morning—assured the rest of us that he and his fellows were doing all right. The brother wrote, "Many are cold, but few are frozen."

For a while, there was talk of buying an airplane. The Trappist abbeys in Iowa and Massachusetts each had one. So when we saw a helicopter land in St. Mary's Field one morning, we weren't too surprised. However, it had only been hired—to lower the new bells into the new belfry of the church.

Many of us, especially Merton, complained to the abbot about the roaring of bulldozers, the pounding of jackhammers, and the hooting of horns that gave the abbey the atmosphere of a shipyard. At one time, the abbot might have listened. There was a time, according to Merton, that the abbot would never have permitted such materialism. That was before he became the abbot of Holy Ghost Abbey and when he had serious thoughts about becoming a Carthusian. He figured, when he was elected abbot, that God had given him a sign that his vocation was not to solitude. He told me this, and I believe he meant it. But Fox believed lots of things that I held as incredible. For example, he maintained that anything—conducive to a person's spiritual life, of course—asked of Christ while praying at the thirteenth station of the cross, would be granted. No question about it. He also taught that, although the abbot (meaning him) may be fallible, the monk in obeying the abbot is infallible. The implication is pretty clear: Anything the abbot says is the will of God. Although obedience is only one of the five vows a Trappist monk takes, according to Fox he need only obey and he can forget about the other four. And Fox used this axiom to vindicate all the changes he had made at Gethsemani. Despite spiritual books lauding silence and solitude as means to contemplation, when I protested the noise at Gethsemani, he said something much like, "Accept it. It will make you a saint."

Even if we doubted that Fox's tenet that the will of the superior is always, for the subject, the will of God, he seemed so certain of its truth that we had diffidence in acting on our own contrary convictions. Perhaps he was simply a good salesman or actor. There was a story about the abbot in confrontation with his own superior, the abbot general. The latter imposed some restriction upon Fox and pointed out that such was the will of God, to which Fox remarked, "It must be his will, for it surely isn't mine." Perhaps he said it as a joke. But my grandfather always said that at least half a joke is the simple truth.

I have always thought it marvelous that the Pope and all superiors in the church are completely dependent on the faith of their subjects. Consequently, should we agree to renounce the faith, we could destroy one of the most powerful institutions on earth with impunity. We could stay away from mass and the sacraments, refuse to fund our parishes and missions, and even tell the Pope to jump into the lake. The church has no sanctions except in the spiritual order.

On the other hand, should our faith be strong, we, paradoxically, obey the tenets and leaders of the faith with fear and trembling. To the faithful, there are no sanctions to disobedience more formidable than the spiritual, since they diminish or destroy our hope for eternal life. Even though the gospel and most spiritual guides emphasize love—love of the Church, its hierarchy, its teachings—the element of fear is ever present. We still do not know God, the object of our faith, and loving the unknown God is much harder than fearing him.

And we Trappist monks of noisy, materialistic Gethsemani had faith. Consequently, we did what the abbot told us to do. But we began to speculate upon the reason behind the abbot's bent for making money, erecting new buildings, and gaining publicity. It certainly wasn't the trait of a man seeking anonymity; rather it suggested ambition. But where could Fox, as superior of the largest, richest, and most famous abbey in the world, ascend to? Within the Trappist order, there was only one post higher than his own—abbot-general. But that was invariably held by a Frenchman.

We noticed that Fox rarely missed opportunities to attend ecclesiastical gatherings, such as ordinations and church dedications, where dignitaries as high as cardinals usually were present. Also he often invited members of the hierarchy to the abbey. He could show them an institution on the rise. Although Gethsemani was already growing when he became its abbot, and the many talented monks under him were also responsible for its success, he was the chief administrator. And if administrative ability is an essential quality looked for in a prospective bishop, Fox could point to material improvement; to the many retreatants the abbey hosted each year; and to the testimonies of celebrities, such as Fulton Sheen, Evelyn Waugh, Robert Speight, Jacques Maritain, and others, concerning his monks' piety.

At least on one occasion, Fox joked publically (in chapter) about hobnobbing with prelates and the possibility of—to use his phrase—"someone touching me on the shoulder," which meant recommending him to Rome for a bishopric. But Fox never became a bishop. Moreover, during the sixties, the wheels of industry at Gethsemani slowed down by order of the Trappist abbot-general. Both novices and monks were leaving because of the tension that existed then between the abbot and his coterie, on one hand, and those monks who wanted to return to the old simple form of life, on the other. Eventually, Fox resigned his post and did the supremely ironical—he became a hermit. I had left Gethsemani by that time, but I have heard that many monks considered Fox's retirement the best change he had made during his sixteen-year reign.

10

In St. Joseph's Infirmary

On the morning of March 21, 1950, in the chapter room, Abbot Fox put on me a black scapular and hood, a shiny tan leather belt, and a white woolen cowl. Afterward, in the refectory, Brother Adam served me a platter of fried eggs smothered in catsup, the traditional reward at Gethsemani for making profession as a Trappist monk. Just before the conventual mass, Father Walter, the assistant master of novices, cut my hair. It was the most perfect monastic crown I had ever seen.

I felt great having become a monk. I knew my mother and Sister Veronica were proud of me, although sad that I had isolated myself from them. I wondered if Father Finn had learned about my new lifestyle. He would probably say something like, "I always felt he had something good in him." (Even though I don't even recall what Finn looked like, I still cannot think of him without feeling displeasure. The situation is different in regard to Fox; I remember quite well what he looks like. But in both cases only feelings are involved, not a deliberate ill-will.) I figured that Maggie had heard of the event, since our mothers were friends. And the day before I made profession, I speculated on what I would do if Maggie wrote, begging me to come to her. It had been over three years since I saw her, but the memory of her still sent a shiver up my spine. And in the midst of my sentimentalizing, I had a most rational reflection concerning celibacy apropos of the spiritual life: Having a good woman wouldn't hurt it.

But what really let me free to take vows was the fact that they would last only three years. By that time, I would have finished my studies prior to ordination. Then if I still wanted to be a monk and a priest, I could leave and join the order both Merton and I esteemed so highly—the Carthusian. Quitting Gethsemani in such circumstances would not imply that I couldn't make it as a Trappist. Even should I make solemn (perpetual) vows to remain a Trappist, canon law would still permit me to pass from my order to another, so long as the transfer involved embracing a form of religious life that offers the best means to contemplation. The best means is, of course, solitude. And, in the Roman Catholic Church, only two religious institutions provide it: the Carthusians and the Camaldolese. I thought I had drawn up a rather wise plan.

Even though Merton no longer gave spiritual orientation to the novices, he still taught mystical theology to the young monks. As one of them, I could talk to Merton even outside of class. His office, where he both wrote and met with monk-students was in the "vault," so-called because it had a steel double door. In that room, containing the abbey's collection of rare books, we often discussed mutual interests and attitudes. We loved literature and loathed machinery (except typewriters), and we had an attraction to solitude. Neither of us cared much for "manure spirituality," the Trappist order, or Abbot Fox. We often quoted, derisively, Fox's favorite adage concerning the proper disposition of a Trappist: "To die unknown, unheralded, and unsung." Yet Merton was already one of the most popular, praised, and publicized religious writers in America, and I wouldn't have minded a little fame myself.

Talking to Merton in private was always a pleasure. He seemed to concentrate so hard on what you were saying that you wondered if he were counting the syllables. And I often marked the difference in speaking with him and the abbot who, apparently, heard only half of what I said, so intent was he in couching a response to what he thought I was going to say. Moreover, Merton always encouraged me to choose a topic and helped me stick to it until we exhausted it. After that, Merton started squirming in his chair, a sure sign the tête-à-tête was over.

Some of our longest conversations took place at St. Joseph's Infirmary in Louisville. Merton had already been there for two weeks when, on the vigil of St. Martin's Day, while I was trimming a felled hickory tree during a rare excursion to the woods, my ax slid off the trunk and slashed through my left shoe and into my big toe. Our infirmarian sewed up the gash but, dissatisfied with the results, arranged for me to see a doctor at St. Joseph's.

When I got there, a nursing sister (a nun who was a nurse) took me to a private room. After about ten minutes, a gorgeous, blond nurse, the image of Carol Lombard, entered. She smiled, said "Hi," pushed a thermometer into my mouth, and began to take my pulse. My heart started to race, and the more I tried to control it, the faster it went. I could see a slight grin form on her cupid-bow mouth. I was as helpless as cobra caught in the mesmerizing rhythm of a snake charmer's fluting. However, she soon departed leaving me with only the scent of her perfume and diffidence in my allegiance to celibacy.

Several hours went by without my seeing anyone. Back in the abbey, I would have welcomed such an interval in a private room. Maybe that was the trouble: I had privacy but not solitude, a state related to the presence of God rather than the mere absence of people. It always occurred, as far as I was concerned, between the ringing of bells—a duration in which consciousness of time does not exist, like that experienced (or *not* experienced) while attending a good drama or concert. At the abbey, solitude was also an escape from work or the choir or lectures. But in that hospital room, solitude was not a natural end of an activity; and in it I was out of place, out of rhythm with life. I was isolated and, what was downright humiliating, I was lonely.

Lucky for me, that evening Merton came to my room. He was looking rather defeated: face swollen from an operation on his nose, another enamel facing off his denture, badly in need of a shave, and the circle of hair on the back of his partially bald head standing up like a mantilla. He had been working all day in the chaplain's office writing a book called *Bread in the Wilderness*. I teased him about having nothing else on his mind but wilderness and bread, and that led to his attempt to justify our having dinner together, based on the fact that the desert fathers occasionally visited one another to enjoy a few leaves of lettuce and some edifying conversation. As he started on his salad, he began a parody of one of *Cassian's Conferences*. I cannot remember his exact words but they were something like these:

> After abating the hunger spasms menacing their emaciated bodies, the monk Geraldus, recently come to the desert of Scete from Sodom and Gomorrah, bespoke himself to the old man Ludovicus:
>
> "Father, what shall I do?" Whereupon the latter slowly opened his eyes—first the left and, after a considerable interval, the right—and, after deliberating until morning, turned to the monk Geraldus and said, "Eat but one loaf a

day, sleep only three hours—standing up—and gird thy loins with barbed wire. And when temptations of lust come upon thee, contemplate yonder dung heap, which is thy brother."

I laughed and agreed that the dung heap did bear a family resemblance. Toward the end of the meal, one pork chop remained upon the platter and we both insisted that the other have it. Merton proposed that we debate the issue in the manner of the two monks featured in the *Vitae Patrum* who, unfamiliar with contention even after thirty years of living together, decided to experience that vice by arguing over the rights to a piece of tile. Merton and I had discussed the story so often that we knew it nearly by heart. Merton began:

"Brother Geraldus, I cannot rest from the curiosity taken hold of me concerning the pastime of arguing, so prevalent among the brethren in this desert. Therefore, let us contest the ownership of this single porkchop. I shall say it belongs to me; and, on the contrary, you shall avow that it is yours."

"As thou knowest full well, good brother, I have no skill in debate and it would please me for thee to have the porkchop. However, since thou art intent to wrangle, I shall attest that the viand is mine," I replied.

"Verily, it is my own, brother."

"Wouldst thou deprive me, scoundrel?"

"By my faith, no. Yet I shall eat the porkchop."

"Glutton, thief, liar! I claim the chop," said Merton and winked.

"Very well, brother. If thou sayest it is thine own and that I am a glutton, thief, and liar, surely thou art right. Take it with good grace and let us live in peace."

"Thus," said Merton by way of epilogue, "the two holy men settled their differences, fulfilling the injunction of the Apostle: 'Guard the bond of peace, preventing one another.'"

Then we both stabbed at the porkchop with our forks and Merton got it.

My toe began to heal after three days at the hospital. However, one afternoon while I was drinking a Budweiser one of the sisters gave me and reading the maxims of St. John of the Cross, my heart started to bounce around in my chest. After examining me, Dr. Roth said, "Fibrillation. You know you have a heart murmur?" I said I knew that. "You'll be here for a while," he said. It took three weeks of EKG tests before Roth thought of letting me go home. Consequently, I saw Merton at dinner very often.

One evening, we were interrupted by a commotion down the hall, just outside the doors of two other sick Trappists, Brother Leo and Frater Joachim. We stepped into the hall and saw Joachim, a middle-aged ex-captain of the United States army, lantern-jawed and stiff-spined, standing outside Leo's door and yelling "Obey! Obey!" Next to Joachim stood a sister wringing her hands and probably wishing that she had not appealed to "the Captain," as the monks referred to him, to persuade Leo to take his medicine. I doubt if Joachim gave a fig about Leo's health, but since he had given him an order, he expected Leo to obey it. But Leo—old, bearded, deaf, and probably mad—had not obeyed anyone for years. Whenever the abbot or cellarer even approached him, he would turn off his hearing aid, hiss at them through his teeth, and cross one arm over the other, signifying "useless." About thirty years before, he had learned the routine at Gethsemani, geared himself into it, and just followed the exercises mechanically. He was in charge of the wagons and horses all that time, and even when farming became mechanized, no one attempted to replace Leo's equipment with trucks or to give him another job. Not that he was fond of hauling logs or hay or vegetables; not that he was fond of horses. In fact, no one and nothing seemed to please Leo. He was in the hospital because one of his horses kicked him in the knee—probably, as Merton suggested, after Leo had kicked it.

How the infirmarian at the abbey got Leo into St. Joseph's, I cannot say. Certainly Leo volunteered no information. I cannot imagine him coming peacefully unless he had been sedated. And Leo disdained the sisters as much as he did the monks. He hissed, snarled, and growled when those ladies greeted him in the hallway, when they served him meals, and especially when they tried to give him a bath. Whenever he did smile, you expected him to follow it up with a declaration that he had just murdered your family. Yet, as boorish as Leo was, the sisters apparently loved him. He ate very little, rarely looked at anyone, let alone spoke, and spent nearly the entire day in the chapel, saying his rosary. To the sisters, I guess, Leo was the epitome of the Trappist, the long-awaited, extraordinary man of God. Moreover, even though Merton and I joked about Leo, I believe we rather admired him—at least, his contempt of socializing and material comforts. No one we knew fit our image of St. Jerome, St. Arsenius, or other desert fathers more than Leo.

As rude as Leo was, he never really offended people, once they knew what to expect from him. But Merton, for all his affability, could hurt. For example, on Thanksgiving Day, while we were having dinner together in Merton's room, two elderly nuns knocked on the door. They explained that they had the day off and had taken a bus across town to St. Joseph's, hoping to see Merton and receive his blessing. I expected him to say a few kind words, autograph their copies of his book *Seeds of Contemplation*, and send them away ecstatic. But when he opened the door, Merton declared that he was forbidden to have visitors and closed it again, abruptly.

Another conversation with Merton taught me his lack of courtesy. One morning he came into my room, leading by the arm a man about sixty, wearing thick-lensed glasses and hobbling along aided by a cane. While Merton attempted to introduce me, the man resumed his story about skiing at Mt. Moritz, indicating that he was not only blind and lame but hard of hearing as well. I don't know how he found Merton at St. Joseph's. His name was Sir Arnold Lund, recently awarded the K.B.E. (Knight of the British Empire) for promoting good relationships between England and Switzerland through his establishing skiing tournaments involving athletes of both countries. I could imagine his being knighted for training seeing-eye dogs or inventing a better hearing aid or performing some heroic deed that resulted in his lameness, but never for doing anything connected with skiing.

After about ten minutes of Sir Arnold's droning, Merton asked to be excused and left the room. Sir Arnold went on about people and events that I had no knowledge of or sympathy with. Certain that he could neither see nor hear me, I ate breakfast, brushed my teeth, and even recited matins and lauds of the divine office with only an occasional "Is that right?" and "How extraordinary!" and "Really?" Eventually Merton returned with Sir Arnold's chauffeur, and together they hoisted the old man out of his chair. Without interrupting his "monologue," he shook my hand and allowed himself to be led out of the room. I was not pleased with Merton that evening.

During the last conversation Merton and I had at St. Joseph's Infirmary, we were in my room again when the door opened and in walked a tall, handsome priest in a black overcoat and homburg, both covered with snow. Merton burst out laughing and led him to the bathroom where he shook the snow off his clothes into the bathtub. His name was Father Finnegan, I think, and had been a novice with Merton at Gethsemani before he left with the other pioneer monks to found a new abbey in Utah. He had just left the Trappist order with permission from Rome for the purpose of working with the lepers on Molokai. His idea was to transform the colony there into a kind of monastery and thereby give a spiritual dignity to what was a physical necessity. I could not imagine myself doing anything so heroic and felt moved by the young priest's generosity. Merton, however, said something like "Aren't the lepers miserable enough?" Throughout our conversation, Merton teased the priest about his wild schemes as if Merton hadn't a few himself. However, his always involved solitude and silence and the mystical. Yet when I eventually read *The Seven Storey Mountain*, I learned that Merton once thought about dedicating his life to helping the sick, downtrodden, and exiled at the Friendship House in Harlem. He chose, instead, a worthy profession but one directly oriented to his personal sanctification. And as I got to know him better, I realized that God, mankind, and nature seemed more attractive to him as objects of his personal contemplation than anything else. Later, in his books he referred to himself as a "bystander," a "marginal man" in society. Although he touched many people with his prose and poetry, few people ever really touched him.

On the day scheduled for our return to the abbey, the snow that had fallen the night before turned into ice. Father Osborne, the chaplain at St. Joseph's, offered to drive us to the train depot, and Merton telephoned the abbot to ask that he have a car meet us around 5:00 p.m. at the station in New Haven. During our conversation while going through Louisville, Merton was in high spirits. He remarked at the number of billboards and window signs advertising corn whiskey and concluded, facetiously of course, that Kentuckians regarded it as their supreme good against which everything else of value must bear an analogy.

Passing the stores downtown, he kept us laughing with remarks like, "Buy our shoes. They fit like whiskey." And, "Got sore muscles? Rub them with whiskey." And, "Go Delta to Aruba. Our planes fly on whiskey." He kept up this chatter until we said good-bye to Father Osborne and boarded the train. Then he lapsed into silence. I had a feeling that he was embarrassed by his own levity, remembering his reputation as a monk.

At New Haven, the son of a history professor of Georgetown University met us. He worked for room and board at the abbey and, though brilliant, had emotional problems. That morning, despite the ice and snow on the roads, he had not put chains on the tires. Merton remarked on this fact and told Tibor to drive carefully. After we got in and drove off, Merton signaled the end to conversation by closing his eyes and fingering the rosary he held. But Tibor seemed insensitive to Merton's silence and began to tell us about the wreck he almost had on the way to New Haven. I listened apprehensively as he removed one hand from the steering wheel to gesture. He was looking back at me when a yellow truck approached us, skidded, and went into a spin. I yelled and Tibor put on the brakes, but too quickly, and lost control. Like a pair of revolving doors, the truck and our car spun in unison, fenders to fenders, in a full circle, and then stopped. "Wow!" said Tibor and smiled. I looked over at Merton. His eyes were still closed, but his face was as white as the snowdrifts along the road. Tibor started the car again and, going about five miles an hour, brought us safely to the abbey. As we walked through the garden in front of the guest house, a retreatant tried to strike up a conversation. But Merton walked right by him.

11

Among the Have-nots

I really didn't need to spend so long at St. Joseph's Infirmary. But, in those days, the sisters who ran it never charged monks and nuns, and even coaxed them to stay as long as they liked. Sister Helen Elizabeth, the supervisor of the floor I was on, even plied me with ice cream and beer. Yet, back at the abbey I had no trouble readjusting. Not that I had come to appreciate Trappist life more, but I liked it better than that of a hospital patient.

Merton, on the other hand, had fallen in love with Gethsemani again. As in his earlier writings, his lectures to the monk-students seemed premised on the assumption that the abbey was one of the few happy places left in the world. He said that the human race could do worse than unite into one huge congregation of nuns and monks. He even declared that all men and women are called—not to contemplative orders but, at least, to contemplation. And he suggested that, of all the religious institutes a man or woman might enter, the Trappist order is the best. His reasoning was like this: Since the ordinary way of life is fraught with obstacles to the spiritual life, a person should choose an extraordinary way to perfection, such as that offered by the Benedictines, Jesuits, Franciscans, and so on. However, the members of such orders do share with laymen and laywomen many ordinary things, such as full diets, street clothes, entertainments, vacations, and regular communication. Since the Trappists forgo even these everyday pleasures, theirs is the least ordinary way of life and, therefore, the most conducive to holiness. And almost every book, article, and poem Merton wrote in those days of his regained fervor was tantamount to his sending to humankind a postcard from Gethsemani inscribed with the words, "Having a wonderful time. Wish you were here."

But Merton presented his students—and his readers—with an idealistic picture of Gethsemani. Not all the monks shared in the euphoria that sprouted from *Seeds of Contemplation*, a book of reflections on contemplative experiences which, Merton said, might have been written by any of his confreres. I sat in chapter while that book was being read aloud to the assembly each evening for two weeks and, judging from the blank, and even embarrassed, looks on many of the monks' faces, I doubt that even a tenth understood what they heard. A few even made signs to Merton, facetiously begging him to levitate.

Perhaps the monks unintentionally confirmed Merton's rosy view of Trappist life. Most of the old ones had been trained in the "manure spiritually" of Dom Vital, which demanded not only acceptance of humiliations but even a joyful acceptance. In this doctrine, "long faces" reflected troubled consciences and despondency. Therefore, the monks kept stiff upper lips. Since they had been trained to welcome suffering as a means of expiating sins, even faces known to be contorted from physical pain received little sympathy. I had never complained to a superior of a toothache or back pain without his telling me to "offer it up." Of course, Abbot Fox's "All for Jesus,through Mary, with a smile" took manure spirituality to its apogee (or nadir). Although Merton acknowledged humiliations, obedience, and sheer boredom as a part of the Trappist ascesis, he never stressed them. Perhaps he presumed that any person who perseveres long enough to become a professioned Trappist monk will be sustained through the rough times by heavenly favors. I know that, right after his ordination, he took a certain pleasure in his dryness by reading himself or his situation into "The Dark Night of the Soul" and assuring himself that he was being "purged" before rising to a higher spiritual plane.

Whether or not Merton ever received mystical graces, I'm not sure. But I rather doubt he would have remained at Gethsemani—even with them—had he not been permitted to write and publish. And when, in 1949, he found consolation neither in praying nor in writing, I wonder if he would have stuck it out had not the abbot made him a teacher, an occupation he had always wanted.

But not all Trappist monks had Merton's gifts and privileges. It was only after leaving St. Joseph's that I began to realize what a burden a boring job is for a Trappist. Dr. Roth, my physician, sent word to the abbot that I should not do heavy work. Consequently, I ended up in the gate house filling orders for books, rosaries, holy cards, and other religious articles. I didn't particularly like the job, but, as a student, I worked there only two hours a day, four days a week.

But for Brother Isidore, my assistant, working in the shipping room was his temporal salvation. At the time he was over forty years old and had spent fifteen years at the abbey. He was less than five feet tall, his physical growth having been stunted by a congenital disease of the spine that had twisted his torso into an "S" and required him to wear a heavy metal brace from neck to hips. Not only did Nature give Isidore a misshapen body; she dulled his wits as well. He could count, accurately, the items of merchandise he packed for shipping and wrap a carton so artistically that you would think it done at Tiffany's. Yet he had little power of concentration. While pulling out books for packing, he often lost count and had to repeat the process several times until he got the correct number. Moreover, his judgment was poor. He often chose cartons far too large or too small for the space his merchandise demanded. Either he would have to change boxes or cut a large one down to the proper size, wasting much time. He was whimsical too. He loved to tie a certain kind of slipknot and often, in securing a carton, used enough twine to moor a yacht. And he had no sense of order. Instead of stacking the books and pamphlets, he left them strewn over the floor and counters. Now and then, Brother Alexander, Isidore's boss (but not mine since I was a choir monk), stormed into the shipping room and scolded the little fellow for his bad housekeeping. Isidore took the abuse with a smile, but when Alexander had left, he pantomimed blasting the post office and its master with a machine gun. I then realized that Isidore's cheery countenance served only to mask his anger and plead for acceptance.

As well he should have been, Isidore was terrified that he might offend someone able to take him out of the shipping room. For years he had been in charge of the chicken coop, which, during winter, was as cold as a meat locker. Consequently, from the end of autumn until the beginning of spring, Isidore suffered chills, fevers, and dizziness resulting from the disagreeable atmosphere. Each Sunday morning he took his miseries to the infirmary where the abbot and the infirmarian listened to the complaints of the sick monks. Whenever they saw him coming, Isidore said, they began to comment on how well he looked and what a fine job he was doing the chicken coop. He had neither the courage nor the rhetoric to challenge the judgments of such eminent authorities on health, so he simply asked for a new supply of aspirin—which he ate like peanuts even while working in the shipping room—and went on his way wearing a toboggan cap under his hood, a bathtowel (in lieu of a scarf) around his neck, and several cotton shirts under his robe. After getting his story—through signs, of course—I suggested that the next time he wanted a better job or more rest or tastier food, he should tell the abbot he had a bellyache. Fox, who had an ulcer, sympathized with anyone afflicted by stomach ailments.

Fortunately for Isidore, one summer the chickens died of some pestilence, and he went to the shipping room. He decorated the walls with crispy new holy cards, crystal-beaded rosaries, silver medals, gold crucifixes, and statues of the Infant of Prague. But the real object of Isidore's veneration was none of the holy people represented by the pious paraphernalia. Sitting in the middle of the room, like an ill-fashioned Buddha, was a pot-bellied iron stove that, during the winter months, he propitiated with so many contributions of coal that it glowed red. I was sure that, rather than let the temperature drop below seventy degrees, Isidore would have fed the iron deity every combustible item in the room. But for all the physical comfort Isidore enjoyed in his new job, he lived with the chilling fear that someday he might lose it.

Another member of Gethsemani's group of forgotten men was Father Lambert. Isidore used to seek out Lambert to bless the rosaries bought by visitors at the store (also operated by Brother Alexander) across the entrance way from the post office. Lambert was usually found in the library or the church even during work periods, since his trick knee that supported, precariously, 250 pounds of brittle bones and amorphous flesh incapacitated him for following the regular exercises. One day, for some reason, I got excused from choir during a conventual mass and sat it out with Lambert in the benches of the infirmed. Lambert was singing the mass and seemed to be enjoying himself. Suddenly we heard someone hissing from behind. It was Isidore. He stood just outside the church doors, in the cloister, with a coffee-bean rosary dangling from his fingers. Without interrupting his singing or even turning around, Lambert extended one arm backwards and made the sign of the cross. Whether or not the Annie Oakely shot of benediction "hit" the rosary, God only knows, but Lambert would not be denied one of his few moments of community living for a mere sacramental. Unlike Merton and me, who considered a legitimate excuse from the monastic routine a special grace, Lambert's misery was having been created a gregarious man and being forced into solitude.

After about a year in the shipping room, I was sent to work in the bookkeeping room on the first floor of the guest house. My boss was Father John, the same gangly, bald, old monk who had pushed, blocked, and twisted Merton during solemn high masses, while both functioned as masters of ceremonies. Like Isidore and Lambert, John was a smiler—at least while he was communicating. But John's smile put a person at ease about as much as Dracula's sneer. I always felt more comfortable with him when he assumed his dark and ominous but natural scowl. Not that John ever exhibited any vicious behavior. His pushing people around during religious rituals and slamming the door of his office and exaggerated grinning resulted from tension. Actually, during the free intervals, when John had nothing to do, he seemed quite relaxed.

The considerable difference in John's demeanor while at leisure and while on duty led me to believe that behind his forced smile was fear of or distaste for responsibility. Of course, being of the old Trappist school of unquestioned obedience, he accepted all assignments without a murmur. However, there was one task connected with his job that he could not manage: opening the mail. That was my obligation. Each afternoon Brother Alexander knocked on the door three times (John's highly imaginative secret signal). After I let him in and he dragged two mail sacks to my desk, John seemed to cringe. He would wait until I had slit open a few letters; read the contents; marked the passages referring to mass stipends, donations, or payment for merchandise; attached the checks with paper clips; and put them upon his desk. Then he would type up the information on a recording sheet marked at the top with the initials "J.M.J." (Jesus, Mary, Joseph). On days that I did not work, he managed to open the letters addressed to the abbey in general. However, he never touched those addressed to individual monks. I suppose he did not want to violate their privacy, although he knew the abbot had the right to censor all incoming mail, either personally or through a delegate. I often wondered what John would have done had he seen the photo contained in one letter to a novice. It depicted a chesty young woman in a bikini and was signed "Your *sister*, Jeannie." I passed it on, although I think the abbot might have torn it up. John never saw any photos or read any letters sent to monks as long as I worked with him in the bookkeeping room. In the winter of 1953, he came down with influenza and was sent to St. Joseph's Infirmary. After several weeks there, he returned to the abbey hollow-eyed, yellow-skinned, and shakey-kneed. He never resumed his responsibilities as master of ceremonies and bookkeeper, and he ceased to smile altogether.

That spring I took over the bookkeeping room with Father Leonard as my associate. Leonard often laughed, grimaced, sneered, but never really smiled. My hardest task was keeping him from reading the monks' letters, since he had a reputation around the cloisters as being an inveterate quidnunc. I could have gotten him out of there had I mentioned his curiosity to the prior, and I suppose I should have. However, I hoped that he would be given full range of the bookkeeping room and would leave me free for another job. He would have liked that too, since he had once been the president of a small bank. And every afternoon, before coming to work, the well-groomed executive spent about a half hour standing before two mirrors, applying hot towels, fragrant lotions, and talcum powder to his unprepossessing face. But just as his own brother Benny had fired him at the bank, so the abbot, eventually, took away Leonard's bookkeeping job.

Once in a while the abbot sent me to the cheese lockers to help Father Idesbald, an old Hollander. He knew before anyone else that loony Brother Gabriel had painted the church steeple yellow (and then repainted it silver by order of the abbot). He promulgated reports on how the fish in the abbey's lakes were biting (he angled with a safety pin at the end of a string), and he kept records on every "proclamation" (accusation made by one monk against another) during the chapters for the previous twenty years. However, for all his years at Gethsemani, he had not mastered the English language. Of course, he rarely spoke it, but he used most of his free time memorizing the English words he had written on slips of paper arranged on his desk in the scriptorium. He rarely reviewed them all in one interval. Usually something—such as Leonard's perfumed lotion—would irritate Idesbald's nasal passages and provoke a sneeze loud enough to rattle the windows. The slips of paper would fly everywhere and, by the time he collected them, the bell would ring for work or choir. As unproductive as Idesbald's hobbies were, he was the fastest cheese washer in the business. Although his work was mechanical and took place in a cold, damp locker, he loved it. In the cheese factory he was his own boss and, whenever I joined him, mine as well.

On Wednesday afternoons, the abbot decreed one morning in chapter, all monks would participate in the "common work." Usually that took place in the renovated cow barn that housed not only a slaughterhouse but a packaging plant. There, even the sick could stuff advertisements for cheese, ham, fruitcake, and so on, into envelopes. But now and then, by special request of the older monks, the abbot himself put on a blue denim work blouse and led us out to the woods. On one such occasion, I was teamed with Father Arnold, a dumpy, middle-aged man who spent his free intervals roaming the cloisters looking for someone to make signs with or sitting at his desk in the scriptorium translating a German translation of Mabillon's *Vie de Rancé* into English, unaware or unconcerned that the abbey had one or two English translations of the work in its library. Just as Idesbald's hobby was learning English, Arnold's was perfecting his German. On my first day in the monks' scriptorium, Arnold waved at me, pointed to himself, and placed one hand on his head with the forefinger sticking up. He was describing the spiked helmets worn by German soldiers during World War I. It was the unofficial, but commonly recognized, Trappist sign for "German."

Arnold's regular job was pressing the altar linens in the former laundry room with the aid (or hindrance) of old Brother Stanislaus. And anytime we wanted to hear a German monk swear (in whispers) at an Irish lay brother, we had only to walk in on them and wait until Arnold's helper shoved an altar cloth into the mangle the wrong way.

I experienced his wrath one Wednesday afternoon. For a while he sat down on a log and began gossiping in sign language, since no superior was around. I ignored him and began stacking logs with the feigned complacency of a Tom Sawyer whitewashing a fence. Arnold must have interpreted my fast pace and apparent satisfaction as a challenge. He could not bear for someone to outdo him. Toward the end of work, each of us had stacks of logs over five feet high, and all the wood had been gathered except a tree stump that must have weighed two hundred pounds. Arnold picked it up and hoisted part of it onto his stack, looking quite smug. Suddenly the log began to slip. With his one free hand he signed for help. At that very moment, the abbot, somewhere nearby, clapped his hands, ending the work. I signed to Arnold that it was time to go and walked away. He became furious, stomped the ground, and blurted, "You call that charity?" I laughed but quickly sobered up when he let the log drop, picked up his ax, and shook it at me. On the way home, he walked directly behind me, now and then kicking the heels of my shoes to spur me on, and sucking, audibly, on his ill-fitting dentures. He had nothing, not even an interesting job or hobby, to compensate for the tedium of Trappist life.

When the weather got warmer, Frater Joachim, who had been in the hospital with Merton, Leo, and me that winter, asked the abbot for a helper. He had just inherited seven hundred rose plants from his brother's estate and wanted to plant them in the monks' garden as soon as possible. Since it entailed no heavy work, I got the job. But I had no sooner got the roses planted when Joachim became ill again. There I was, the head of the garden and cemetery, out in the sunshine and fresh air, without anyone to bother me—but Father Stephen, the old monk who ate fruit and candy bars in his cell at night.

Each morning after mass and breakfast, Stephen put his blue-denim work blouse over his robe and slipped on a pair of galoshes. On rainy days he usually went to the tailor shop where he made church vestments out of the materials his sister sent him. He finished only one garment I know of: a fiddle-back chasuble about the size of a baseball umpire's chest protector, embellished with a picture of a white lamb carrying a white cross in its mouth. It looked like a whippet gnawing on a bone. On very cold mornings, Stephen joined the lay brothers in the warm cannery. Eventually, he was barred from the place because he ate almost as many tomatoes, peaches, and plums as he skinned.

But Stephen's favorite work—his passion—was gardening. As early as five o'clock in the morning, he could be seen in his blouse and galoshes, pushing his little wheelbarrow loaded with tools, dirt, and fertilizer toward one of his many plots of cannas, marigolds, and zinnias scattered within the enclosure. Stephen did not mind having to walk far to his work, but he deplored the fact that very few monks ever had the opportunity to see and admire his flower beds. Joachim had forbade him from even setting foot in the monks' garden during worktime, for Stephen liked to theorize on horticulture. But with Joachim gone, Stephen often dropped by to praise my efforts and propose a spot or two where he thought a flower might look well. I finally gave him a few square feet in my bailiwick to cultivate as he pleased. That spring we worked together in the afternoon in a kind of laissez-faire harmony, having agreed not to offer each other any advice or criticism. Only one thing about Stephen bothered me: He smiled too much.

I suspected that Stephen's grin indicated a touch of encroaching senility. One day my hunch was confirmed. By coincidence, both of us had appointments with the same doctor at the new hospital in Bardstown. On the morning we were to leave, Stephen made the driver and me wait for him while he wrapped a potted gladiola in tinfoil and watered it. Halfway to the hospital the water seeped through the foil and onto Stephen's lap, leaving a big, brown blotch on the front of his white robe. Luckily, his black scapular hid it when he stood up. At the hospital, while the doctor and I were talking, we happened to glance out a window to see Stephen digging around some bushes on the lawn with the fury of a forty-niner who had just struck a vein of gold. On the way home, Stephen directed the driver to a house on the outskirts of town. After we parked in front of it, Stephen picked up his gladiola and got out of the car. Standing on the front porch, he rang the doorbell, and waited. After quite a long time, a woman, wearing a pink bathrobe and a white towel on her head, obviously just out of the shower, opened the door. The driver nearly choked from laughing at the sight. The old elephant in his white robe, black scapular, and tan galoshes stood there eulogizing the beauty of the gladiola while the woman listened and rubbed her hair with the towel. At last she took the plant and closed the door. Stephen came down the steps, smiling like a little boy who had just sat upon Santa Claus's knee.

I cannot recall who told me the history of Stephen's monastic career—possibly he himself or Merton. When he came to Gethsemani, thirty years before, his superiors put him in the choir novitiate and later permitted him to study for holy orders. In those days, monks did not have to be very bright to become a priest, since they were not ordained to become pastors or missionaries or teachers. Even as late as the sixties, some monk-priests at Gethsemani had never administered any sacrament but the eucharist. Stephen was one of them. He had been ordained merely to earn mass stipends and to share the burden of singing the conventual masses. He got through his sacerdotal studies through the leniency of his instructors and by virtue of his prodigious memory. (He knew the entire psalter—150 psalms—by heart.) But Stephen had never been happy either as a priest or as a monk. In fact, he spent most of monastic life trying to get out of the abbey. He wrote hundreds of letters to bishops for their acceptance of him into their dioceses (a requirement for monk-priests to be dispensed from monastic vows), but they did not want him. Naturally, the bishops had to have recommendations from Stephen's superior before they could assign him to a parish. What could the superior say? Consequently, Stephen languished for decades in Gethsemani Abbey until he acquired the peace that comes with despair.

Merton's enthusiasm over Trappist life during this period derived, I believe, from his new attitude toward life in general. His health was certainly better. And, as I mentioned before, he had sublimated—as the psychiatrists say—his acedia. Moreover, his ability to write had returned. He had just finished *Bread in the Wilderness* while in the hospital. He was enjoying his lectures to the monk-students. He certainly was not among the underprivileged Trappists, such as Isidore, Lambert, John, Leonard, Arnold, and Idesbald—just to mention a few. He seemed to believe himself called to fulfill a mission at Gethsemani. He thought he had the knowledge, experience, and grace to revolutionize the spiritual life, first at the abbey and eventually throughout the world. A man with such hopes certainly was not leading a quiet life of desperation.

12

A Family Reunion

In March of 1953, Gethsemani had another flu epidemic. Of course, it had one about that time every year, but this time I was one of its victims. It needed no formal announcement. I knew it had arrived one morning about 2:00 a.m. when only thirty or so monks appeared in the church choir. I considered myself lucky that morning. But on the next, I could not get off my couch when the bell rang for matins.

As a result, the Lenten fast was canceled—a sane measure, to be sure, but only the healthy monks benefited. We sick ones couldn't eat anyway. By noon, our small infirmary was filled. So the infirmarian, Frater Eudes, got all the healthy monks and brothers to nurse those forced to stay in the cold dormitories. It was rather touching to see one part of the community helping the other half—bringing soup to each cubicle and carrying away bed-pans. I marveled at the number of bedpans we had in stock. They must have accumulated over the many years of flu epidemics.

For a few days, I remained in the dormitory. One night I heard a cry from some monk nearby: "O Lawd! O Lawd! Help me, Gaud!" I could tell by the New York City accent that it was Father Lawrence, the former assistant master of novices. He loved to mimic Groucho Marx and often went into his act while supervising the novices working in the workshed. As I lay there, I expected to hear, "This is the most ridiculous thing I ever hoid of." I rather liked Father Lawrence; no matter how cold it got in that woodshed, he stayed in good humor.

I was too weak to go to Lawrence, but within seconds I heard the prior and some other monks whispering quite audibly. One kept saying, "Take it easy. Take it easy." Another recited what I supposed was the formula for absolving sins. As I lay there on my straw mattress, alternately sweating and shivering, I hoped we would both die. All I thought of was relief from my misery. Later, when I recalled how I felt at the time, I realized that my death wish was as rational as it was emotional. After all, what did Lawrence and I have to look forward to by recovering? More epidemics in the winter and heat rash in the summer and consummate boredom all year round? We had no dependents, no close friends (at least, in the abbey), no property. If St. Teresa of Avila could complain, "I die because I do not die" while she was healthy, surely I could long for death while I was sick.

The next morning, Father Lawrence and I both left the dormitory. He was placed on a bier in the church; and I, because of my heart murmur, was given a private room in the infirmary. I never attended poor Lawrence's funeral. I just lay staring at the dirty, green walls of my room and listening to the sizzling of the old steel radiator. Once in a while, the assistant infirmarian, Brother Wilfred, entered, took my temperature, went "tsk, tsk," and left the room. I first encountered him the previous summer while we both worked in the refectory one Sunday morning. He had just entered the brothers' novitiate, having transferred from some other religious congregation—the Marists, I believe. He had thick gray hair, watery blue eyes, a chubby body, and a touch of lavender in his manner. At the time, he was applying a cube of margarine to the squeaking wheels of a cart he was pushing. I knew immediately that he was one of a kind.

Through Wilfred I learned that, so widespread was the epidemic, several guest rooms had been converted into an extension of the infirmary. I could see from my window the snow-covered pasture below the choir novitiate, and a sycamore tree, stripped of its bark, standing near the duck pond. It looked like the arm of a giant who had been buried alive.

After about a week, I began to get up for mass in the infirmary chapel. My old friend, Father Stephen, usually said the five o'clock mass. He often wore the chasuble depicting a lamb carrying a white cross in its mouth. Stephen, because of his weak ankles and bunioned feet, supported himself with one hand on the altar and paged the missal with the other, reading from it in a kind of whistling whisper. Brother Leo, his deaf acolyte, knelt at Stephen's side so that he could read the priest's lips. The rest of us either sat or knelt during the service, depending on how sick we were. The chapel was clean enough but, like the rest of the infirmary, it smelled of urine.

Being alone in my room was a pleasure. Nothing to do but

read and say the rosary. I finished one book called *The Sands of Tamanrasset* in one day. It was about the life of Père Charles de Foucauld, soldier, cartographer, Trappist monk, and founder of Les Petits Frères de Jesus. His example, however, did nothing to settle my mind about my own vocation. On the twenty-fifth of that month, I was scheduled to take my solemn vows as a Trappist monk or leave the order. De Foucauld's life seemed to suggest many alternatives, but I veered particularly toward solitude. However, I realized that if I didn't make solemn profession, and if I joined the Carthusians as I had planned, I would interrupt my studies. I would have to spend two more years in a novitiate—the Carthusian novitiate—and without any guarantee that I would like that order or that it would like me.

I enjoyed my studies very much: philosophy, theology, Latin, chant, church history, and canon law. It was not the subjects that fascinated me so much as my newly acquired ability to learn anything with ease. One day, in the library, I found a little book on memory training written in the early nineteenth century. The author based his system on the use of fixed ideas. With it I eventually became able to recall everything I heard in a class or read in a book. Even though I confessed that I did not have a photographic memory but simply a method of recall that anyone could master, my professors and classmates regarded me as a sort of genius.

It is not easy to leave a place where people admire you. It is even harder to leave an organization that not only enjoys respect among religious circles but even inspires awe. I realized that people tend to romanticize about Trappists, yet I could not help liking being thought of as heroic. Moreover, it did not occur to me that the many outward changes in my life might not indicate changes in my character. If it had, I might have despaired, having worked so hard to fit the image of a monk that both the order and the public demanded. Of course, there were times when, alone in the woods, I sang Cole Porter songs, and times when I clowned with other monks, and times when I imagined Maggie in my arms. But I interpreted these instances of failure as evidence that my transformation had not been completed. I had only to avoid such slipups and I would become perfect. I never really understood how ridiculous such a notion—that outward changes produce inward changes—was until many years later I saw a cartoon in

The New Yorker. It depicted two monks standing outside their abbey and looking down at a valley at sunset. One says to the other: "Strange. Twenty-four years later and I still think of this as the cocktail hour."

Another reason for staying at Gethsemani then was the fact that I was too weak to go anywhere. So I declared my intention to make solemn profession to the abbot, and he set the date—March 25, the Feast of the Annunciation. About five days before the big event, I went on retreat, an exercise that consisted in doing what I had been doing since I entered the infirmary: going to mass, reading spiritual books, and meditating. Ordinarily, an older monk-priest would have directed my activities, but the flu epidemic had changed that. Most of the old-timers were still sick. Father Odo, the most popular retreat master for monks, had the flu and lived in the infirmary. Moreover during his illness, he had become senile. He just walked around, wearing leather slippers, a woolen shirt, and a pair of the old-fashioned Trappist underpants, held up by suspenders.

On one of his visits, Merton gave me a copy of *Le Paradis Blanc* (The White Paradise) by Pierre van der Meer de Walcheren, a Dutch Benedictine monk who had a fascination for the Carthusians. It featured several of their monasteries (not abbeys, since their superiors are not abbots) and I especially liked Val Saint in Switzerland. There was a photo of the church covered with snow, some parts reflecting the sunlight and others draped in long, purple shadows.

Also there was a photo of La Grande Chartreuse near Grenoble, France. That's where Frater Alberic, a fellow Trappist, had entered just after he finished his third year as a monk of Gethsemani. Everyone thought he would fit right in at the abbey, and he became our bookkeeper after Leonard was fired. It seemed an appropriate job for him, since he had been a successful broker on Wall Street before joining the monks. But he never wanted to get mixed up in finance and commerce again. And I think his leaving Gethsemani especially embarrassed Abbot Fox, who admired Alberic for his talents and maturity.

I also read *The Cistercian Dictionary*—at least the section on the monastic vows. Most religious orders require their members to take three: chastity, poverty, and obedience. But Trappists must also vow conversion of manners (which I never fully understood) and stability in the same abbey in which they made profession. The latter bothered me, for I was certain that I did not want to end my days at Gethsemani. But I knew that I could still join the Carthusians, or even the Camaldolese, since the Church recognizes these orders as providing the most direct means to perfection: solitude. And there was a handy axiom I had learned in canon law: "No vow can impede a greater good." That settled my mind and, on the 25th of March, during a pontifical high mass, I vowed to remain a Trappist forever while fully intending to leave Gethsemani and the Trappist order within four years.

After the ceremonies, I went to the gate house where, in the visitors' room, my mother, Aunt Mary, and Uncle Frank awaited me. I was still rather weak from my bout with the flu, but Brother Alexander built a fire in the Franklin and I enjoyed sitting before it and chatting with my folks. Mother delivered all the messages from my friends in St. Louis. They wished me well, but most of them said they had hoped I would leave the abbey. Mary, the chemist at Scullin Steel, actually dropped by the house to introduce herself. According to Mother, when Mary learned I was going to stay at Gethsemani, she started to cry and said, "He was such a sweet boy." I just shrugged my shoulders after hearing that account. But I loved it. As for Maggie, she had sent no message, since she was in a hospital having her third child in three years.

It was the second year my aunt and uncle had accompanied Mother on her visit. They felt very comfortable at Gethsemani. Frank knew several brothers—Alexander, Matthias, Isidore—and loved the big evening meals, which he took with some retreatants and other visitors. Afterward, they walked and smoked in the guests' garden or had Father Francis, the guest master, take them to the monastic library. On the previous visit, Frank had read Merton's *The Waters of Siloe*, a history of the Trappist-Cistercian Order. Then about six-thirty, everyone went to the church for the Salve Regina service.

Mother and Aunt Mary said the highlight of their day was walking back to the women's guest house across the highway from the abbey after the Salve Regina. In the early spring, at that hour, the stars appear just as the sun begins to disappear behind the range of hills towards the west, and the only sound along the road flanked by sweetgum trees are the shrieks of skylarks diving and soaring above the church like Shelley's unbodied joys.

The next morning, Merton said mass for my family, and I served. He seemed to enjoy doing this favor for his students because he liked being paternal and, I think, because he got to wear the most lavish vestments in the abbey's wardrobe: the lace alb with crimson cuffs, the silk cincture with golden tassels, the crocheted amice, and a chasuble covered with more figures than a painting by Hieronymus Bosch.

That afternoon was warm and sunny. Earlier, Mother had gone shopping in Bardstown and made a picnic lunch. So we all piled into Uncle Frank's Thunderbird and drove up the road running through St. Stephen's Field, leading to the big lake where we planned to eat. On the way, we passed Herman Hennekamp, an ex-Trappist who, thirty years before, had become sick—with tuberculosis, I think—and was allowed to retire on the abbey's property. He lived alone in a dugout, except for a half-dozen goats and the mule he rode that afternoon. Merton, in one of his lectures, described Hennekamp as a Trappist whom God had drawn away from community life to solitude. But I never could think of Hennekamp as a hermit in the religious sense of the word. Whenever he saw a group of monks working, he hooted at them and clapped his hands, as if celebrating his escape from the thralldom of manual labor.

For the first time in weeks, I ate heartily. I stuffed myself with deviled eggs, potato salad, and apple pie. I even ate a ham sandwich and drank a bottle of Budweiser beer. Aunt Mary watched me with an expression that seemed to reflect her delight and astonishment. And when I refused the cigar Frank offered me, I noticed that she breathed a sign of relief. Mary had adopted the traditional view of how a Trappist should behave and wanted me to conform to it.

After three days, the visit was over. I had enjoyed it as much as my family did. Even though they had been at Gethsemani only a few times, I knew that the place had become a part of their lives. It was their conversation piece and a kind of permanent vacation spot. Frank talked to his workers about it during lunch at the shoe factory. And Mary showed slides of me and the abbey during her sodality meetings. Mother saw me as her "sacrifice" to the Almighty. When they drove off, I had another reason to be glad that I made solemn profession. We would have missed a good time had I left Gethsemani that year.

13

The Scholasticate

In April, Dom Louis Gonzage le Pennuin sat upon the abbatial throne in the chapter room. He was about forty and recently installed as abbot of Melleray Abbey in France, from which the founders of Gethsemani had come. His small, crepe-soled shoes barely reached the floor, and he shyly glanced at the monks as Abbot Fox, sitting before a table next to the throne, introduced his guest. The latter looked like a little boy having his picture taken on a pony and worried that he might fall off. On his first time in America, unable to understand English, only a few days as an abbot, he was obliged, in virtue of being the superior of Gethsemani's "motherhouse," to pass judgment upon the biggest, richest, and most renowned abbey in the world. But when, after a signal from Fox, Merton left his seat along the wall and went up to Pennuin, the little abbot smiled. Merton had spoken to him in French.

All during the week of the "visitation" (interviewing the monks with the intent of finding out abuses of the rules and of promoting enterprises), Merton stayed with Pennuin in a room of the guest house, interpreting, translating, and providing companionship. It was not unlikely that, over a private meal of broiled trout and a bottle of Pinot Noir, Merton convinced the Frenchman that Gethsemani needed a scholasticate and that he, Merton, was the right man to supervise it. At any rate, when the visitation had ended and Pennuin's decrees were read in the chapter room to the community, Merton was named master of scholastics.

I had known for a long time that Merton wanted such a job. He had given lectures to novices and students, but the lectures were not permanently on the monastic agenda, nor was attendance mandatory. What's more, I never thought Merton would ever get such a position. He was not a model of monastic observances, with his special food, special work, special sleeping quarters. Had Fox himself appointed Merton, the older monks would have complained. As it was, Pennuin was responsible.

In his first lecture as the official master of scholastics, Merton told us that he honestly felt God had arranged his appointment. He had the facility for interpreting the permission of a superior as a mandate of God, even though, had he not received what he wanted, he would have thrown the house out the window. During these lectures, he often expanded upon the mystical experiences he described in *The Seven Storey Mountain*. He said that, at the age of four, he had worshiped the gaslight jet in his mother's kitchen and, as a student in Rome, had felt the presence of his father who had died in London several years before. Moreover, since his college days, he had been practicing yoga and what Hubert van Zeller called "The Prayer of the Blank," a kind of meditation that involves falling asleep for a few seconds and then awakening with a heightened awareness. And, of course, Merton had been an ardent student of mysticism, both Christian and pagan, since his youth.

Naturally, he wanted to use his knowledge, and he knew that his lectures would not be attended by the older members of the community unless the abbot ordered them to do so. And the latter certainly would not do that. So, as master of scholastics, he knew he would have a captive audience of about thirty young monks totally receptive to anything he might say. Through them, Merton hoped to accomplish his mission: to change the spiritual orientation of Gethsemani from ascetical practices to mystical contemplation.

Merton declared that most people don't know about mysticism, yet have mystical experiences anyway. He tried to prove that statement by referring especially to the biographical writings of monks and nuns of all times and all places. He felt that most people who enter religious orders had experienced an insight into the vanity of living in the world and an impulse to leave it. And often such an experience ends there—just enough to sustain a person when he breaks with normal life. But others go on. Some go through what St. John of the Cross called "the dark night of the soul," which entails continuing prayer and good works despite feeling disgusted with them. Those who persevere are given an illumination, an insight into the nature of God.

Merton thought he, himself, was surely being "purged" of

spiritual consolations. He kept talking to us about being reduced to the "nada" (nothing) described by St. John of the Cross and the "impersonal nothingness" of Aldous Huxley. He would have liked to suffer patiently, passively, like some Hindu fakir. But that was not for Merton. He was more suited to a more aggressive, active way to God. No fasting and wearing a hairshirt for him. Instead, he followed the path of St. Thomas Aquinas, who, Merton believed, came to illumination through writing, preaching, and intense study. Merton hoped to so preoccupy his mind with study that he would forget himself (and his sufferings) until he found himself on the blissful threshold of mystical union.

Merton continually attempted to reconcile the mystical teachings of St. Thomas Aquinas with those of St. John of the Cross. His effort culminated in the publication of *Ascent to Truth*, which proposes that the illumination of the mind as described by St. Thomas Aquinas is the product of theological study and contemplation; yet, since it comes only as a result of a person's union with God, and union with God comes only through affection, as St. John of the Cross believed, so the union is had through love and not understanding.

I totally agreed with Merton regarding the disparity between the experience of mysticism and the understanding of it—at least understanding it as he described it. But his lectures were often baffling. It seemed that after "mining" many books on mysticism, he presented ideas on the subject the way buckshot comes out of a shotgun barrel. It seemed that he could not structure an argument without writing his ideas down and speaking them out loud. Consequently, he pursued the "cons" as vigorously as the "pros," without letting the audience know he was really trying to find his point of view. Like his favorite poet, William Blake, he progressed toward his conclusions by citing opposites. But when he arrived at the conclusions, they seemed to pop out of a box.

Consequently the works of Merton—for the most part, bound volumes of linked reflections—can be used to argue for or against many theories. Some critics have said this amorphous style of Merton's works is due to the fact that he wrote in spiral notebooks, leaving some pages, but ripping out the rest without worrying about logical connections. It is no wonder that all three of his novels were rejected by his friend Robert Giroux. Merton could not maintain a theme or a tone in his writing. He would spin around a point like a Fourth of July pinwheel until it just fizzled out.

Hence, his enthusiasm rarely reached his audience, and when he noticed it, the tone of his voice would mount to a shrill and he would gesticulate wildly trying to evoke in us interest and approval. Despite his insistence on peace of mind—*solitudo mentis*, he called it—as a requisite for mystical experience, he often had those old urges to become a hermit, to seclude himself in an honest-to-goodness physical solitude. Of course, when such temptations arose, he tried to resist them by doing what he was expected to do: praise the cenobitic life of the Trappists. However, he was often unconvincing.

I shall never forget one Sunday afternoon—the time for his lectures—when he mounted the podium with undisguised reluctance as if someone had marched him up there with a pistol in his back. He began with a quotation from St. Matthew: "If anyone say to you, 'Behold, he [Christ] is in the desert,' do not go forth; 'Behold, he is in the inner chambers,' do not believe it." He then attempted to use the line as an argument against those who aspired to the eremitical life. We suspected that he felt guilty about having put such notions into our heads on other occasions. But we responded by denouncing his tropological interpretation of the text and yelled out other scriptural references in defense of solitude, such as "I shall lead him into the desert and there I shall speak to his heart," and "he [Christ] went up to the mountain to pray, and when evening came, he was there alone," and "I am the voice of one crying in the wilderness"—all habitually used by spiritual writers (even Merton himself) to argue for the sublimity of the solitary life. As usual, he attempted to defend his point but finally capitulated and joined us in making monkeyshine remarks about himself.

Once we began to regard Merton's lectures as entertainment rather than spiritual exercises, and to think of him as our "Uncle Looie" (his religious name was Louis) instead of a spiritual director, we enjoyed both. In fact, many students who disdained Merton for his vacillating opinions, his abhorrence of asceticism, and his use of us as sounding boards for his new theories started to regard him as a wit. The younger students admired him as a celebrated author and also as a father. He brought them extra food in the refectory, gave them permission to take naps, led them to the woods to plant seedlings and to mark timber for cutting. Certainly, Merton enjoyed being master of scholastics. As such, he had permission to use the vault as his private office, and he could lead his students outside the enclosure to work or to walk in the woods. In fact, Fox named Merton the abbey's "conservationist," which entailed planting pine seedlings. It was a job "made" for Merton. Often, he rode out to his work sites in the back of a jeep driven by one of the students, a volume of Migne's *Patrology* under one arm and a writing board under the other. He looked like a five-star general out on maneuvers. However, this privilege was eventually revoked, partly because the older monks complained that Merton was violating enclosure laws but, principally, I think, because the abbot needed the students during working hours, to wash cheese, peel tomatoes, and wrap smoked hams. Although Merton had many shortcomings as a master of scholastics, he nevertheless geared us closer to the goal we all thought should be ours as monks. As time went on, this fact became more evident and Merton's teaching exerted a greater influence on my life.

14

Merton As Novice Master

Merton's "mission" at Gethsemani was to put more solitude into the Trappist routine. He tried to prove, from the writings of Jerome, Augustine, Origin, Athanasius, Tertullian, and Gregory of Nyssa that solitude was a time-honored means of lifting a person out of the mire of sensual pleasure and cultivating his taste for spiritual things. In the fourth century, men and women set up hermitages in the deserts of Scete, Nitria, and the Theibaid, where

Thomas Merton in cowl.

they made baskets to sell and meditated on the scriptures. They believed that the Christian ideal was to die for Christ who had said, "Greater love has no man than this, that a man lay down his life for his friends." But the age of martyrdom had passed. The Romans no longer tossed Christians to the lions, so the latter proposed for themselves a kind of "daily martyrdom" that consisted of practicing asceticism in solitude.

As time went on, the practice of living in solitude became popular in Western Christendom. Many hermits in Europe, tired of the deprivations peculiar to a life in the wilderness, began roaming around the countryside like vagabonds. In Nursea, Italy, a hermit called Benedict thought he could help his wayward brethren by gathering them all together into one place—a monastery. But even after he had established the Benedictine monastic order, the founder still provided opportunities for the monks to live in solitude from time to time.

Since the Trappists follow the Benedictine Rule, Merton argued that hermitages should be built on the grounds of Gethsemani for those who wanted them. He insisted that the longing for solitude itself is a sign of the eremitical vocation and that, so long as a person is kept from answering that vocation, he will remain static in the spiritual life. Moreover, since Merton felt himself unable to mount any higher on the mystical ladder, in 1953 he was ready to abandon his mission and leave the Trappists.

By that time, the Carthusians of France had founded a kind of religious center for recruits at Sky Farm in Wittington, Vermont. The superior, Dom Humphrey, replied to Merton's request to join the Carthusians by inviting him to Sky Farm for a visit. But Fox forbade it. He argued that Merton's writings had identified him with the Trappists, and for Merton to quit the order would disillusion Merton's readers and disgrace Merton himself.

Eventually, Fox relented and Merton did apply for admission to La Grande Chartreuse near Grenoble, France. The prior (highest superior) invited Merton to come, providing he would keep the fasts, attend the vigils, and limit or even eliminate his writing. The Carthusians do not compromise. They give no special treatment to any of their candidates—not even celebrities. That backed Merton up. He needed lots of good food to control his stomach problems and plenty of opportunities to satisfy his need to write and lecture. He did not join the Carthusians but returned to his mission to introduce the solitary life into the Trappist order.

During the middle 1950s, the State of Kentucky built a fire tower at Vineyard Knob—on the abbey's property—and asked the monks to maintain it. When Merton heard about it, he decided that, as Gethsemani's conservationist, he should be in charge of the tower. Fox agreed and, for several weeks, Merton spent long intervals in the small cabin of the tower, watching for forest fires, to be sure, but also reading and writing. Eventually, Merton begged Fox to let him use the cabin as a hermitage and to excuse him from monastic exercises. Fox must have anticipated that request, for when Merton made it, Fox had the right answer prepared. He told Merton he could have the cabin as a hermitage, providing he stay in it day and night. He knew that Merton would never take up a Simon Stylites form of solitude in a bare cabin, swinging in the air one hundred feet above the ground.

And Fox was right. Merton backed out of the proposition. Moreover, as paradoxical as ever, Merton begged, as an alternative, not the privilege of building himself a hut instead but of occupying the most gregarious post in the abbey: master of novices. And what is equally curious, Fox agreed—despite the fact that Merton had broken his promise never to apply for admission into the Carthusian order and that canon law demands in a novice master the highest degree of stability and regular observance.

Fox possibly felt that Merton would be content as a master of novices and consequently cease bothering him about becoming a hermit. But in asking for that job, perhaps Merton was a bit "foxy" too. He must have known that with those new duties would come new privileges. He would have a private office and bedroom in the novitiate. He could redecorate the novitiate chapel as he wished. He might miss monastic exercises with impunity, since novice masters are on call for spiritual direction at all times. And he could use the most talented novices as researchers, proofreaders, and typists. In fact, from 1955 to 1965, he used them to produce over a dozen books, such as *Thoughts in Solitude, The Silent Life, New Seeds of Contemplation*, and *The Wisdom of the Desert*, which, incidentally, reflected his way of life as much as the *A* does the *I* on the Square of Opposition.

Seemingly, Merton found his niche as master of novices. Yet, at times, the desire to become a solitary gnawed at his soul. I'm not sure if he tried to join the Carthusians again, but he did attempt to enter the Camaldolese *laura* (group of hermits) founded by Dom Agosto Modotti in Big Sur, California. Modotti, despite his magnificent property overlooking the Pacific Ocean, was hurting for postulants and would have accepted Merton without any conditions. But Fox knew that Modotti was in disgrace with the Sacred Congregation at Rome, so he wrote to the prefect of that organization, Cardinal Valeri, asking him to refuse Merton permission to make the transfer. In responding, Valeri used a quotation from Merton's *No Man Is an Island*: "Our Father in heaven has called us each one to the place in which he can best satisfy his infinite desire to do us good." Valeri must have had a sense of humor. He must have seen the irony of using Merton's own spiritual bromide against him.

Although Fox never fired Merton from his post of master of novices, he was certainly fed up with Merton's persistent preoccupation with solitude. About that time, 1956, one of Merton's former scholastics, Frater Eudes, returned to the abbey after finishing a course of study in psychiatrics at Georgetown University. Fox saw in Eudes a possible buffer between Merton and himself. Fox, a *sui juris* psychoanalyst, received Eudes with great fanfare. He gave the young monk a blanket permission to speak to any monk seeking his professional help. For a while Eudes had a considerable clientele. But the fad soon waned and only a few extroverts came to our doctor for companionship. Eventually, Fox permitted Eudes to give lectures to the community. I attended a few and enjoyed them. However, listening to all those symptoms of abnormal behavior, I began to wonder about Eudes himself. I was shocked when, during one of the lectures, Eudes attacked—verbally, of course—one monk who disagreed with him on the eccentricity in Mahler's music, and I noted in the cloister that whenever he walked behind Father Alphonsus, Eudes would lift one shoulder higher than the other and sort of drag his left foot in imitation of the older monk.

Nevertheless, Fox had great confidence in Eudes and proposed that they both attend a symposium called "Religion and Psychiatry" at St. John's University in Collegeville, Minnesota. They asked Merton to accompany them. When the sponsors learned that Merton was coming, they asked him to do a paper and he readily agreed.

Before the trio left for Collegeville, Fox arranged with one of the slated speakers, Dr. Gregory Zilboorg, to do an analysis on Merton based on his paper and the rest of his writings. Of course, Merton knew nothing of the intrigue. And when they arrived at the symposium, and had met Zilboorg, Merton even asked for an analysis. Well he got it. Zilboorg criticized Merton severely, calling him "An exhibitionist who wanted a hermitage in Times Square." He also ranted about Merton's disguised egotism and his manipulative obedience. I feel that Zilboorg, and Fox as well, intended merely to discourage Merton in his pursuit of an unattainable ideal; nevertheless, Merton was so humiliated by Zilboorg's dressing down that he burst out crying.

But Merton did not break. In fact, looking back on the situation, I think his experience at St. John's Abbey was, as Zilboorg might have said, "therapeutic." Even though Merton continued his quest for solitude, he seemed to regard it with less reverence than before; in fact, he began to consider the eremitical life as a kind of pleasant make-believe. Moreover, he gradually—at least in our private conversations—talked about hermits as people of leisure. He even started to use the mundane term *privacy* rather than the hallowed *solitude*. Of course, I had often seen the happy-go-lucky side of Merton; otherwise, I would not have found him so charming. But after the incident in Collegeville, he seemed more consistent in laughing at himself and his eremitical ideals. And although I liked him best in his playful mood, I felt as if he had undermined something very important in the spiritual life. My respect for solitude hadn't changed.

15

Ordination in Louisville

As interested as I was in Merton's misadventures and in my own progress in the mystical life during these years, most of my energy went into study. I was so preoccupied with theology, philosophy, church history, and Greek, that I almost forgot the end of these disciplines, namely, the priesthood. As a novice, I didn't reflect much on the matter, since I believed—perhaps even hoped—that my heart would give out on me before taking holy orders. Considering the nature of the Trappist life, wanting to die early in the order does not imply heroism. But it does indicate faith. As a novice, I believed, absolutely, in God, heaven, and the Catholic Church.

Even though the study of theology challenged my faith and made me wonder if I could ever actually convince others of Catholic dogma, I paid little attention to the question. Trappist priests, for the most part, have no ministry. After being ordained the only change in my life, it seemed to me, would be my offering mass every morning rather than serving it. I would not be embarrassed with a sacerdotal dignity or be encumbered with pastoral obligations. So, during my last year as a scholastic, when the abbot asked me if I wanted to receive holy orders, I said yes.

My only consolation in ending my scholastic program was the prospect of getting away from Father Arsenius, my dogma professor. In his teaching he was what theologians call a "probabliorist," that is, a person who, faced with two courses of action—one being more likely conformed to the standard of morality than the other—feels obliged to choose the former. I, on the other hand, was a "probablist." I felt justified in following one probably moral action, even though the opposite was more probably upright. Also, I remember how upset he was when he found out that I had learned all the prayers of the liturgy by heart and had boasted that I could "say mass with my eyes closed." I think he seriously believed that omitting a word of the text or even garbling one while saying the prayers of the mass from memory constitutes a mortal sin of negligence. I suppose I should have respected his scrupulosity and followed his direction or at least kept my opinions and intentions to myself. Even though I had the highest grades in my class, I knew that he would never recommend me a as candidate to study in Rome and that he would feel even obligated to deny me that privilege.

Early one frosty morning in December, the abbot, a few other monks, and I were driven to the cathedral in Louisville. Archbishop Floersh had decided to ordain all the candidates for the priesthood in his diocese at the same time. Though the ceremonies began at eight o'clock, the place was full of people. As we filed into the presbytery I tried to find my family, but the dense incense smoke and glaring lights cut off my vision. At the sound of the MC's "clicker," we lined up and knelt at the foot of the archbishop's throne. He sat leaning on one arm looking sour and as if he could use an antacid tablet. At that point I decided that I had to go to the bathroom. In fact, for the following hour and twenty minutes, nothing but this ever-increasing need entered my mind. I shifted from one foot to the other while standing and, by so doing, maintained a small degree of comfort. But just before the ordination itself, we were required to lie prostrate on the cold marble floor. I focused all my attention upon blocking the urge. I began to think of the old story about the little Dutch boy who stayed awake all night jamming up a hole in a dike. I thought of the axiom "Every analogy limps" and had to laugh at the absurdity of the situation. And just as I was about to surrender to nature, the clicker sounded again, and we all rose to approach the archbishop. It seemed a kind of minor miracle that I regained composure and completed the ceremonies without incident. However, because of my intense concentration on keeping dry, I recall hardly any other details of the ordination. The only time I really reflected on what had happened that morning was after the mass while in the bathroom. Later, at the reception in the archbishop's palace, when I heard other members of the newly ordained describe themselves as feeling "ten feet off the ground" during the mass, I realized that I had missed the significance of the experience. In fact, to this day I don't recall having been ordained.

After the ceremonies, the abbot said he wanted us, as soon as possible, back at Gethsemani. It was as if he considered the abbey a kind of sterile bubble and the monks fragile patients without immunizing white corpuscles. Yet before escaping from the corrupting influence of Louisville, Fox had us drop in on the Carmelite nuns who lived in the suburbs. There we were, the silent monks conversing with the secluded nuns, both groups separated by a kind of grill. As we started to leave, the Mother Superior behind the grill asked for a blessing. I heard a lot of kneecracking and thudding on the floor, and I made a sign of the cross toward them. On the way home, I felt felt uneasy, even depressed. Again, the notion of playacting came to my mind and I seemed conscious of preparing myself to smile, to gasp, to sympathize as the foreseen occasion arose. Like Eliot's J. Alfred Prufrock, I teetered on the verge of asking the "overwhelming question" but never let myself do it. I had, after seven hard years, put too much into my profession to want to doubt its value.

At the abbey, I went directly to the visitors' room in the gate house, where I thought Mother, Aunt Mary, and Uncle Frank would be waiting. But Brother Alexander told me he received a phone call from my mother saying they would be late. It seems that Uncle Frank, driving Mother's Buick, had skidded on the icy streets in front of the cathedral in Louisville and crashed. Frank had a history of light, almost negligible car accidents resulting, he admitted, from dozing off at the wheel. But this time he tore off the whole fender of Mother's sedan, smashed the front of a mailbox and, in so doing, threw dozens of Christmas letters and packages on the street. Consequently, my family spent the afternoon partly at a garage and partly at a police station.

The next morning, about eight-thirty, I went to the sacristy to get ready for mass. One thing Father Arsenius would have praised me for, had he known of it, was my refusal to accept any presents given me for my ordination. In fact, I told the sacristan that I wanted to use the simplest silver chalice and oldest vestments he could find. I had even asked the abbot to excuse me from offering my first mass on the high altar according to custom. I wished, rather, to say a low mass on one of the little altars at the rear of the church reserved for visitors and attended only by my family. But Fox wouldn't have it. In fact, he had the sacristan set out for my use a new gold chalice studded with rubies, and a gorgeous set of white silk vestments imported from some Benedictine abbey in Belgium. When he entered the sacristy and glanced my way, I smiled back at him as if I were delighted.

Brother Isidor, dressed in a blue-white surplice, stood nearby watching. He set down the candelabra he was holding and passed the palm of his right hand in front of his face. He meant to say that I looked "beautiful." As we proceeded into the church, I recalled the first time I had marched in a religious ceremony. That was the occasion of my first holy communion held at St. Ann's. Aunt Mary had given me a memento: a white patent-leather prayer book and a white mother-of-pearl rosary. As I knelt at the communion rail with the other children, I had no doubt that each little white host Father McGee put on the children's tongues was God. Yet there I was a Trappist monk with seven years of theological training behind me, about to consecrate bread and wine into the body and blood of Christ, and wondering if I could really do it. I had to keep reminding myself that I didn't want to doubt my power and that speculations of that sort came with the office. After all, I told myself, without the possibility of doubt there can be no faith, and faith was what religion was all about.

During the mass I was almost entirely preoccupied with remembering the rubrics. But there were times when I seemed to leave my body and, as it were, to hover above myself while watching all that was going on. As I chanted the preface of the mass, the Latin words seemed to leap out of my lungs, soar to the roof of the presbytery, and bounce around the pillars surrounding the apse like a ball in a squash court. I was startled at the power of that voice. It was as if I had suddenly recovered from a long period of laryngitis and had forgotten how it sounded. As I lifted the host from the altar, the church became as silent as outer space. I recalled Dom Vital's injunction that I keep only the edges of my two hands on the altar cloth. Just as I was pronouncing the words of consecration, the great bells in the tower began to ring. "Hear it not Duncan for it is a knell/ That summons thee to heaven or to hell" came to mind. I was in Marshall McCluhan's English class at St. Louis University, back in 1943. Like Walter Mitty's, my mind vacillated from one memory or imagined situation to another.

At last the bells stopped and I could hear the older members of the choir gasp as they hoisted themselves up from their kneeling positions. I turned to face the choir and noticed a girl in the front pew of the chancel, high above the rest of the congregation, in the rear of the church. She stood with one hand on her hip as Marcy used to do when she pouted or flirted. If I was ever glad not to see someone, it was Marcy. She would have reminded me of the summer mornings when we should have been in church but had sneaked off together to swim or collect shells near Emerald Bay. I recalled once having said to her, "Maybe we should go to mass" and hearing her tart reply, "Go ahead. Pray for me, jerk!" Then she ran down the beach shaking her pretty, pear-shaped behind. In a way, I feared and respected her as I did God. Both, I felt, could see through my pretenses and both, it seemed, punished me for them with humiliations. She was still on my mind as I followed the other ministers in procession back to the sacristy.

That afternoon I rather wished the sarcastic, irreverent Marcy were there. She would have tempered the adulation showed me by the family. Even Uncle Frank seemed a little in awe of me. He actually stood up when I entered the visitors' room at the gate house. Aunt Mary just sat in a corner saying, "It was wonderful. It was wonderful," whenever Mother mentioned the ceremonies of that morning. I guess they believed I had reached the apogee of the spiritual life and the only thing keeping me from bursting out in celestial glory was my encumbering mortal body.

16

My Rebellion

By 1958 my studies were over and my goals were reached as far as Gethsemani was concerned. Life at the abbey had become as stagnant as the water in our duck pond. There was nothing to look forward to but death—either my own or that of another monk who would leave open a good job or a desk near a window in the scriptorium. But the covetable monotony that usually results from peace and quiet and prepares the soul for contemplation was not there. Rather, the atmosphere at Gethsemani was a mixture of boredom and annoyance, resulting from ceremonies, lectures, and noisy work in the factories.

And it didn't help when the new Pope, John XXIII, began his *aggioramento*, his bringing the Catholic Church up to date in respect to policy and organization. I was all for working for peace and social justice. I was enthusiastic about having a dialogue with other religions and beginning a reformation of monastic orders. However, I feared that his urging orders, such as the Trappists, to give more retreats to laymen and to help out in parishes would compromise the contemplative life. But Merton didn't mind at all. In fact, he persuaded the abbot to invite the faculty and students of seminaries—Catholic and Protestant—to Gethsemani's ecumenical activities. He argued that taking care of those people would be no more distracting to the monks than having them operate the machinery in the cheese-ham-sausage-bread factory. Fox gave into Merton's insistence, aware also that the Pope might learn of this innovation and appreciate the abbot's efforts to cooperate in the new adventure. Many of us suspected that Fox would like to become a bishop and wanted to be in a good position when the Pope began raising many of his supporters to high ecclesiastical dignities.

It wasn't long before people from many walks of life reached the hallowed portals of Gethsemani Abbey. They had come to follow the monastic exercises, to meet others interested in ecumenism, and to listen to the words of the famous Thomas Merton. He told them what they wanted to hear. War clouds hung over many countries, even America, during those years, and Merton was an aggressive pacifist. He even disparaged St. Augustine's "just war" theory, renewed his Oxford pledge never to bear arms, and proclaimed himself the eternal conscientious objector. Many ideas from these talks went into the composition of *The Original Child Bomb*, *Seeds of Destruction*, and *Confessions of a Guilty Bystander*. He openly condemned President Truman for atom-bombing Hiroshima and Nagasaki, and disgraced himself with many bishops who sympathized with the American government's part in the Vietnam War.

Merton said much about social justice as well. He had been interested in minorities since his days at Oakham Grammar School in England, where he defended the social and political views of Gandhi. Later, in New York, he worked for Friendship House, helping the poor of Harlem. And after that, he became a white liberal, allied in spirit with Martin Luther King, Jr., James Baldwin, and Eldridge Cleaver. Once, he professed his desire to resign from the human race and be naturalized a Negro.

Merton considered himself quite apt in establishing a rapport with people of all religions. He had studied Anglicanism as a youth in England and, at Columbia College in New York, had taken courses in Western and Oriental religion and philosophy. In all of them he recognized a common ground, a mysticism that leads to *satori*, an enlightenment, not in respect to divine truth, but to self-knowledge. Much later, this research helped him in his collaboration with the Buddhist scholar Dr. Dasetzi Zuzuki, which formed the basis of Merton's *Mystics and Zen Masters*.

To bring the Pope's ecumenism in accord with his own ambitions as religious reformer at Gethsemani, Merton proposed to his many guests a rather unlikely proposal—I thought—on the contemplative life. He envisioned three distinct categories of monks in the abbey. First, those who practice contemplation, whether they live in the abbey itself or in hermitages on the abbey's grounds. Second, those monks who undertake the government of the monks, occasionally preach retreats, and even do missionary work in the area. Finally, those monks who concern themselves with the material needs of the abbey. Certainly, these three kinds of activities go on and must go on in every abbey.

However, no person enters a religious institution denominated "contemplative" with the intention of assuming one of these roles exclusively. People enter a contemplative order to contemplate and should view all other duties as unfortunate impositions. At least that was Merton's teaching when he was master of scholastics.

Although Merton won the Peace Award one year for his efforts in promoting social justice, he said his mind was still set on becoming a hermit. And so was mine. At the time, I was professor of Latin and often had occasion to speak with Merton on the progress of his novice students. But we also discussed other subjects, among which were hermits. He told me about the Camaldolese who had settled in Big Sur, California, and promised to recommend me to Dom Modotti, should the abbot let me go. But the abbot became so angry when I asked to apply to the Camaldolese that he fired me from my teaching job.

I might have persisted in my efforts to join Modotti's group, were it not for the day providence or coincidence threw Merton and me together. Early that morning, we set out in one of the abbey's cars for Louisville, where we were to have physical checkups. Joe, our driver, let Merton off at the Carmelite monastery, where he said—grinning—he intended to lecture on "dark nights." Then Joe and I continued downtown, where we had lunch in a Walgreen's drugstore. I was the center of attention, since I had been tonsured recently and had only an inch-wide band of hair encircling my head. And that was an era when even a beatnik crossing the street could hold up traffic. On the jukebox Frankie Lane was singing "Moonlight Serenade," the old Glenn Miller theme song. While I was waiting to see the doctor, the receptionist kept glancing at me over her typewriter and smiling. I wondered whether or not she would have been so overtly attentive had I been just a young man in a tweed suit and a duck-tail hairstyle. Probably not. She most likely didn't think of me as a man at all, but as some benignly insane monk from the Middle Ages. I distinctly recall having had an identity problem that morning.

Having decided that I was neither a threat nor a challenge, the receptionist stopped looking my way, and Dr. Mulligan called me into his office. On his desk were photos of his wife and children, as every good family man should have. Yet from his devotion to Gethsemani, I imagined that he was a frustrated monk at heart.

He spoke of his profession as if it had been a regrettable second choice. It seemed that he was not quite comfortable with his prospects of salvation, since his scientific persuasion was at odds with the doctrine of the Immaculate Conception. Despite my distaste for carrying on philosophical and theological discussions, I grunted negatively or positively at Mulligan's complaints or suggestions, knowing that the abbot was paying him nothing for his services.

It was only two in the afternoon, and I wasn't to meet Merton until dusk. I strolled up Broadway, intending to visit the library, where we would all meet and go home. I hadn't been in that part of town since 1948, and I felt in the mood for some sightseeing. What I saw most were women. Even the nuns rushing around the streets doing errands were gorgeous. As I rounded one corner, I found myself beneath the marquee of a burlesque theatre featuring a star with the exclamatory name of Ann Howe! A life-size poster, depicting a tall, narrow-hipped female with an enormous, partly-bare bosom, stood near the entrance. Were it not for my clerical clothes, I might have lingered—out of curiosity, I would have assured myself—to marvel at that spectacle. But grace cooperated with embarrassment to urge a quick retreat.

In the library I sat down at the same reading table as a tall, long-haired man dressed in a tattered overcoat. He wore thick-lensed glasses. I imagined him to be some scholar, too intellectual to worry about appearances. But when I noticed the title of the book he held—Zane Grey's *The Thundering Herd*—I felt like a fool. He reached his free hand into the pocket of his overcoat and pulled out a greasy brown bag filled with jelly doughnuts. When he began to eat, I moved to another table.

For hours I read Hemingway's *Death in the Afternoon* while listening to Shostakovich's taped concertos through earphones. I hadn't had such a cultural orgy since the night Robert Spaight read *Murder in the Cathedral* in the chapter room before compline. As I sat there enjoying myself, I thought how natural it would have been to have a cigarette in my mouth and a whiskey in my hand. But despite the good time I was having, I could not help reflecting on how incompatible my present activities were with my intent to become a hermit. And I rather envied Merton, for such an ambivalence would not have bothered him since his meeting with Zilboorg. Merton had learned to handle ambivalence, obscurity, even contradiction.

Merton, Joe, and I met at the front desk of the library as planned. Under his arm, Merton carried six oversized books on Shaker architecture that the librarian had ordered for him. He said that he intended to "Shakerize" the novitiate chapel and described the present altar there as so vulgar that should one drop a nickel in it, out would come "Swanee River." He joked with us all the way to Bardstown, where he insisted that we stop at Jones's Restaurant and have dinner. Merton knew all the waitresses by their first names, since he frequently went there with visitors. We ate fish sandwiches, drank beer, and listened to the jukebox play "Sophisticated Swing" five times, thanks to Merton's investment of a quarter.

We had a lot of fun that day, but it was the trip back to the abbey that made it memorable for me. We both agreed that entering the Carthusians or Camaldolese should not be our goals but that we should find a bishop willing to accept us into his diocese as missioners—way out in the boondocks somewhere—and, after winning favor with him, convince him to keep us on as hermits. It was a radical plan since following it would eventually lead us out of the Trappist order. We made a pact, then and there, to the effect that whoever got to the "desert" first would blaze the trail for the other.

I thought Merton would be the trailblazer, since he was so well known and so highly regarded by the American bishops. But months passed and Merton, apparently, had not contacted any bishops. It seems that he was having too much fun giving his ecumenical lectures. So I gave up on him and began writing to bishops myself. But all my letters were followed by others from the abbot, saying that I was an invalid and therefore a possible liability for a diocese. Some bishops didn't even acknowledge my inquiries; others offered their sympathy and regrets. After about a year of frustrated efforts, I gave up.

My first direct step toward rebellion against the Catholic Church, the Trappist order, the abbot of Gethsemani, and my conscience, was taken during the summer of 1960. The entire abbey was preparing for the feast of Corpus Christi, and of all the feast days of the church that I disliked, I guess I disliked that one the most. It involved dreadfully long hours of work preparing for a dreadfully long procession and mass. I thought about both as I rode with some other monks in the back of a truck on the way to St. Gertrude's Field to gather flowers. The next morning we would depetal the blossoms and use them to cover the designs made of wet sawdust situated at various places on the floors of the cloister. And during the procession, the abbot, carrying the Blessed Sacrament, would tread upon those pelicans, lambs, doves, and chalices as if they had been pine needles wind-fallen from the pine trees rather than elaborate time-consuming creations.

In the woods I filled my wicker basket with daisies, tiger lilies, and goldenrods. Near the lake, a few hundred yards from Merton's new hermitage, built by his novices but used—ostensibly—as a conference center, I brushed the lichens off a log and sat down. I could hear the other monks moving about in the bushes and some creature in a thicket crying plaintively, "Angh, angh, angh." I threw a rock in its direction and suddenly the woods were silent as if petrified. Then I saw a squirrel and some chipmunks staring at me like trophies in a hunter's den. With time, I thought, I might be accepted there.

In the chapter room the next morning, I knew, Dom Vital would speak about the coming procession and exhort the thurifer—the monk in charge of burning the incense—to have plenty of "nice, red, glowing charcoals" and to carry the censer—the vessel containing the incense and charcoal—in the right hand "even if he has the right hand on the left side." That was his perennial joke on lefthanders. The year before, he advised us on the ways to put on an alb—a long, white garment worn by ministers during the liturgy. In doing so he read from the enormous tome on rubrics lying before him on a table. "When you put on the alb, you must tie the strings at the neck with a bow." Vital spoke pretty good English, but homonyms often gave him trouble. Obviously, he understood the word *bow* to mean an inclination of the head or body but never as a kind of knot. He ended that directive saying, "My brethren, I don't understand this. Why must you bow after tying the strings of the alb?" Most of us just grinned, yawned, and went back to sleep.

Vital read a note from Father Placid. The latter wanted to know about liturgical kisses made during a solemn high mass celebrated by Eskimos. "Good God," I recall whispering aloud with a sigh, aware that Placid was up to his nonsense again. Again those weak smiles appeared on the faces of the somnolent brethren. Vital read, "Since Eskimos kiss by rubbing noses, should not the ministers of a solemn high mass at the North Pole rub their noses on the abbot's hand when presenting him the crosier instead of touching it with the lips?" Vital shoved the note into the sleeve of his cowl and scratched his head. He probably suspected a trick, knowing the reputation of Placid as a wag. At length, however, he looked at the ceiling as if he hoped to find the answer written there and said, "My brethren, we must respect the customs of the Eskimo faithful, even if what they do seems disgusting." I looked at the quotation from St. Bernard inscribed on the wall opposite the one against which I was leaning: "Bernard, why hast thou come here?" And I asked myself, "Why in the name of heaven did I come here?"

Later, the monks bustled about the cloister making their designs. I worked in the préau with the others, pulling apart flowers and filling baskets with the petals. When the bell rang, ending the morning work period, I hurried to the showers. However, six or seven sweaty monks had the same idea, and I had to wait my turn.

I knew I had little time before the procession started. And as soon as I was under the cold water, the bells began to ring. Ordinarily, I would have rushed to dry off and get dressed. I had even gone to church wringing wet rather than be late for a religious service. I reacted to bells like a Pavlovian dog. But that morning I felt one instinct pulling against another. Then a familiar, almost uncontrollable, perhaps Irish, one predominated. Once again, I was the college student, fleeing or refusing to attend Finn's sodality meeting at St. Louis University. When I finally got dressed, instead of joining the community in the cloister, I ducked out a side door and headed for the woods, knowingly and willingly breaking a rule. Of course, I had broken rules before, but never with such deliberation. I was really quite afraid, aware that snubbing the voice of conscience gets easier with repetition.

I passed several brothers coming in late from the fields as I opened the gate leading to the cedar hills. They looked at me, I thought, as if they wondered why a choir monk was going away from the church instead of toward it. After all, the bells were ringing in the church tower calling all good monks to worship. I damned my scruples and tried to rationalize. Merton did this sort of thing all the time, so why should I feel guilty? I began to think that this experience was really good for me; perhaps, afterward, I won't consider myself the perfect monk any more. To add to the humiliation, I could not even boast that my disobedience was the resolute *non serviam* of Milton's hero in *Paradise Lost*. My previous determination had left me. Yet I couldn't change my course. I couldn't go to that boring, annoying Corpus Christi procession because I couldn't will it if I tried. I remembered Dom Vital's "manure saints" and tried to think of myself among their number. At length I reached the end of my debate and came to a cliff overlooking a large grove of cedars with a perfect view of the church.

About an hour later, the bells rang to announce the consecration. I knelt down but couldn't pray. I picked up the book I had brought along, *The Cloud of Unknowing*, but soon put it down after coming to a part that demanded obedience even to the point of self-abandonment. I recalled reading about the French writer Peguy, who couldn't say the "Our Father" because it contains the words "Thy will be done" and because he didn't do that will. So he prayed the "Hail Mary," which doesn't contain any tit-for-tat clauses.

That evening I returned to the abbey, knowing that I was caught in a maelstrom of rebellion and unable to swim clear because of my abulia. I arrived at my place in the empty refectory—for dinner was over—and sat down to the cheese, fruit, and bread remaining at my place. By then the community was in the chapter room, listening to the reading before compline and the Salve Regina. I ate and then went directly to my cell in the dormitory annex, reconciled to the fact that I would probably drop out of the community for good—unless, of course, the abbot commanded me to return in virtue of my vow of obedience. I didn't learn canon law for nothing. I could break all the little rules I wanted without getting into serious trouble. But fooling around with the vows was another matter. If Fox simply asked me to come back, I could remind him of all his letters declaring me to be an invalid, too weak to carry out the normal duties of a monk, be he Carthusian, Camaldolese, or Trappist. Fox was a cautious man, and I knew he would not compromise his image as a prudent and even benign administrator.

17

The Recluse

One morning Father Calistus, the new prior, appeared outside my cell. He wanted to know if I was sick, since no one had seen me at the "regular" places for a long time. I assured him that I was not in pain but that the "poor health" ascribed to me by the abbot had not altered. I explained how I had written to several bishops asking admission into their dioceses as a hermit only to be refused because the abbot wrote them saying I was sick. Calistus was an unsophisticated country boy unaccustomed to the casuistry used by subtle urbanites such as Fox and me. He said he would talk to the abbot about the matter and hoped I would change my mind.

I really thought Calistus would return that afternoon with some kind of message from the abbot, but he didn't. Several weeks passed before I spoke with him again. Whenever I encountered other monks, they neither heckled me nor asked about my absence. They simply smiled—sympathetically, I thought—as if resigned to the fact that I was no longer among them. Eventually, I learned that the abbot, during a meeting in the chapter room, had announced that "the doctors at the hospital said our good Frater Gerald had better take it easy for a while." The doctors had done that several times, but Fox never took their advice seriously enough to force leisure upon me. I suppose he needed a reason for his permissiveness should anyone demand that he recall to duty. Moreover, so long as I kept to my cell, on the grounds that I had a health problem, I implicitly confirmed his diagnosis.

I'm sure Fox believed I would soon tire of living alone in my cell. However the life of a recluse suited me very well. During working hours I tended my flower garden as I had been doing for the past two years. The only person I saw there was old Father Stephen, who begged me for small plots in which to plant his petunias. For meals I had to come to the refectory like everybody else, since nobody was going to bring food to my cell. And that was agreeable to me; after twenty hours of seclusion, being with the community was a pleasure. I enjoyed listening to the reading and seeing my companions.

Following Merton's example and an old impulse, I began to write. I did a book on the spiritual life called *Within and Without*. It was filled with maxims gathered from dozens of other spiritual books which, I believed, had only to edify to become worthy for publication. After I had typed the manuscript, I considered asking the abbot to have it published. But I let it rest for several weeks and read it again. It was unoriginal, uninspired, even unedifying. I threw it away.

I also undertook a serious study of the Pentateuch—the first five books of the Old Testament. At the time, form criticism of scripture was popular, and I read almost every book and pamphlet on the subject available in our library. Eventually, I got the yen to read the Bible in its original languages, Greek and Hebrew. I was amazed when the abbot gave me permission to study with Father Augustine, a middle-aged, British gentleman who had entered Gethsemani two years before, despite his having but one leg. Meanwhile, he had grown enormously fat and could no longer get his stump into his artificial limb. He adopted the use of a peg leg and crutches but, with them, could not get around sufficiently well to keep up with the monastic routine. Consequently, he was retired to a room in the infirmary where he wrote, painted, sculpted, and had—what seemed to me—a very good time. I once remarked that he too was a recluse, but he assured me that he was the the most sociable of all men and missed being with the community. The most important thing I learned from Augustine was not how to read the *Anabasis* in Attic Greek but that solitude can be tolerated by anyone who follows a strict schedule of agreeable work and that nothing is heavier than time on your hands.

Very few of the monks knew where my cell was, and those who did rarely visited me because they weren't allowed in the dormitories during the daytime without special permission. So most of the time I remained free of distractions. Whenever I needed some, I went to the window opposite my cell to look down at the abbey compound where the brethren went from garage to cheese factory, to food-packaging plant, to cannery, to blacksmith's shop, to vegetable garden. Because the monks below talked with their hands, I could follow the conversations. Beyond the compound I could also see the field where a blackbird frequently dived at my head whenever I came near his nest and, farther on, the hill above the cedar grove where I spent my first day away from the community.

It is difficult to write about the long hours I spent in the solitude of my cell in such a way as to evoke in readers the experience of such a duration. There were few events, and the recounting of those events, despite the long intervals between each, ends up sounding—or reading—as if they followed one another with such rapidity that every minute was filled with action. In reality, solitude is best measured and described, not by the quantity of minutes passing, but by the quality of those minutes. There were afternoons, especially at the beginning of my retreat, during which I could neither reflect nor study. Yet I couldn't sleep the time away either. Those afternoons were especially heavy during the winter, when I had to stop working in the garden because of the foul weather. And in my dormitory cell I had only a feeble gray light to read by while I lay on the straw couch under blankets to stave off the cold. However, I eventually got over what I refer to as the "hump." I never really understood the term, even though I use it. I suppose it's something like a "second wind" that tired runners can look forward to as they start on the last leg of a marathon. I knew from experience that as soon as I sank to the nadir of listlessness and melancholy my spirits would crest again. And they did, even though the weather stayed gloomy. I thought of the dreary services in the choir and the fatuous lectures in the chapter room. I was free to miss them and to continue my reading.

As time went on I became so used to my way of life that I forgot all about its renegade quality. I no longer felt guilty or threatened. Consequently, I gained enough peace of mind to contemplate. It was a pleasure, after a day of study and manual labor, to kneel on the terrazzo floor, leaning against the bed, and to let myself go into the Blank. It emptied my mind and relaxed my body and gave me a healthy perspective in regard to the solitude. I had no doubt my life had a purpose, and I figured the times I doubted it did resulted from my inability to see clearly what it was, despite my feeling obliged to fulfill it.

Although the purpose of my life seemed painfully vague while imprisoned by conscience in an abbey, it had been no clearer while I lived in ordinary society. *Is there indeed a purpose to life?* I thought at the time that I had answered it affirmatively and that I had begun to fulfill my own when I entered Gethsemani. And after all the time invested in the monastic life at Gethsemani, it was hard to persuade myself that I had been wrong. Instead of questioning whether or not I belonged in the religious life at all, I decided to try another form of the religious life—reclusion.

That spring I felt my tenure in solitude in jeopardy. It was time for the annual visitation again. I thought that maybe Fox had let me alone those ten months to see if I could stand the loneliness and, if I stuck it out, to let the visitator demand that I return to the community. One morning Father Idesbald sneaked up to my cell to tell me that the visitator had arrived but was not Le Pennuin. The latter had resigned for reasons of health and was currently living in the Trappist house of studies in Rome as master of students.

I shall never forget the day I was scheduled to confer with the new man, Dom Columban Bisset. He was in a room of the guest house talking with another monk and his translator. Outside in the corridor, Fathers Amandus and Arnold and I awaited our turns. Amandus had also dropped out of the community ever since the last flu epidemic when, one evening in the chapter room, he fell over. For several weeks afterward, he walked around the cloister with a bandaged head. Yet there seemed to be a smile on his face as if he were sure some great plan had almost reached fulfillment. Eventually he managed to get a room in the infirmary and a sedentary job in the warm bookbinding shop. Usually, while the monks were in church or at work, he appeared in the cloister to read the bulletin board and in the scriptorium, where he searched the wastepaper baskets for the monks' discarded letters from home. Whenever he met someone, he simply closed his eyes behind those thick-lensed glasses of his and continued on his way. Only Father Raymond demanded a proper salutation from him. Raymond would hold him with one hand and wave the other in front of Amandus' face. But the latter would simply wait until the obstacle removed itself and then, like a patient turtle, carry on.

As we continued to wait, Arnold practiced his greeting to Abbot Columban. Pacing the floor and then kneeling to mimic kissing the abbot's ring, he said—under his breath but loud enough for us to hear—"Comment allez-vous, mon révérend père?" Arnold did this several times, seemingly unaware of our presence, so intense was his concentration. Arnold then walked toward Amandus, genuflected, and asked, "Comment allez-vous, mon révérend père?" and winked at me. Amandus, sitting on the low windowsill, opened his eyes for a second, smiled, and brought forth a long, whining flatulation. Arnold's face and bald head turned pink. He grabbed Amandus by the neck and drew back his fist. Amandus neither resisted nor cringed, perfectly confident that his helplessness made him invulnerable. Then with movie-manuscript timing, the door to the abbot's room opened and the monk leaving beckoned to Arnold. He relaxed his grip and signed to Amandus, "I-cut-you-down," meaning that he was going to tell the visitator all about Amandus' slackness in monastic observance. As Arnold closed the door behind him, Amandus turned to me, crossed one arm over the other, signifying "useless."

When at last my turn came, Abbot Columban and I talked for several minutes about nothing in particular. He seemed to understand my college French well enough. Then he looked into his log resting on the table. He mentioned that "someone" had complained that I no longer lived in the community. My heart skipped a beat, and I tried to prepare myself for some unpleasant directives. But he said nothing more and looked as if he awaited an explanation. So I described my attempts to take up the eremitical life and Fox's efforts to frustrate them. He smiled at me, rather sympathetically it seemed, and offered me his ring to kiss—a hint that our discussion had ended. But as I started out the door, he said to me in English, "Let us pray for one another." I returned to my cell to do just that.

18

The Duping of Abbot Fox

In 1961, after nearly a year in seclusion, I stopped thinking about leaving the abbey. I was happier than I had been in all my thirteen years of monastic life, and I began to think that my purpose in life was to stay at Gethsemani as its in-residence iconoclast. I was the living statement that community life is not for everyone, and I even wrote on the nameplate hanging on the wall of my cell: "Recluse." I found living on the margin of Trappist life quite enjoyable.

One morning in my cell, it struck me that so long as I *hoped* to become a hermit—or anything else for that matter—I could never be free. Even though hoping implies a possible goal to attain, it does not guarantee that the goal is worth hoping for. Having reached the age of thirty-seven, I discovered that all those things I yearned for so badly when I was young, I really didn't want at all. Free of what Sartre called the "dirty hope," I gave little thought to the ambitions and the fears they engender. I didn't even speculate upon what I would do should the abbot demand that I return to the community. But my peace had nothing to with Browning's "God's in His Heaven,/ All's right with the world." Like the existentialist Jean Camus, whose works I had been reading, I learned to disregard the fatherly and brotherly aspects of God and, consequently, the temptation to arouse my hopes by asking for divine favors. As I did during my childhood, I thought of him as something—in the true sense of the word—"awful." And only because I found God awful and remote did I find him a consolation.

As far as people outside the abbey were concerned, my position had not changed at all. My family and friends—according to their letters—still venerated me as an example of piety and self-renunciation. The monks in the abbey seemed to have the same opinion. None complained that I had dropped out of their midst; in fact, I believe many were edified that I had chosen seclusion. I suppose I should have felt embarrassed at being such a bogus object of admiration, but I reached an inward peace in which it didn't bother me.

One afternoon, while absorbed in the Prayer of the Blank, I thought I had a true mystical experience. I neither levitated, nor saw a vision, nor heard celestial voices. If I had, I would have seen a psychiatrist, for I knew enough about mystical theology to consider such phenomena as symptoms of hallucination. Rather, I seemed to been in a kind of delightful half-conscious vision that must have lasted twenty minutes or more, although it seemed but a second. Abbot Dunne once spoke to me about this experience. He called it "coeternal," something that happens in time but seems beyond the duration of successive events. He talked of St. Thomas Aquinas, the Dominican theologian who grew quite fat because, while at table, he pondered so intensely on theological questions that the cook kept filling his plate without his being aware of it. Thomas just kept on thinking and eating. Abbot Dunne ended this little story with one of his pithy sayings, "It's better to use pleasures distractedly than to concentrate upon ascetical practices."

The closest analogy that I could draw concerning that experience was the way I felt the evening I spent with William Inge at the Kiel Auditorium in St. Louis. As Lily Pons sang, I became completely immersed in her voice, unaware of how long the concert lasted or where it was taking place. I don't recall the effects that voice produced, other than elevating my taste in music above Benny Goodman's swing and Duke Ellington's jazz. But that afternoon in my cell, the Blank left me with the clearest impression that I still was—essentially—the same irreverent Irish-American kid on Grand Bahama Island, the rebellious upstart at St. Louis University, the enthusiastic lover of books and art and Maggie. I might have covered my sense of humor, my dilettantism, my phobias and prejudices, with the habit of a Trappist, but I didn't eradicate them. And I suspected that all the religious practices and attitudes of my early monastic career had never made me virtuous since, at the time, I wasn't really myself. I had been putting on the same act I started while a postulant in the guest house back in 1948. It was the act we all played under the spiritual direction of well-meaning but benighted men who said we would become humble by looking humble, by casting our eyes continually upon the floor. A poet once wrote, "They give, they do to get esteem/ Until seeming blest, they are like what they seem." I had even heard preached in the chapter room, by a professor of theology, that if a person has no faith, he need only act as if he has and all will be well. It doesn't work. At least it didn't on me. Of course, every now and then I would recall St. John of the Cross's teaching that those destined for the mystical life had to be purged of all spiritual consolation by suffering doubts. Consequently, through this dirty hope, I kept alive my feeble faith.

Theologians say that a person loses his faith, not all at once, but gradually, by willful skepticism or by living in a manner incompatible with religious laws. Yet I knew Trappist monks, apparently not only regular in their duties but even devout, who left the abbey after twenty years of service. And I have heard of Catholic lay people, unacquainted with the austerity and monotony of Trappist life, who gave up their religion after many years in the church. I had read of a Christian woman of Nero's era who, shaky in her allegiance to the cult of Jesus, offered herself to the Roman executioners as candidate for the arena. She seems to have jumped at the chance to be a martyr, hoping to win the reward of faith before losing faith itself.

I don't think my faith grew weak through the breaking of any serious laws. We were obliged to go to confession frequently, and I always had trouble coming up anything interesting to tell the priest. Possibly my problem began in my third year of the scholasticate, when I learned about the new *form* criticism of the Bible as well as other ways of interpreting the Scriptures. I had no trouble accepting these teachings; in fact, I found them refreshing. But once I discovered controversy in the church, I lost my esteem for what I considered the Catholic tradition and joined the other radicals in seeking alternative doctrines. Also, many of the theological journals in our library contained articles on situation ethics, existentialism, ecumenism, and humanism, which seemed to challenge infallible teaching espoused by the old Pope Pius and his equally old cardinals, described by the young theologians as behind the times.

Then the new pope, John XXIII, came on the scene and opened the windows to what many considered rays of enlightenment, which to me, heretofore guided comfortably by tradition, became shadows of obfuscation. Imagine. It was no longer a mortal sin to drink or eat before receiving holy communion. Now, how would that change affect all those who had broken that law and died without being absolved? Many other church regulations, once thought to be "laws of the Medes and the Persians," toppled. A pious Catholic could eat all the ham and eggs he wanted before communion, so long as an hour intervened. Many pastors no longer regarded missing mass on Sunday a mortal sin. Some even began to instruct their flocks that contraception was a matter of the individual's conscience. As for traditional devotions, the young lions of ecumenism stressed the liturgy and seemingly despised the rosary, stations of the cross, solemn benediction, and first Friday communions. There was even talk of changing the traditional and universal language of the Catholic Church—from the sublime Latin to the vulgar tongue of each nation.

Except for doing away with Latin, I favored all these changes. I cheered the ecumenists for their efforts to "purify" the church of nonessentials. However, in so doing they made the same mistake Mallarmé did when he attempted to purify poetry. In reducing the material aspects of both, they emptied religion and art of emotion. As a consequence, Catholics for whom the mystical held attraction began to turn, in ever-increasing numbers, to the lure of Zen and other Eastern philosophies.

One afternoon, while I was thinking such deep thoughts, who should come to my cell for a visit but Father Idesbald. His light-blue eyes sparkled with excitement. I prepared myself for his weekly account of those monks proclaimed on Thursday in the chapter of faults, or the progress being made on the cave the brothers were blasting out of a hill to make a storing room for cheese, or his most recent catch of sunfish at Abbot Dunne's Lake near Merton's chalet in the woods. But the news he brought me that day would change my life entirely.

Idesbald announced the arrival of Father Jean Leclerq, a friend of Merton from St. Maurice's Monastery in Luxembourg. Merton had told me, several years before, that Leclerq's former abbot Dom Jacques Winandy had renounced his post and settled in a hermitage on the island of Martinique. My first reaction was apathetic. Wonderful! Another middle-aged infant who loves to play hermit. I considered myself having outgrown religious ideals just as one grows out of susceptibility to chicken pox. In fact I wished Leclerq's coming had not reminded me of the eremitical life. I was a happy recluse or monastic dropout and didn't want to think about vocations anymore.

Nevertheless, I did attend Leclerq's opening conference held in the novitiate scriptorium. That was the first time I had been there since 1950, when I made my simple profession and happily waved good-bye to Father Urban, the novice master. I recalled those cold winter mornings at five o'clock, the radiators that started clanking with hot water, and the tiny pencil stubs we used to write with in the notebooks we made out of used envelopes. It was the same room where Dom Vital gave his famous lectures on "manure spirituality," and where he introduced me as the "pig shot American postulant."

Leclerq lectured in English, but his accent was so bad that I could hardly understand anything he said. But another former aspirant to solitude stuck out the entire series of lectures and even met Leclerq personally through Merton. He was Frater Sylvanus, the current librarian. It seems that Sylvanus had also tried to join the Camaldolese hermits in Big Sur, California, but the abbot foiled the attempt. So Merton persuaded Leclerq to write Winandy on behalf of Sylvanus, asking him to recommend the latter to the bishop of Martinique. Should the bishop accept Sylvanus into the diocese as a hermit, there was nothing Fox could do about it. Moreover, since Leclerq was not under Fox's jurisdiction, the letter went off without being read by the abbot. Also, since the bishop's positive response arrived at Gethsemani before Leclerq had departed, Fox could not intercept it. Leclerq received the letter and gave it to Sylvanus, and one fine morning Sylvanus presented it to Fox. The old abbot was beaten. He was forced to to let Sylvanus go as soon as he had obtained an indult of exclaustration, that is, permission from the Sacred College of Religious in Rome to live away from the abbey.

I learned about the great ruse one evening after work, when Sylvanus appeared at the entrance of my cell, almost beside himself with joy. He said he had permission to show me letters from the bishop, Winandy, and a Canadian hermit named Jean Paré. The latter was about to leave for some seminary in Holland to study for the priesthood and offered Sylvanus the use of his hermitage in a place called Canton Suisse during his absence. According to Paré, living expenses on the island were practically nothing. Since the temperature was continually mild, the flimsiest housing and lightest clothing would do. And no man would starve if he could content himself with the food he could pluck off the trees or pull out of the rich volcanic soil. Moreover, Paré said, the people are friendly and often bring presents of fish, milk, eggs, and bread to the hermits.

I thought it most strange for the abbot to let Sylvanus show me those letters, unless he had become so frustrated with the malcontents of the abbey that he had resolved to encourage us all to leave. This was my chance. So I asked Sylvanus to help me get to Martinique once he was established there, and he said he would.

About a month later, in April, Sylvanus came to my cell before dawn, dressed in a black clerical suit and Roman collar. It seemed rather ridiculous to communicate in sign language, for we could hardly see each other's fingers. But we did, yet not without the help of whispers while discussing critical points. He was to leave that very day for Salem, New Jersey, where his father was to undergo a serious operation, even though the indult of exclaustration had not arrived. In other words, the abbot had given him a temporary leave of absence, valid for just under six months.

Sylvanus and I speculated awhile on the unaccustomed generosity of the abbot. Not only was he tired of the malcontents, as I suspected, but Sylvanus believed that, with the many new ideas coming out in reference to monasticism, he was no longer sure of his stance against the solitary life. But neither of us would have dreamed that, two years later at the annual meeting of Trappist abbots in Rome, he would argue successfully for introducing the eremetical life into the usages of the order and, a few years after that, quit his post and become a hermit at Gethsemani himself, in fulfillment of his ambitions as a young monk.

That noon, in the refectory, I looked at the place where Sylvanus ordinarily sat. It was empty. He had done it.

19

The Near Sin

Throughout that summer the abbot's strange behavior continued. He even permitted a regular correspondence between Sylvanus and me, even on days not slated for writing. Eventually, a lettergram from Sylvanus reached me with a note from the abbot pinned to it. He informed me that, on the following Friday, I would be taken to Louisville by one of the drivers to get a passport, visa, and inoculations. I could not help mark the irony of the situation. I finally got what I had wanted so long, but only after I had convinced myself that I could be happy without it.

I had to go to St. Joseph's Infirmary for the inoculations, so I decided to get a complete physical examination at the same time. When I walked up to the admissions desk, a beautiful young woman greeted me. We talked and joked with one another for a few minutes. Then one of the sisters in the back office called her, and she pulled up from beneath her desk a pair of crutches. With them under her arms, she stood up, swung around, and propelled herself away from me. Then I saw her legs—two spindly appendages, supported by steel braces. Under my breath, I cursed as vehemently as I might have after hitting my finger with a hammer. She must have been one of the many student nurses at the hospital back in 1952—while I was there with Merton—who had come down with polio. And she must have stayed on as a clerical worker, since she, like many of the others, could never hope to become a nurse. When she reached the sister who called her, she turned herself around awkwardly and smiled. She must have noticed the shocked expression on my face and remembered she was a cripple. She hobbled back and signed me in without another word.

On the way to my room, I wondered if the parents of that lovely girl still went to church. Perhaps their faith had been deepened by the tragedy. But had she been my sweetheart or daughter, I think my religious sense would have suffered. Even St. Teresa of

Avila remarked that few people find loving God easier when confronted with sorrow or misery. When my grandmother died, I was told, Father McGee, trying to console my grandfather, quoted a passage from Job: "I shall love Him [God] though he kill me." Grandfather took the pastor by the arm and pushed him though the doorway. Somehow, even as a child, I sympathized with Grandfather.

I sat back in a sumptuous chair and picked a *Life* magazine out of the rack. The cover depicted another beautiful woman—Queen Elizabeth II. Again my mind returned to my stay at St. Joseph's ten years before. One afternoon the head nurse of the wing insisted that I sit in the visitors' parlor—where the television was—to watch the coronation of the new queen at Westminster Abbey. Since I enjoyed the show immensely, I felt guilty about such self-indulgence. Since the new queen was quite beautiful and only two years younger than I, there followed hours of speculation on what would happen should we meet. One possibility was that we would fall in love with each other. In my fantasy, she was ready to abandon her throne should I agree to leave the religious life. I thought about what my answer should be but, without making a definite commitment, broke off the daydreaming and fled to reality. However, as I looked at the queen's picture again—she was older but still handsome—I realized that, confronted with the same question at that time of my life, I would have to answer, at least, "Maybe."

That afternoon, Dr. Mulligan sent me down to the cardiology room for an EKG. The lab technician, one of the sisters, smiled pleasantly as if sticking those rubber terminals on my chest were an amusing game. And the more she smiled, the prettier she seemed. I was fascinated. I could not help wondering why a woman with her beauty should enter a convent. She had a way of looking at a man that made him feel both superior to, and yet dependent upon her. As I was leaving, she said that she might drop in on me sometime. She didn't bother to ask if she would be welcome.

After visiting hours were over that evening, she knocked on my door. When I let her in, she said hello and placed her hand on my shoulder as if to assure me. I suppose that I seemed nervous, for the corridors were dark and only one lamp shone in my room. There was something about the atmosphere that suggested a secret rendezvous. But she immediately assumed the role of a revering nun and insisted that I take the lounge while she drew up a straight-backed chair. At first we talked about the Trappists and her cousin who intended to become one. She hung upon my words as if they had been revealed on Mount Sinai. Later the subject switched to mysticism and, whenever I described some mystical phenomenon, such as "the dark night of the soul" or "the spiritual marriage," she looked at me as if she believed I was talking about my own experiences. Of all her attractions, the most seductive—I now realize—was her admiration of me.

Two nights later, about nine in the evening, she visited me again. This time she brought a copy of St. John of the Cross's *The Ascent to Mount Carmel.* We sat on the divan reading it together and, despite the mystical words, I felt her knee pressing against mine. I froze, afraid to move lest moving away from her signal my puerile fear, afraid not to move lest she interpret my passivity as a tacit invitation to go on. Melodramatically, "in the nick of time," a nurses' aid pushed her cart into the room, waved perfunctorily, and changed the ice water. My companion arose and thanked me for a pleasant evening. Alone again, we stood at the door, talking. Then she suddenly took my right hand in both of hers, squeezed it, and bolted out of the room. The gesture carried the promise of another, more eventful meeting, I thought, and I regretted that I would not be there to share it. I felt ashamed, of course, but rather than torture myself with thoughts of guilt, I had recourse to Dom Vital's old manure spirituality and reflected that the experience might make me at least humble. It had confirmed what I had forgotten. I wasn't really chaste; I was simply cloistered.

Back at Gethsemani there was a rumor going about that Merton was ready to leave for a Benedictine monastery in Mexico, where he had been offered the post of superior. Merton was quite aware of the speculation on his stability, which had spread not only among the monks of Gethsemani but throughout the world. In the preface to the Japanese edition to *The Seven Storey Mountain*, he wrote, "Many rumors have been disseminated about me since I came to the monastery. Most of them have assured people that I had left the monastery, that I had returned to New York, that I was in Europe, that I was in South America or Asia, that I had become a hermit, that I was married, that I was drunk, that I was dead." Although later in the text he denies all these possibilities, it is remarkable how close he was in verifying every one of them. I am not sure he ever got drunk on his short excursions from the abbey, but the evening we spent together drinking beer at Jones's Restaurant, he was "happy." Also, he did leave the abbey for a short while to keep an appointment in New York City with Dr. Daisetz Susuki, the Zen scholar. In 1965, Merton did become a hermit on the grounds of Gethsemani. And though he never got to Europe or South America, in 1968 he journeyed to Asia, where he died. After his death I learned that what seemed the most extravagant of the public's theories on Merton's adventures—that he got married—nearly happened. While a patient at St. Joseph's Infirmary, he became romantically involved with a student nurse. Consequently, not just one of the rumors about him was true, but almost *all* of them!

Merton's ambivalence toward becoming a solitary, on one hand, and a cynosure, on the other, is evident in most of his biographies. He had entered Gethsemani both to renounce the world and, at the same time, to become a famous personality. And when he became a star, he could not renounce his monasticism without losing the basis of his popularity. By identifying himself with solitude, he became mysterious. Yet unless he wrote about himself, his mysteriousness could not have sparked the imagination of his readers. Nor could he have enjoyed his solitude and his mystery without others knowing about them and admiring him for them.

Perhaps the explanation of Merton's ambivalence can be found in one of the theories propagated by his favorite poet, William Blake. The latter believed that all progress takes place through the confrontation of opposites. Just as Blake divided his best poems into *Songs of Innocence* and *Songs of Experience*, one group viewing subjects one way, and the other group viewing them in the opposite way, so Merton might have believed that all progress in knowledge of himself, the Trappist order, and the spiritual life depended on his assuming—for the sake of study—opposite attitudes toward them. Although his worst writings are serious—deadly serious—others are quite lighthearted—even funny—and good. Not only the style but even the subjects of his writings show his bifurcated tendencies: For example, those espousing seclusion and those advocating social action. And what always seemed to me the supreme irony in Merton is the fact that, after convincing the abbot to let him live the eremitical life, he began planning a trip to the Orient. And what did he do once he got there? He visited the cells of Indian solitaries to talk about their mutual love of silence and to argue about the attainment of peace of soul.

Perhaps my understanding of, and sympathy with, Merton's ambivalence derived from the awareness of some ambivalence in myself. There I was, eager to leave the abbey with its noisy construction and its embarrassing commercialism—both distractions from the contemplative life—yet I had redeveloped my taste for secular literature as a means of coping with the tension produced in awaiting my release. The opportunity for my indulgence in this type of reading had been furnished by Frater Francis de Sales, the former librarian with a penchant for spending money and immersing himself into any project assigned to him. His ambition had been to turn Gethsemani's bookshelves into the equivalent of a university library. Before the two months of his reign had ended (Fox fired him), we had all the novels of Hemingway, Faulkner, Fitzgerald, Dos Passos, and so on. I knew that most of those books had no more place in the abbey than Gypsy Rose Lee, yet in the silence of my cell I read *Farewell to Arms, The Great Gatsby*, and even the very unsanctified *Sanctuary*. Their topics did not arouse my desires for women, money, and adventure, but their exquisite styles made me disgusted with the unctuous rhetoric of most devotional literature.

Moreover, to confirm my ambivalence, I began to have mixed feelings about going to Martinique when I learned that the abbot-general had invited Gethsemani to send some monks to Rome for graduate studies in theology and philosophy. Fox complied and began selecting candidates for the venture. The event was unprecedented at our abbey, since abbots of the past had been too poor to pay for passages to Europe, and the order usually forbade Trappists to study in American universities. Moreover, the old abbots didn't believe monks needed academic degrees. As for instructors of Trappist candidates for the priesthood, there were always qualified people to enter the order as novices. And when I saw the names of the monks chosen—many of whom I had helped to pass examinations, I felt shamefully outraged.

And there was something else I wanted that opposed both the monastic and eremitical vocations: a child. I was unable to clearly understand this longing. But I remember that it was more poignant than my desire to study in Rome and certainly unrelated to a passion for women. Perhaps it was a matter of self-perpetuation that had come on with middle age, or the curiosity of a celibate who wonders if he indeed could generate an offspring, or the loneliness of the jaded solitary who would create a companion, or—and this seems the most probable—the ordinary person who realizes that he needs to love and be loved. At one time I felt that all a monk should (or need to) love was God. The emphasis is upon "felt," for nothing I had heard or read insisted that I should believe this notion to be true. My idealism led me to consider friendship and family ties as concessions to beginners in the spiritual life. Consequently, the urge to have children after nearly fourteen years in an abbey was not only a surprise but an embarrassment as well. I was still a human being and the same individual human being I had always been.

20

The Exodus

I had been happy at Gethsemani because I had nothing better to hope for. But throughout the summer of 1962, I could look forward to starting a new life on the island of Martinique. Nevertheless, the exciting prospect routed my peace and left me anxious lest the indult not be granted or the abbot change his mind about letting me go. Every noon I went to the refectory, hoping to see a letter from Rome at my place. But instead of reading the Scriptures or *The Imitation of Christ* for consolation, I lost myself in novels, such as *L'Etranger*.

For a while I tried to emulate the impassivity of Camus' hero Meursault, and when I arrived at my place in the refectory I refused to look down to see if the letter had come. I was cool, invulnerable to surprise or disappointment, I thought. But when at last the letters came—one from Rome and another from Sylvanus—it was like Christmas, Easter, and the Fourth of July. I stuffed them into the pocket of my robe while I ate, but before the dinner had ended I could not help pulling them out to read them. The indult said just what I knew it would—that I could live out of the abbey for a period of two years. So most of my attention fell on what Sylvanus wrote. Of particular interest was the fact that one of the hermits, a young Dutchman named Vandoorne, had become ill and was recuperating at the convent of the Dominican sisters in a town called Morne Rouge. He had offered me the use of his hermitage at Canton Suisse until his return. The word *hermitage* kept popping up in the letter, and I found it amusing. Soon people would be referring to me as Gerald the Hermit, and the thought made me burst out laughing just as we began to chant the *De profundis*, the regular prayer after meals. I had always imagined hermits to be emaciated and melancholy like those described by John Moschus in the *Pratum Spirituale*. But apparently, plump Sylvanus and the other hermits felt comfortable with the title. Yet I wondered what St. Antony of Egypt or St.

Macarius the Elder would think of a modern hermit arriving in the wilderness on a jet plane.

In Martinique it seemed that all one needed to be a hermit was to live in a hermitage, and now I had one—for free. Moreover, Sylvanus assured me that I would never want for food so long as I could be contented with whatever I found on trees or bushes or under the ground. However, I figured I should have some cash in case of emergencies, and I knew the abbot would give me no more than the price of a one-way plane ticket and a few dollars for expenses. So while I waited for the abbot to return from a business trip, I began an article entitled "Fourteen Years with Thomas Merton" and planned to send it to William Shawn, the editor of *The New Yorker*, my favorite magazine, hoping he would pay me well. I knew full well that I was exploiting a famous name, but I was grateful for the opportunity.

One morning in September, about five o'clock, while the monks were still in church, I went to the refectory. A few lights were on, since some brothers were there having breakfast early before going to work. I found Merton's place and slipped the note I had written under his napkin. It was an invitation to join Sylvanus and me in Martinique. I knew he wouldn't accept, but I felt the gesture was called for. Then I got a cup of soybean brew from the aluminum urn at the back of the room and sat at my own place to drink it. I glanced up at the pulpit in the middle of the refectory and wished I had a dollar for every book I had heard read there during the meals. And I recalled coming in from the woodshed, after splitting logs all morning in zero weather, so hungry that I could have eaten even Brother Fabian's macaroni-celery-tomato casserole, and wondering with fear and trembling whether the servant of the refectory had given me my main portion of vegetables in that dreaded small, green galvanized bowl. I recalled too those mornings during Lent when, by order of the abbot, all students were obliged to eat breakfast instead of fasting with Fathers Raymond, Timothy, Arsenius, and the other ascetics. I had felt ashamed to be associated with . . . eaters! I think I must have been a little crazy during those days. I was continually keeping records of my ascetical practices—no taking hot baths, no wearing winter robes, and—above all—no eating breakfasts. I reminded myself of Kafka's protagonist in *The Hunger Artist*. And as I left the refectory—for the last time of my monastic career—I thought about the time when, as a postulant still in my street clothes, I dropped a saucer into the big aluminum urn that served—in the evenings—as a garbage can and Merton rolled up a sleeve of his cowl to retrieve it.

At dawn I strolled through the cemetery. It was quiet, since Father Placid was not there with his Winchester shooting bluejays and crows. The first rays of the orange sun fell upon the aluminum-painted crosses marking the graves. There was a funereal poem I had found, as a novice, in an old book about Trappists and their alleged preoccupation with death. It went:

Je suis revenu de la Trappe
Cette maudite trappe à fou
Et si jamais le diable m'y attrape
Je veux qu'on me casse le cou
Ce maudit trou n'est qu'une trappe
Ce maudit trou
n'est qu'une trappe à fou.

Translated, it goes something like this:

I just returned from La Trappe,
That cursed, foolish trap.
And if ever the devil catches me,
I hope someone will break my neck.
That cursed hole is only a trap;
That cursed hole
Is only a foolish trap.

According to that same book, the Abbey of La Grande Trappe was founded, in the twelfth century, by Rotron, the Count of Perche in Normandy. Although actually named Maison-Dieu, the natives called it La Trappe because in the patois of Perche, *trappe* means "step," and the monks had to go down many steps or levels to reach the marshes surrounding the abbey, where they fished. However, the name "La Trappe" was never linked with death until the seventeen century, when Armand de Rancé obtained the abbey as a benefice and, after a (for a priest) rather libertine life, assumed the role of abbot. The monks living there at the time had been less than edifying; in fact, they had turned the church into a bowling alley. Despite their resistance, De Rancé reformed the community, which at his death numbered fifty or more fervent monks.

Legend has it that those Trappist monks and their successors became identified with death, that they even greeted one another with the cheery salutation, "Frère, il faut morire" ("Brother, you have to die"). Of course, the story isn't true, since Trappists never greet anybody with words; they simply bow their heads. Another legend accounts for De Rancé's conversion to monasticism. While in Paris one day, he learned that Madame de Montbazon, famous for her beauty and easy morals, was ill. Since he loved her, the abbot went straight to her house, where he learned she had just died. When he entered her room he found her body stuffed into a coffin. It seems that the box was too small to accommodate all of Madame; consequently someone had decapitated her and placed her bloody head next to it on the floor. Moreover in his *Vie de Rancé*, Chateaubriand suggests that the grieved lover-priest took that head with him to La Trappe and put it in his room to contemplate.

Probably that story isn't true either. Yet the Trappist's *gout de l'horrible* is still evident in the enormous deathhead that adorns the refectory in the Abbey de Port-du-salut and the inscription below it:

Fut-il roi, fut-il pâtre?
(Was he a king, was he a shepherd?)

—as well as in the picture, still visible I am told, above the entrance to the dormitory at the Abbey de Mont-des-Olives. Below an image of the Grim Reaper armed with a scythe, his boney hands resting on the lintel and gazing at all who pass, is written:

Diese Nacht Vielleight
(This night perhaps)

Much has been written about the dubious practice at La Trappe regarding the digging a bit of one's grave each day. I noticed it mentioned in the French novel I referred to earlier, called *Les Memoires du Comte de Comminge* by Madame de Tencin. In the story, the hero is forbidden by his parents to marry his cousin Adelaide. So, heartbroken, he enters a Trappist abbey to spend his life in melancholy reflection and preparation for death. Adelaide, married to someone else against her will, disguises herself as a man and joins the same abbey. They live there together without one recognizing the other. But one day Adelaide finds the count weeping while gazing at a small portrait of her, which she had given him years before. From then on she is happy, for she had found her beloved and knows that he loves her. Only after he dies does she confess being a woman. For her penance, the abbot—so the story goes—commands her to dig her own grave.

I tried to imagine a Trappist cemetery where, every day each of the sixty or seventy monks digs up a few shovelfulls of earth from his grave. That custom would soon produce a lot of deep holes. It was ridiculous and besides, the Trappist usages never, even in De Rancé's time, prescribed such a duty. Yet it was such legends that had attracted me to Gethsemani, and, on that last morning in the cemetery, I regretted that I would never be buried as a Trappist—without a casket, embalmed in that gray-white solution, and placed under one of those aluminum-painted crosses. I smiled at the romantic thought and said to myself, "Well, you can't have everything."

When the bells rang for prime at six o'clock, I went to my cell, took off my monastic clothes, and put on a black suit, white shirt, Roman collar, and a yellow panama hat, very much like the one Father Barnabus wore back in the forties when I was at St. Anthony's Hospital in St. Louis. I put it on and flipped up the brim, baseball-fan style, just as he had done. I made a final check on my valise: passport, visa, inoculation papers, underwear, socks, extra shirt, my manuscript "Fourteen Years with Thomas Merton," and the cover letter. Then I counted the 250 dollars in my wallet—the biggest sum of money I had ever owned—and stuffed it into my breast pocket.

At the guest house I waved to Brother Isidore who smiled and made signs asking where I was going. When I responded with "Over-big-water," he looked rather sad. Then I placed my manuscript in the basket for the outgoing mail lying on Brother Alexander's table in the post office. For my return address I had written on the envelope: Bellefontaine, Martinique. Out in the driveway, in front of the main gate, I looked up at the statue of Our Lady holding the Infant Jesus on her broad hip and at the inscription written on the wall underneath: *Pax Intrantibus*. I decided the words conveyed the author's wish, not his conviction. I threw my valise into Brother Giles' van and got in after it.

On the road to Louisville I thought of Arnold, Leonard, Idesbald, Amandus, and the other quidnuncs of the abbey speculating on where I had gone. Arnold would have signed, "Who-cares-useless-monk." Leonard would have ventured, "Over-big-water-Rome." He thought I was bright and would have been sent to study. Idesbald would propose, "I-think-joined-white-monks" (Carthusians). Amandus, always concerned with health problems, might have commented, "Sick-near-death-go-home." Merton, of course, would tell the novices and soon the truth would be out.

In Louisville, Giles drove up Broadway and eventually turned in at the Brown Hotel, where I had spent a very expensive night fifteen years before. I had no recollection of the restaurant inside, so I decided it had been remodeled since my last visit. But the food seemed just as good then as it did in 1947 and the waitresses even prettier. Giles ordered ham, eggs, grapefruit, toast, Cream of Wheat, and coffee. He smiled like a man-about-town when he directed the waitress to bring the coffee right away. I was too confused to know if I were hungry or not, but I ordered the same.

All through the meal a plan kept taking shape. There was no reason for my leaving the country immediately. The abbot hadn't obliged me to do so, and it seemed natural that I visit my mother before going off to Martinique. When we left the hotel, I told Giles I wouldn't be going to the airport but to the train station instead. The depot was only a few blocks away, and when he dropped me off he wished me luck and slipped a pack of spearmint gum into my jacket pocket. Then he gave me his sinister smile. He had large teeth and one of them was missing in the front. With that smile and shaved head he might have passed for an escaped convict.

At the depot I sent a telegram to my mother and boarded a coach bound for St. Louis. Then I found a seat next to a window and looked out trying to recall that cold February morning fourteen years earlier when I was there on my way to Gethsemani. During that time I had been out of the abbey several times, but only to the hospital in Louisville. As the train moved out of the depot, I moved into a totally new world. Had I been in jail rather than in the abbey, I might have kept up with events through newspapers and television. But at Gethsemani, the only news we received was by way of the abbot's remarks in the chapter room. I knew that Elizabeth II was queen of England and that John F. Kennedy was the president of the United States, but I could not recognize the different makes of cars, the names of actors on movie marquees, or the titles of songs coming over my fellow passengers' radios. Like Rip Van Winkle, I had awakened in a strange environment and the entire decade of the fifties had been lost to me.

Late that afternoon the train rumbled over one of the trestles that spans the Mississippi River between Illinois and Missouri. The muddy waters below were carrying barges and yachts toward Cincinnati to the east and toward Memphis to the south. Beyond the Eads Bridge, near the levee (Grandfather used to pronounce it "le-VAY"), a steamer was moored. It looked like the *Admiral*, once used for moonlight cruises to Alton. Maggie and I had spent many summer evenings in the cool darkness of the upper deck. And then I realized that she still lived in St. Louis. Her mother and mine were friends.

In Union Station I stood on the quay and could almost feel the presence of Abbot Dunne, bent and frail, with the breeze tossing the hood on his black scapular like a windsock. I surrendered to a few moments of what-might-have-been speculation. Had I never met the abbot that afternoon, or had he not invited me to make a retreat at Gethsemani, or had I simply never gone, and so on, I might never have become a monk. I might have married Maggie and raised a family. I would be coming home from a business trip with presents for the children, wondering what my wife was preparing for dinner.

I almost gave the taxi driver my old address on Evans Avenue but remembered in time to direct him to mother's current home in south St. Louis, where she had been living for the past seven or eight years. She wanted to be near Aunt Mary and Uncle Frank. But she probably would have moved from the West End anyway, since most of the Irish had abandoned the old neighborhood and left it to the poor blacks who couldn't afford to live anywhere else. Many of our Jewish neighbors were still in that part of town but farther west, in University City and Clayton.

We pulled up before a tan-brick bungalow built in the early fifties, I guessed, with a two-car garage suggesting the modest affluence of that era. I had read of such homes built by the survivors of World War II, happy with the middle-class splendor of American life, which they had fought for and won. Such homes were the artillery from which the conventional and fertile ex-warriors had launched the baby boom. But many of the babies grew up revolting against their parents' bourgeois materialism, and they beat paths to San Francisco and New York to form the beatnik subculture. I suppose many of them found their way to the monasteries as well, since there had been a great influx of postulants in those days.

Of course, Mother was glad to see me. But I couldn't account for the hysterical welcome shown me by her latest cocker spaniel, which barked and wagged its behind and peed on the floor from excitement. On the wall opposite the front door hung the same picture of the Sacred Heart, reflecting the afternoon light and the piety of its owner. Dominating the front room was, I imagined, the largest Philco television set in the world, and on the screen appeared a nattily dressed man who identified himself as Paul Harvey.

In my bedroom was the copy of Zurburan's *The Standing Monk* that I had bought at the Forest Park Art Museum years before. I never noticed until then that the monk was St. Francis of Assisi, although he wore the habit of a Carthusian except for the rope around his waist. With that observation, I condemned it as not only melodramatic but phony. I had paid less attention to the picture's historical and aesthetic details when I first saw it. Piety, like love, I guess, dulls one's critical sense. Next to it hung a photograph of Maggie and, beside it, a framed picture of me sketched by William Inge. Under the triad stood the old Philco radio-phonograph mother had bought at the Union-May-Stern Furniture and Appliance Company in 1941. It featured the "revolutionary" beam-of-light playing arm. Mother had thought that the beam actually called forth the sound from the grooves, replacing the conventional needle. Next to the phonograph were four racks of recordings, going as far back in production as the twenties. There was Whiteman's rendition of "Rhapsody in Blue," Cab Calloway's "The Man from Harlem," Benny Goodman's "Sing, Sing, Sing," and hundreds more. I felt that Merton would have asked if I had "Sophisticated Swing." I would have loved to play it for him. I looked for my collection of books, but all I found were those on the dresser—*The Three Religious Rebels, The Garden of Allah, The Razor's Edge*, and *The Imitation of Christ*. I picked up the last one and turned a few pages. Out of it fell a holy card depicting some artist's conception of St. Jude, the patron of the dying. On the back was written, Sister Veronica

O.S.F. She was in some Catholic hospital in Chicago, near sixty but still nursing. I had never met a more lovable woman.

I sat at the kitchen table before a plate filled with a Porterhouse steak as thick as a doormat. But I started on the bowl of wilted lettuce with that sweet-and-sour taste I liked so much as a boy. Beside it was another plate covered with roasted potatoes and creamed corn, right out of a Libby's food container. All that made up my birthday meal since I was three years old or as early as I can remember. With each bite of the steak I seemed to feel the muscles in my arms double in size. As Proust would have reminded me, despite the years of fasting and abstinence, I had not lost my taste for good food or the capacity for consuming a lot of it. Afterward, I even wanted one of my mother's Chesterfield cigarettes but didn't dare ask. That evening we sat on the divan together watching "Gunsmoke" followed by the "Gary Moore Show" and then by a movie starring Betty Grable and Victor Mature, the title of which I have forgotten. It occurred to me that I could easily get used to such a life, and I felt both embarrassed and even a little scared.

The next morning I drove Mother's car to Brentwood, a suburb of St. Louis, where I knew Maggie lived. I passed her house about six times hoping she would appear. But I couldn't make myself stop the car, mount the steps of her front porch, and ring the doorbell. What could I expect her to do—rush into my arms? Then I realized that the proper thing to do was ring her up and inveigle an invitation. I rode around a while looking for a drugstore or service station with a phone and thinking what I'd say to her. On Lindbergh Road I pulled into a Toddle House snack bar and ordered coffee and one of those enormous cinnamon rolls. After couching what I thought to be a reasonable line of conversation and assuming a casual tone, I looked around for a public telephone. Unfortunately, it was attached to the wall behind me and not in an enclosed booth. She would know I was calling from a restaurant, for the jukebox was playing and people were talking.

As I drove the Impala through Clayton, I passed the Shaw Park pool, Clayton High School, the Shady Oak Theatre—places existing, as far as I was concerned, only by virtue of their association with Maggie in my sentimental reveries. I knew I was going to leave St.Louis without seeing her, without even speaking to her over the phone. And I recalled the other senseless things I had done while dating her back in the forties. I would pass the entire week thinking about her and yet never call her to say hello. I even let the weekends go by without arranging a rendezvous, simply because I felt so miserable after kissing her and saying goodnight. I broke dates with her—stood her up—with the intention of ending a relationship I felt would never last. I couldn't determine why I had such diffidence about myself in regard to Maggie. With other girls I had no such problem. Yet after all those years I hadn't changed. Despite my intention to contact other old friends, to visit some of my old haunts, spend several more days with my mother, I left for Martinique the following afternoon.

21

In Martinique

Flying south above the Mississippi River in the plush Delta D-C 10, I lamented my not having contacted Maggie and my other friends as well. I had missed enough opportunities by entering the abbey at twenty-three and should have been making up for lost time. And I might have continued reprimanding myself for breaking my St. Louis ties forever, had I not recalled my mother's parting words, "Remember, if you don't like it down there, just leave. But whatever happens, do try to get home for Christmas." She had given me the same advice the morning I left for Gethsemani. Pious though she was, she took lightly resolutions, promises, and even vows that proved inconvenient. She assumed they were rashly made and therefore unbinding. She felt confident that her God of consummate common sense regarded it quite enough that his fatuous creatures keep the Ten Commandments—at least most of the time—and didn't worry about their observance or nonobservance of ecclesiastical laws. And some of the younger priests she confessed to confirmed her theory. When she told one that I was trying to leave Gethsemani and join the Camaldolese, he said, "Tell your son to walk out of that damn place. I'll fix it with the archbishop."

After a five-hour wait at the New Orleans airport, I changed planes and flew to San Juan, arriving at about six in the morning. I was sleepy and the terminal was hot, so I decided to get some air. I had missed two mornings of not hearing mass during my stay at home so, to satisfy my conscience, I began to look for a church. A taxi driver said there was none within walking distance, so I had him take me to the Carmelite Monastery of Santa Teresa. Within ten minutes we pulled up before a white-stucco edifice, California-mission type, just as the bells were ringing.

Entering the front portico I noticed that the side walls were punctuated every seven feet or so with arched doorways, through which came and went parishioners, dogs, cats, chickens, birds, and mosquitoes. Six or seven priests, wrapped up in chasubles and hoods, carried covered chalices with arms extended, led by tiny boys in white surplices and red cassocks, to the altars, already lighted by long, yellow candles. Over the slapping sounds of the acolytes' bare feet on the terrazzo floor, I could hear the unified murmur of Spanish petitions from the congregation—mostly women kneeling in the pews. Over the high altar in the apse, I noticed the white paint peeling off the wall like bark off a sycamore in midwinter. The wall itself had a crack, two inches wide, running from the dado to the ceiling. Again I thought of Eric Hoffer and his word for civilization: *maintenance*.

After mass I took another car back to the terminal, thinking of the despicable priests who had let their church fall into such disrepair. Of course I realized that, despite having lived many years on an island among Bahamians, lackadaisical about order and sanitation, I was thinking American. Even at Gethsemani in the forties, where deprivations were taken for granted, squalor and dilapidation were not tolerated. Suddenly my heart leapt into my throat. I had forgotten to ask Sylvanus if my hermitage had a bathroom and running water.

The Pan-American "prop" I took from San Juan itself suggested that it was headed for an airport too small to accommodate jet planes. The plane flew so slowly that I had plenty of time to think about it. And by the time I had convinced myself that I would never make it in an underdeveloped country and that I would soon take my mother's advice and "just leave," I fell asleep. When the stewardess awakened me, it was almost dusk and the captain was announcing the beginning of our descent upon the airport at Lamartine. From the window I could see the landing strip and terminal and several planes on the ground. No evidence of a step up on the ladder of technical progress, but adequate.

At the ticket counter I saw a monk in his late thirties wearing a gauzy white robe, scapular, and hood. I walked up to him and introduced myself, figuring that he was from the Benedictine monastery where Winandy lived. He smiled, shot out his hand, and said, "Ah, Père Gerald, l'ermite." I surely must have blushed at that salutation, although he didn't seem to notice. Then he picked up my valise, and I followed him to his little Citroen pickup truck parked in the lot. It occurred to me that I had had more adventures in the last fourteen hours than during the past fourteen years.

The monk's name was Alexandre and, to compound the coincidence, served his community as porter, postmaster, and clerk in the monastery's gift shop. But unlike Brother Alexander at Gethsemani, this one was quite friendly. In fact he was so friendly that, as we drove down the Littoral (coastal road), he stopped at a bar where, after greeting everyone with handshakes and embraces, he bought two bottles of Bière Lorraine and popped a straw in each. I had never drunk beer through a straw before, but it seemed appropriate for French drivers who had to keep both eyes constantly fixed on the road while they raced around hairpin turns as if competing in the *Grand Prix*.

In Fort-de-France, the capital, the driving was even more hazardous, not because of the fast pace, but because the narrow streets were drained by canals, about a foot wide and a foot deep, next to the curbs. They were aptly designed to break both the axles of cars and the legs of pedestrians. The only caution was the policing by gendarmes on motorscooters—one driving and another riding piggyback. I couldn't imagine streets more dangerous other than, perhaps, those in Pamplona during the running of the bulls.

Alexandre blessed himself as we passed in front of the Cathedral de St. Louis—another coincidence—and its savanne with benches and royal palms bordering the walks, mulatto children in smocks that did not quite cover their bare behinds playing *touche* and dancing to a kind of music I had never heard before, coming out of a loudspeaker above the display window of a store called Roger Albert. Later, I learned that the music was rock and roll, and the name of the man depicted in a life-size photo pasted on the store window was Jackie Gleason.

Back on the Littoral, I watched the sea below turn dark blue and as calm as a lagoon. Near the Pitons du Carbet, a mountain range, the stars and fireflies seen against the ever-darkening woods seemed like a great shower of sparks. Farther down the road, at Bellefontaine, long fishing boats lay on the beach beneath nets hung from tall bamboo poles sunk into the black sand. Alexandre pointed out one of the Petites Soeurs de Jésus coming up the road with a bag of bread loaves and wearing a high-crowned straw hat called a *bakua*. She was one of the new breed of religious women coming out of France those days. She lived in a convent but, from nine to six, worked in a bakery for a salary that she surrendered to her community each week.

The next town was St. Pierre, the second largest and the original capital. But only three streets remained in it. The rest had been destroyed on May 8, 1902, when Mont Peleé, a volcano a mile to the north erupted and spit out of its fumerole chunks of lava the size of automobiles. Finally we turned up a steep driveway, passed the tombstone of d'Artagnan the Mousquetaire, and stopped before the gate of the monastery. Instinctively, I looked above the gate for the inscription *Pax Intrantibus*. It was not there, and I took its absence as a favorable sign.

Jacques Winandy, a small man with a large, bald head and a brindle beard that reached to his waist, met me in the visitors' room. He greeted me with a hearty though whispered "Bienvenue" and touched his bristly cheek against mine. I followed him over a cinder path through a garden by means of the flashlight he carried. We stepped over dozens of great toads, out to enjoy the evening dampness, and picked our way toward the guest house—a quadrangle of concrete blocks, roofed with sheets of corrugated iron. Then he left me with the promise of returning early that morning to bring me to the church for matins.

I lighted a paraffin lamp and looked around the room. On the bed lay the white Benedictine outfit Winandy said I should wear to choir. It must have been placed there before I arrived, but I had no idea how the wardrobe keeper knew my size. I took off my clothes except for my underpants and prepared to go to sleep. However, mosquitoes started cruising through the unscreened windows, keeping me on the alert. From my doorway I could see the lights far below in St. Pierre and could hear a steel-drum orchestra tapping out a beguine. It seemed I had returned to bed for only a few minutes when Winandy knocked on my door. I put on the monastic clothes, surprised to find them only about one size too small. Without a greeting, I followed him and his flashlight to the church. As we entered, I noticed that the older monks were already there in the semidarkness, kneeling against the stall and stroking their long beards.

For two days I followed the community exercises with reluctance. Yet I tried not to lose my sense of humor, for I could see the irony in a prospective hermit leaving his secluded cell at Gethsemani and finding himself leading a community life at

Notre Dame de Pelée. However, although I disliked the religious services, the monastic buildings and gardens, and the sound of Creole French, I didn't want to appear unappreciative of the monks' hospitality. So I didn't press Winandy to bring me to Canton Suisse. But on the third day, Sunday, Vandoorne, the Dutch hermit, paid me a visit. I could understand why the Dominican sisters of Morne Rouge took him in during his illness. He looked no older than seventeen and had blond peach fuzz for a beard, a tailored blue hermit's robe, and shiny black sandals set off by a gold St. Andrew's cross—perfect for some motherly nun to cosset. He quickly informed me that he had no intention of ever returning to the eremitical life. I thought he might have some chronic illness, or that the sisters had spoiled him too much, or that he had resolved to go back to school. Rather, he winked at me and said he had decided to become a "peregrinator," a kind of pilgrim who roams about the Holy Land. I wondered why he chose to tell me his plans. Then he proposed that I buy his hermitage. He wanted 20,000 old French francs for it, about $400. It seemed cheap enough, but I wasn't going to buy anything unseen. Besides, I didn't have $400. Since his departure wasn't imminent, I suggested he let me occupy the place for a month or two before deciding. He agreed to that.

Hermitage at Canton Suisse, Martinique.

22

The Hermitage at Canton Suisse

The next morning, Winandy and I packed the monks' Citroen with my valise, several boxes of food and wine, some old mass vestments, and a large hoe. I was about to begin my first day as a hermit. Before leaving the monastery, however, I said good-bye to the brethren, many of whom were at work hoeing stringbeans, sweet potatoes, and okra, undisturbed by the large black ants crawling out of the volcanic soil and over their bare feet. It struck me that most of them in the gardens were native Martiniquaise, doing just what they and their ancestors had done for generations on the plantations of the originally white *bekis* or landowners. Entering the monastery had raised their social status from peasants to monks, but it had not changed their way of life very much.

At Bellefontaine, Winandy turned off the Littoral onto a narrow road that led by Fond Capot—a hamlet with a house and a grocery store—and upward and onward to Canton Suisse. There we stopped at an old farmhouse. The screech of brakes flushed chickens and pigeons from the windowsills. The door opened and we were greeted by three dirty-white mongrels that yelped a few times and then, duty done, returned to the corner where they had been eating chunks of breadfruit.

Felicien Madkaud sat at a table covered with a white linen cloth and burdened with chipped and mismatched china cups, saucers, bowls, and plates. Our host arose, smiled, and began the Creole ritual of handshakes, bows, embraces, and exchange of pious axioms. Then he asked us to sit down and rang a small silver bell. From the darkness of a hallway appeared, like some dreadful jinni, a nearly seven-foot-tall black man wearing a patch over his left eye. He said nothing but waited for Madkaud's order. That given, he disappeared for a second and then returned with a bottle of Hennessy cognac. The whole scene seemed a burlesque on lost nobility. Madkaud had not forgotten his roots, though his house and everything and everyone in it suggested defeat and surrender. Nevertheless, he still owned about fifty acres of arable land, from the cobblestone road leading from Bellefontaine to Mont Vert, to the pastures far below. But rather than farm that land, he offered it to prospective hermits to build on, making him a kind of religious patron. Before Winandy drove off in his Citroen, Madkaud ordered his giant servant Pierre to bring all my things to Vandoorne's hermitage, just fifty yards away from the old farmhouse, beyond a grove of cocoa trees.

The hermitage was a small three-room building made of long but thin concrete blocks held together by mortar and a series of steel reinforcement cables, and covered with sheets of corrugated aluminum pitched toward one direction. One of the rooms—the kitchen—was really a part of the veranda and therefore entirely open on the side overlooking the valley. Sitting on a stool at the square wooden table, one could imagine being at a sidewalk cafe. To the right of the table was a cupboard of two shelves laden with Vandoorne's supply of canned coffee, chicory, Nestlé's condensed milk, a loaf of molding French bread, boxes of salt and pepper, jars of honey, and about six coconuts. Below the shelves was a Coleman single-burner stove resting on a brick oven, which, judging from the residue in it, burned charcoal. The oven butted against a partition made of concrete blocks, which I assumed to be a shower. But when I looked in, I saw only a white, galvanized portable toilet. There was no running water. If a plane were taking off from the cobblestone road nearby, I would have gotten on it.

The kitchen door led into the combination bedroom and study, lighted on opposite sides by unscreened windows. Next to the one, offering a view of the cobblestone road, were a chair and desk facing a narrow shelf that supported a large paraffin lamp. I noticed the wide plank on the concrete floor that Vandoorne had used for a bed, and the window that looked out to the veranda and garden. The next room, the chapel, was entered by sliding to one side a heavy monkscloth drape. Inside, the midday sun shone through the small art-glass windows framed in the broad Dutch doors, casting yellow and pink reflections on the rosewood altar and gray flagstone floors. I opened the Dutch doors and stepped out to the veranda, which, I decided, would be a fine place to sit and read once I had it sheltered from the sun. I took five steps and was in the vegetable garden. The breadfruit stakes holding up the wire fencing had actually sprouted branches and were growing along with the dozen banana trees, carrots, sugar beets, and okra. Just outside the fence were several guava, mango, and coconut trees drawing moisture, I supposed, from the ravine through which rushed a bubbling stream. The stream was obstructed every ten or twelve feet by enormous red or black boulders that had washed down from the mountains.

I walked out of the garden, past the hermitage, through a small field of high grass, crossed the cobblestone road, and started up a mountain. I could not look at a mountain without thinking of Merton and his mania for them. I made a mental note to send him a photo of the place and then stopped for a moment in my ascent to rest. I turned around and saw the metal roof of the hermitage below, and the great expanse of the valley with its many pastures, and finally the cliffs that rose up about three miles beyond and running along the Littoral. Just above them I could see a ship sailing in the Atlantic Ocean. Then I continued my climb, joined by seven or eight small bulls that kept me under surveillance until, panting and sweating, I reached the top. It was hard to believe, as Sylvanus had written me, that Pierre had carried a trunk full of books up to that elevation.

I quickly spotted, under an immense mahogany tree, the wooden shack Paré had built and Sylvanus now occupied. As I approached it, I recognized the short, plump fellow in a khaki robe with hood attached, girded by a black belt, and shod with brown sandals. In that attire and with a long black beard covering his face, he looked as if he had stepped out of a Giotto painting. Had I not anticipated meeting Sylvanus, I would not have known him. "Oh, you're here," he said as I approached. The tone was not enthusiastic, suggesting that the encounter did not entirely please him. But Sylvanus was not demonstrative. Moreover, I think I might have embarrassed him, since he had been in the process of photographing himself. A camera was mounted against a tree, and a string, presumably attached to the shutter, ran through the branches of the same tree to the spot where he was posing. I must have come upon him just as he was about to say, "Cheese."

Sylvanus made a pitcher of orange juice, and we drank it while seated on the steps of his shack, watching the bulls on the mountain path below and exchanging stories about our adventures during the past few months. His father had survived the operation and was well. Also, since his coming Sylvanus had inherited Paré's friends—Mesdames Paul and Fidelin—who attended his mass each morning and afterward left him all the fish, cheese, bread, and milk he needed. As for fruit and vegetables, he had only to walk a few steps to gather oranges, lemons, pineapples, mangoes, bananas, coconuts, string beans, sweet potatoes, cucumbers, tomatoes, okra, and so on. The only reason, he said, he went down the mountain was to collect his mail, which Madkaud brought each afternoon from the post office in Bellefontaine or to accompany Madkaud on a jaunt to Fort-de-France, where, in the Prix-Unique, he could buy apples and candy bars. Naturally, I asked him how he fared in his solitude. He said okay but that he could use a refrigerator and a radio.

Sylvanus had not been your typical Trappist. Although born in New Jersey, he was raised in Buenos Aires, where he eventually joined a Benedictine abbey. He came to Gethsemani as a monastic "transfer" while I was in the second year of the novitiate. I never realized that he was a foreigner until the day he took his turn in the refectory as the *lector mensae* (reader during dinner). He seemed quite at ease with the English language except that he pronounced the word *says* incorrectly. Instead of *sez* he made it *sayz.* Another idiosyncrasy of his was the way he cleaned his glasses. After taking them off, he squirted them with liquid soap from the dispensers in the grand parlor, rinsed them off by holding them under the tap, and finally dried them on his scapular. Also, he seemed incapable of walking slowly. He rushed through the cloisters or the cemetery whistling a samba under his breath—but loud enough to be heard within a few feet of him—and snapping his fingers to the beat. Sitting at his desk in the scriptorium, he continually squirmed on his stool, tapped the floor with his feet, rattled the pages of his notebook, and, when the bell rang for another monastic exercise, closed his desk top with a bang and tore out the room as if it were on fire. Merton used to refer to him as the "hot tamale." As I went down the mountain that afternoon, I wondered what Sylvanus would be like as a neighbor.

After I returned to what I began to call "my hermitage," I sat at the desk by the window looking at the road. For three hours no one came along it except a girl and her donkey bearing two aluminum milk containers. I didn't realize until months later that one person every three hours was rather heavy traffic on such a thoroughfare. However, about four o'clock I got some visitors. The woman was Madame Seville; all the eight children following her belonged to her and her husband and to some of their friends as well. She had beautiful teeth, and long, straight hair that was kind of blue. Later, I discovered that she was known in those parts as "La Coolie," confirming my suspicion that she was Indian rather than West Indian. A century before, many of her race had migrated to Martinique along with a dozen or so pairs of mongooses. She had brought me wild flowers, oranges, and news of a recent murder in Morne Vert. When she noticed that I followed her Creole French with difficulty, she grabbed her oldest daughter and, to illustrate the murder, choked her until her eyes popped.

At dusk the trade winds swept through the valley setting the countryside into motion. The two royal palms just outside my garden bent, twisted, and creaked in the wind. Down in the valley, skylarks, bats, and fireflies darted and soared against the blue sky and setting sun. On the cobblestone road to Morne Vert I passed several cows, so thin they might have stepped out of a pharaoh's bad dream. They were tended by an old man, who, as I passed, was washing his hands and feet in a gorge. He dried his hands on his ragged shirt, removed his battered bakua with an elegant sweep, and introduced himself as "Monsieur Vincent, André, un bon Catholique." He warned me against walking in the tall grass lest I tread upon a fer-de-lance, whose bite, he noted with a broad grin, could kill a man within minutes. He also remarked that the mongooses often killed snakes but that mongooses often killed chickens too. So, he added, he kept snake serum in case he was bitten by a fer-de-lance, and a shotgun in case he caught a mongoose eating his chickens.

After my walk through Canton Suisse I returned to the hermitage, poured out a tumbler of good Beaujolais, and sat at the desk in my study-bedroom. Just as it does in the Bahamas, the sun appeared to almost fall out of the sky, so rapid was its descent. I lighted the paraffin lamp and set it on the desk top and prepared to read my breviary. Suddenly the lamp shade began to tremble under the assault of a convoy of beetles that ricocheted off the glass and fell to the floor. I quickly closed the shutters but not before a bat shot in and slapped himself against the ceiling in the darkest corner of the room. For a while I stood watching his loathsome body heaving and falling with each breath. I slipped out of the door and into the kitchen, where I found an old broom. With it I returned, leaving the door open, despite the possibility that some other creature might fly or wander in. I placed the business end of the broom against the ceiling just behind the bat and swept with all my strength toward the opened door. Like a hockey puck the bat shot through the doorway and into the kitchen, knocking over a couple of saucepans. I slammed the door shut, panting with effort and fright. After a few seconds I heard the bat shriek and flap his wings.

Exhausted, I lay down on the plank Vandoorne used for a bed and shoved a bundle of rags under my head for a pillow. I dropped off to sleep but was awakened by a dreadful cry coming from the cobblestone road. Despite the night fliers, I opened the shutter on that side and beheld the unsettling sight of the giant Pierre with a bottle in one hand and a flaming torch in the other running up and down the road yelling some Creole gibberish to the full moon. Then he threw down the bottle, picked up a machete, and, holding it aloft, ran farther down the road that meandered through the forest, ever ascending toward Morne Vert. I tried to stay awake lest he return and murder me in bed, but I eventually fell asleep.

23

A Bad Move

Although the first night in the hermitage aggravated my dislike for Canton Suisse, I decided to give the place a chance. After a few months I got to like it. Pierre was harmless, even when maniacally drunk. As for Madkaud, he annoyed me sometimes with his pious conversations, but he also did me many favors. Whenever I needed things from Fort-de-France, he did my shopping for me. Mesdames Paul and Fidelin brought me bread and milk and even cultivated my garden. Now and then Sylvanus came down from the mountain for a cup of tea and a chat. We even walked to Bellefontaine to catch a bus for Fort-de-France, where we had lunch with Madame Rimbaud and her daughter. They lived on la rue de la Liberté, just across the street from the park where Napoleon's wife Josephine stayed as a girl and which faced the harbor, where ships from every country in the world were docked.

I had learned of Madame Rimbaud through a mutual friend in St. Louis. Many years before—in fact, while her husband was serving in the *Resistance* during World War II—Madame taught French at Maryville College, the same college Maggie had attended after being graduated from Clayton High. Madame and her daughter became another family to Sylvanus and me. On the night I was to leave Martinique two years later, they insisted on my staying on the third floor of their home, in the same seven-foot-long bed De Gaulle himself used whenever he visited them on the island.

Only once did the bishop disturb my privacy at Canton Suisse. One afternoon Winandy came by with a request from *Monseigneur* that I leave the hermitage and spend a few days at the church of Fond St. Denis until the curé returned from a vacation in Holland. I didn't like the idea, but I owed the bishop a favor. Winandy assured me that, except for the housekeeper, I probably would not see anybody all the time I was there. "Except for the housekeeper," he said. I had seen the housekeeper of Ste. Anne's Church on the south end of island, and she looked like Lena Horne. By time I left Canton Suisse, I fear my principal motivation for taking the assignment was to check out the housekeeper.

My second night in Fond St. Denis, I was awakened by a wind that shook the entire rectory, toppling over a case of books and dislodging pictures from the walls. I heard the tin roof tear loose from the rafters and crash upon the sidewalk outside. Just as I got the wooden shutters closed, the lights went out. I returned to bed but could not sleep because of the swaying of the rectory. When at last I saw daylight through the louvers, I opened the shutters and beheld, through the driving rain, a large crack in the tarmac road below, the only road leading into Fond St. Denis. All around the rectory were collapsed shanties and banana trees bent to the ground like a crowd of Moslems at prayer. I had seen many hurricanes as a child in Grand Bahama but never one comparable to that one in destructive force.

I dressed and went downstairs to the kitchen where Françoise, the pleasant but unprepossessing housekeeper, had a large bowl of café au lait and a croissant ready for me. As I ate she told me all she had seen that morning coming from her home to the rectory. It was hard to believe her account of the Martiniquaises nailing their tin roofs onto their houses while the rain kept falling and the wind continued to blow. It was as if they thought another hurricane, such as the one the year before and the one the year before that, would never hit the island again. And there was Françoise's miracle. It seems that the church had been shaken so badly that all the statues had fallen and crashed to pieces on the terrazzo floor, except that of St. Denis who, with his head tucked under one arm, appeared to view the wreckage of his comrades with indifference.

Two days later the weather cleared. A helicopter flew above the post office next to the church and dropped several sacks of mail. In the afternoon Père Maistricht entered the rectory, dirty and exhausted from having walked over the cracked and mud-covered road from the Littoral. He was followed by a dozen black women carrying his suitcases, golf bag, and a water jug. He waved to me perfunctorily and went straight to the kitchen and, like any Dutchman would in times of stress, made himself a cup of coffee and lit a cigar. Then he sat down across from me at the table and introduced himself. He appeared rather hostile until he learned that I was not French but American. In fact he called to Françoise to make me a cup of coffee and offered me one of his cigars. We talked until about four in the afternoon, when the taxi I had ordered—as soon as the road had been cleared—drove up to the rectory and sounded its horn. Just before I started out the door with my bag, Maistricht shook my hand and asked if I knew any rich Americans who would donate some money for the renovation of his rectory. I gave him the address of Nelson Rockefeller in New York and wished him luck.

I suppose I could have stayed a few more days at Fond St. Denis, but I never really enjoyed the company of clergymen. When they assumed their "official selves," they struck me as phony; when they acted natural—and I guess they have to "act" to be natural—they came across as shallow. I often entertained such belittling reflections on bishops, priests, monks, and sometimes wondered if I were not, despite my own affiliation with the church, downright anticlerical. So I was glad to leave Fond St. Denis and arrive at Morne Vert on the summit of the mountain above Canton Suisse. At the village market I bought a kilo of cheese and a "grand pain" (a three-foot loaf of bread) and started down the cobblestone road. The road did have cobblestone paving, but just in sections. There was no car made, not even a Jeep, that could traverse the entire road without breaking an axle, or getting bogged in the mud when it rained, or simply toppling over at certain inclines. Nevertheless, wearing a hermit's robe and sandals, I began my descent.

In front of me was one of my neighbors, an old Creole who lived just beyond the Vincents. He picked his way down the rain-soaked path—at that point that's all the road was—holding his shoes in his hands. Suddenly, as if someone had thrown the cosmic light switch, the sun disappeared. There was just light enough to see the path but not the treacherous holes and soft places. As many times as I had been on that path and delighted in the panorama it offered, I had never thought of how terrifying it would be in the nighttime. And I know I was terrified, because I started to pray. And then I began to laugh because the incident reminded me of my mother who also prayed at "appropriate" times, such as special meals. Grandfather used to comment as he picked up his fork on those occasions, "The Lord always knows when this family has company for dinner."

Twice I dropped my loaf of bread and sank into the mud above my ankles. Eventually I sank so deeply that I could not extract my left foot from the mire. Moreover, it became so dark that I could barely see the old Creole a few yards in front of me. Thoughts of spending the entire night on that mountaintop with my left foot trapped in a hole passed through my mind just the second before I called out, "*Monsieur, s'il vous plaît*!" The old man turned around, came up to me and, apologizing for some possible breach of decorum, pulled me out of the mud and, holding my hand, asked me to follow in his footsteps. Despite the danger and discomfort of our descent, there were times when I had to laugh. Whenever the old Creole slipped or stumbled, he would stop, turn around, lift his beret, and beg my pardon.

When the moon appeared over the Pitons du Carbet, we could see better. However, in spite of the improved visibility, when we reached a point in the road where a concrete bridge had spanned the ravine, we saw nothing but a bubbling torrent sparkling under the moonlight. My heart nearly stopped. However, my guide unhesitatingly led me into the water, as if he were Christ about to walk across the Sea of Galilee. The water came up to my waist and rushed against me so hard that I had to lean against the current to remain on my feet. But within seconds we were safe on the opposite side of the road, with the hard cobblestone pavement beneath our feet. A gentle trade wind began to blow, and the high branches of the royal palms towering above the road commenced to twirl about the trunks. The old Creole brought me to my hermitage and bade me good evening with the air of someone indebted to another for sharing a delightful experience.

In the hermitage I took the bread out of the muddy wrapper and lighted the paraffin lamp. There was an inch of water standing on the kitchen floor, but the bedroom-study was dry. I brewed some coffee, opened a tin of sardines, and cut two slices of bread. After dinner I lay down on the wooden plank and fell asleep.

The next morning, as I passed through the grove of cocoa trees on my way to Madkaud's place, I noticed what seemed to be a broken branch swaying above me. But as I studied the phenomenon, I realized that it was a man—a thin, black man with a rope around his neck. It was *le fou*, as Madkaud referred to him, the father of the little girl who stayed with Madame Madkaud in Fond Capot. The child had persuaded her *patron* to get her father out of the asylum and let him work with Pierre in Canton Suisse. He seemed to have been getting along well before I left for Fond St. Denis. I suppose the hurricane had frightened him so badly that he lost what sense of reality he had left and committed suicide. When I showed Madkaud the corpse, he blessed himself and ordered Pierre to climb the tree and cut the rope. The body fell more than ten feet, arms and legs flailing the air, until it crashed to the ground, nearly hitting two chickens. The scene was horrendous.

Later that day, I sat at my desk near the window overlooking the cobblestone road trying to read a book, when I heard someone chanting the first versicle of the divine office: *Deus in adjutorium meum intende* ("O God, come down to help me"). I saw an old man with a long, gray beard and broad-brimmed straw hat turn into the path leading to the hermitage from the road. In response, I sang out, *Domine adjuvandum me festina* ("O Lord, make haste to help me"). Since the chapel doors were opened, my visitor went in and knelt before the altar. I joined him and, together, we recited the office of tierce without so much as a glance at each other. Afterward, the old man arose, bowed to the altar, and left.

I had met Père Antoine before—at the monastery in St. Pierre. He showed up there, I was told, for the Sunday high mass, dinner, and conversation. That was his nemesis—conversation. Once he started talking, he found it almost impossible to stop. He couldn't even wait for a response from whomever he was speaking with; he just kept babbling on whatever came into his head. He had been a missionary in some French religious order but, not able to follow the rules of his organization—probably because of his compulsion to talk—he quit and became a hermit. However, he had hermitages all over the island, and he spent his days wandering from one to the others, catechizing the Creole children in rural *communes*, praying his office under the trees, bumming food from friends, and having a moderately good time. The monks at the monastery referred to him as *l'è*rmite en chemin (the hermit on the road).

Except for the hurricane and the suicide, life in Martinique seemed very pleasant. Only once more did the bishop ask me to help out in the diocese and that was when the pastor of Bellefontaine, Père Robillard, took ill one Sunday after being bitten by a scorpion. On Christmas morning of 1962, poinsettias bloomed around the veranda, which I had enlarged a month before. I was proud of the ten square feet of flooring I had made with stones from the ravine and mortared with concrete, as well as the bamboo canopy I had fashioned to cover it. The same afternoon Madame Vincent brought me three fried fish and a lemon cake. And Madkaud insisted that I celebrate the holiday with a bottle of Bordeaux and a transistor radio. I sat on that veranda sipping wine and listening to Stan Kenton's "The Little Drummer Boy" and Elvis Presley's "Return to Sender" coming over an English-speaking station in St. Lucia.

That spring the article I had written on Merton was returned by the editor of *The New Yorker* with regrets that his board had turned it down. However, he did ask if I had anything else, without a religious theme, to submit. I didn't at the moment but felt confident from the invitation that my writing itself was publishable. So I retyped the manuscript on the machine Vandoorne had left behind and sent it to a magazine located in Chicago: *The Critic*. Within two weeks I received a check for one hundred and twenty-five dollars and two long paragraphs of praise from the editor. Afterward *Catholic Digest* in Collegeville, Minnesota, bought the right to publish it in condensed form for seventy-five dollars. Then some company that produced books in Braille wrote me asking permission to use the piece. To someone who hadn't earned a nickel for over a decade, the experience was exhilarating. And it was so easy. Moreover, a little later I received a Baxter "funny card" from Merton, depicting a fellow sitting on a pile of calendar pages with an hourglass on his head. I didn't quite understand the joke, but I knew it had something to do with boredom or a waste of time. On the front of the card Merton had written:

> Great article! Have heard favorable comments! Police are in total confusion! Am on my way to the hills. Wish I were there. Gethsemani is in a deep fog.
>
> Blessings and good wishes to all,
>
> Uncle Louie

The envelope had been postmarked "Nerinx, Kentucky," where lived a number of Sisters of Loretto upon whom Merton could always count to provide him with a good meal and a bottle of beer whenever he dropped by while taking a roundabout way to his hermitage from the abbey.

I congratulated myself on being out of that abbey and in the free mountains and valleys of Canton Suisse. There, I took satisfaction in knowing that the religious exercises, through not as many as at Gethsemani, were followed willingly and not out of unconscious routine. What is more, I could enjoy the night out of doors, with the stars and the dawn and the sunsets. At Gethsemani we always seemed to be in choir or at mass during these parts of the day. Although I never thought about fasting, I had but two meals a day—one at ten o'clock and the other at six. In the morning, I would have a piece of bread, coffee, maybe a banana; in the evening, I took a glass of wine with sweet potatoes, carrots, bread, and sometimes a fried fish. In the afternoons, I read whatever books I had on hand or wrote in my journal. Now and then I would receive a visitor—Sylvanus, Madkaud, Robillard—but not often. Mine was a very peaceful life.

However, within a few months about six or seven families moved into the area. They began to repair—even rebuild—the cobblestone road from Fond Capot to Morne Vert. Pretty soon one of those buses marked *Service Occasional* began to run quite regularly. The neighborhood became populated with commuters who worked as far away as Fort-de-France. Winandy, who had been living in his hermitage about a mile away since January, came by one afternoon to discuss moving out of Canton Suisse. He thought about resettling near the summit of Mont Pelée. However, since its volcano had erupted as recently as 1956, he eventually agreed with me that there is no sense in risking one's life for a little solitude. Both Sylvanus and I met with him a few more times about finding a suitable spot for hermitages. We talked about Samoa, Mexico, Montana, and finally Vancouver, British Columbia. In fact, only a few weeks after they agreed on Vancouver, Winandy, Sylvanus, and another American whose name I have forgotten were on their way to "The Great Northwest." Paré and I were to follow later if we wanted.

I realized that Canton Suisse was no longer the isolated place it once was and therefore not the ideal atmosphere for hermits. But I really didn't mind having neighbors, especially since they were so kind. Moreover, I was rather glad to see the back of

Winandy. Not that he wasn't a good fellow, but his eremitical idealism was simply beyond my understanding. Also, having begun so well my second form of religious life and my first few years of middle age, I had adopted the motto of Cardinal Richelieu: *Quieta, non movere*.

But some time after the others had gone, I began to wonder whether or not I had made the right decision. My life was just as pleasant as it had been over the past year, yet I could not dismiss the notion that they were having more fun than I. Though fully aware of my self-inflicted agitation, I hoped my neighbors would call too often, that the buses would made a lot of noise, that the bishop would ask me to do parochial or mission work. I was looking for excuses to leave Canton Suisse. That meant the beginning of the end of contentment in solitude. For living alone is only tolerable when it is actually enjoyable. And it is most enjoyable when it is also considered honorable. But despite the fact that I avoided people who held hermits in awe, I nevertheless depended on their admiration for my existence. My position was very strange. If I stayed in Canton Suisse, I could congratulate myself on my stability or accuse myself of being too lazy to move. If I belittled the eremitical life, I would feel honest but could not persuade a bishop to accept me into his diocese as a hermit. If I admitted that I was a fraud, I could no longer hope that I was merely going though another "Dark Night," which would eventually leave me stronger in the faith.

All this self-doubt was a product of meditation and, as Merton had advised, "If you see a meditation passing by, shoot it." Instead, I practiced the Prayer of the Blank which, in principle, is opposed to any consideration of the self. If I resolved anything at all, I resolved to take one day at a time and, sure enough, one day a friend in the Bahamas sent me a book entitled *The Hermit of Cat Island*. It was about an Australian missionary who had migrated to the British West Indies several decades earlier and had settled on Cat Island. There he built a hermitage on the highest elevation of all the 400 or more Bahamian islands, a place he called Mount Alverna, after the retreat of St. Francis of Assisi. However, a few years before, the hermit—Monsignor Hawes—died and left the hermitage to the diocese. The pictures in the book showed it overlooking the sea and apparently well cared for.

Just for larks, I wrote to His Lordship Leonard Haggerty,

Bishop of the Bahamas, who, despite the title, was an American Benedictine from the same abbey in Collegeville, Minnesota, where Merton had his ego jarred by Dr. Zilboorg. I figured that he would refuse to let me have the hermitage, since the Benedictine order was founded for the purpose of rounding up all the vagabond hermits in sixth-century Europe and stabilizing them in a monastery. However, Catholic prelates on the islands were more tolerant of idiosyncratic clergymen than those on the Continent. Moreover, Monsignor Hawes had set a precedent and a good example. But even as I was awaiting an answer, many reasons occurred to me to stay where I was. I had always challenged Thoreau's claim to being a solitary at Walden Pond, yet I myself had spent less than two years at Canton Suisse. Also, I wanted to learn Creole and had not yet attained anything like proficiency in it. Moreover, there was not much adventure in returning to the Bahamas, where I had already spent so much time. Nevertheless when the bishop's letter came, in which he encouraged me to visit him at Nassau, I sent off a positive reply that very day and began to pack.

One Friday morning in the autumn of 1963, Père Robillard took me and about five banana cartons filled with tools, books, and clothes to the Air France agency in Fort-de-France. I bought a one-way ticket to Nassau through Miami, left my baggage and, after saying good-bye to the *curé*, walked down the street to the home of Madame Rimbaud, where I would spend the night. I had decided to tell her as well as Madkaud and my friends at Canton Suisse that I was only taking a holiday. And for all I knew it might very well be, since, if things did not work out in the Bahamas, I intended to return to Martinique. Even if I had said that I would never return to the island, Robillard would not have believed me. All the way to the city, he kept saying that Martinique is the *Ile des revenants* and that he would keep an eye on my place in Canton Suisse.

I realized that the circumstances of this departure were much different from those connected to my leaving Gethsemani. I was bidding farewell to a place where I had found happiness, a true, simple, natural happiness. Except for the necessary and unavoidable dignity that goes with the priesthood, I had regained that sort of primitive innocence I once had as a child, not completely, of course, but as much as most adults can. Yet the prospect of never returning to that paradise didn't seem to bother me. At another time I might have called my attitude "detachment" and congratulated myself on having acquired that virtue described by St. John of the Cross as the foundation of religious ascesis. But virtue had nothing to do with it, and I feared that somewhere along the way I had lost my sense of affection. Could it be possibly that in trying so hard for so many years to love God that I could no longer form deep friendships?

That night Madame Rimbaud, her daughter, and I sat on the veranda overlooking the harbor and talking, not about solemn finalities but about the happy prospects concerning my trip. They asked me to bring them back a conch shell and cones off a casuarina tree. At midnight, I left them and climbed to the third-floor room, where the seven-foot-long bed of Charles de Gaulle awaited me. I fell asleep with the words of Père Robillard echoing in my mind: *Le coeur est plus importante que l'esprit.*

The next morning, as I climbed the ramp of the Air France carrier in Lamartine, a band was playing a beguine, and my hand beat time to it as it slid along the railing.

24

The Finding of Lost Beach

I landed at the Nassau airport on December 11 and took a limousine to a place on Shirley Street, known as The Priory. As I stood there, I noticed St. Francis' Church on one side and the many palm and frangipani trees (imported from Florida decades before) lining the same sidewalk Marcy and I often took from her house on Holmes Street to the harbor. There were many more motor cars passing by than during the forties, but above their noise I could still recognize people shouting in their peculiar Bahamian accent. "Hey, mon! How you keeping?" yelled my departing taxi driver to a fellow coming out of the church. Our white teachers used to beat us across the knuckles when they heard us speaking in dialect. I am glad they did, since it is not particularly attractive.

The Priory was a kind of rectory-hotel for priests, nuns, lay apostles, and anyone connected with the Bahamian Catholic diocese. The bishop, a rotund, jolly man with a toothy smile, had his

Gerald Groves at Lost Beach, Grand Bahama Island.

office there, although he lived in a large villa out of town. From the book about Monsignor Hawes, I learned that Bishop Haggerty had come to the islands twenty years before to save the inhabitants, not from paganism, but from the Anglicans, Baptists, and Adventists. It was he who had welcomed the Australian missionary-architect and then put him to work building small, dark, Romanesque churches with their disproportionately thick, Doric columns. The architect later ministered to them on Sundays, making his way from one island to another on a small sailboat. While on a business trip for the diocese of Nassau, he took ill in Miami and died. That was ironic, since he had long since built his tomb in the hermitage on Cat Island. In fact, according to the book, he somewhat melodramatically slept in it whenever he was home.

The next morning after breakfast, I left The Priory, that dilapidated, pink-painted pile of sagging floors, rusting water pipes, and cracked-paned windows that often opened into closets. Bishop Haggerty, whom I saw in his office, wished me luck but warned that I might find the hermitage on Cat Island a "trifle small." *Why should I mind?* I asked myself. Didn't I spend over a year and a half in a tiny cell at Gethsemani? But I forgot that I never cooked, ate, or stored my books in that cell. Yet I resolved to be optimistic, since I had spent a lot of money on plane tickets and, after all, was getting the place for nothing.

Standing on the dock at Bay Street, I watched the ships bobbing up and down in the water, their decks piled high with crates, barrels, crates of chickens, timber, motors, bales of hay, all destined for the out islands. I threw my bags and boxes onto the *Lady Dundas* and followed a deck hand to my cabin, which was just about large enough for the two bunk beds. The bottom one was already occupied by a Bahamian who, I learned after a self introduction, was called Reverend Mr. Russell, a Baptist minister on his way to Eleuthera, the island just east of Cat Island. For some reason I took an aversion to him and begged off accompanying him to lunch at the captain's table. Instead, I went for a walk on the deck. But with all the cargo and the Bahamian passengers sitting around eating their lunches out of greasy, brown paper bags, I could hardly take two steps without stumbling over something or someone. By time we reached Arthurstown, Cat Island, early the next morning, I was in a rotten mood.

On the road to New Bight, my destination, one of the natives agreed to give me a lift—for five pounds. As we drove along he cheerfully described the ferocity of the mosquitoes, the sterility of the soil, and the high cost of living. I felt like asking him to take me back to the boat, but I knew it would have left the dock by that time. Moreover, I remembered my first impressions of Martinique and how negative they were until I got settled in Canton Suisse. There was no going back, at least, until I had a reason to do so beyond my bad humor. I knew that I was easily annoyed—which, I suppose, is a trait of people used to discipline. I had hoped that my ascetical training at Gethsemani would have made me patient. However, those virtues I tried to cultivate in the abbey seemed to languish outside their original environment.

But as we rode along, the cocoplum bushes and casuarinas seemed taller and greener. And from the highway I could see, several hundred yards inland, Monsignor Hawes' stone hermitage silhouetted against the morning sun and overlooking the white-sand beach and clear blue-green water of the sea. Even when the driver let me out at the foot of Mount Alverna and I started up the steep path marked by the fourteen stations of the cross, my new optimism did not wane. But before I reached the summit of the hill, near the thirteenth station, the dimensions of the hermitage became more discernible. I couldn't believe my eyes. It was the size of a child's playhouse!

Nevertheless, with the key the bishop had given me, I unlocked the door, bowed under the bright-green lintel, and stepped into what appeared to be the chapel. Only exactly in the middle, where the ceiling vaulted, could I stand erect. On the walls—one foot thick and made of stone—hung a crucifix and a picture of St. Francis. The stone altar was the size of an end table and, behind it—what at first seemed to be a fireplace dug into the stone—lay the sepulcher where the hermit slept. The floor followed the contour of the site and sloped toward the next room, the kitchen, which I reached by crawling downward through a hallway with a radius of about three feet. After oozing through the kitchen door to the outside, I sat down on a large stone, wondering whether I should laugh or cry.

Late that afternoon, I hired a boy with a cart to bring my bags and boxes to the island airstrip. Luckily the five o'clock plane to Nassau had not yet left, and I boarded with the pilot and two large Bahamian women. The trip by riverboat had taken hours, but the plane would make it in fifteen minutes. The relief I experienced in leaving Cat Island lasted until the airport of Nassau came into view. Then the prospect of retracing my steps to Martinique confronted me. If I had only asked the bishop how small that hermitage was.

The next morning, I saw the bishop again and explained why I had to refuse his offer of the hermitage. I thought he might be disappointed, but he simply laughed and reminded me of his warning. Moreover, before I left him, he suggested that I look for another site in his diocese before returning to Martinique. When I suggested Grand Bahama, he agreed and mentioned that a Trappist from England was presently the pastor of Our Lady Star of the Sea in Freeport. I had never heard of that city but, from his directions, decided that it could not be very far from West End. Then it struck me how pleasant it would be to revisit the place where I grew up. And, as I took the BOAC out of Nassau that afternoon, I felt I couldn't wait to see again the cottage my father built at Boodle Bay.

Father Bruno invited me to stay with him in his rectory while I made up my mind whether to settle in Grand Bahama or return to Martinique. Some American Franciscan sisters lived in a large house only fifty yards away from us and, about the same distance from them, stood the ten-classroom school that they ran. In one of those rooms we said mass every morning, then visited the Grand Bahama Clinic—staffed by sisters of the same order—and then had breakfast at the Caravel Club, the only good restaurant in Freeport.

It was there that I first experienced the excitement of that town. On rainy days, with no other place to go to, bank presidents, chiefs of police, croupiers (for the new Lucayan Beach Hotel opening New Year's Eve), construction workers, and people from every walk of life gathered at the Caravel Club two or three times a day to consolidate their pioneering spirit and resist boredom. Many of the hotel workers, especially the cocktail waitresses both from America and England often sat with us to talk about the first Christmas holidays they would spend away from home. They were quite good looking and, with their easy manner, gave the place what I imagined would be the atmosphere of a Playboy Club. Bruno told me that Connie, the assistant manager, had been a member of the Four Lads group before coming to Freeport in 1963. With a silver coffeepot in one hand and a white linen napkin in the other, he moved from table to table, taking orders, chatting with customers, and singing the latest Beatles' hit, "I Want to Hold Your Hand." On Sunday mornings even the Franciscan sisters had breakfast at the Caravel Club, rubbing their chaste elbows with chorus girls, croupiers, waitresses, construction workers, and financiers. This, of course, was after mass held in the classroom designated Mary Star of the Sea Church, where Connie, with his guitar, sang and played every religious tune he knew from Schubert's "Ave Maria" to "Michael, Row Your Boat"; where Keith Gonsalves, Groves' right-hand man in the Port Authority, always dropped a ten-pound note into the collection basket; and where Ginger Mallonig—blond, tall, slender, elegantly dressed—promenaded down the aisle.

On weekday mornings, I often met friends at the post office and from there went shopping in the mall across the street. The supermarket had authentic British bangers and Robinson's barley water. We could get a free cup of coffee at Callahan's dry goods store, which, despite the name, was managed by a charming Jewish couple originally from Miami. For a bit of folklore or profound wisdom, we might drop in on Mr. George, owner of the local hardware store and head of one of the oldest white Bahamian families on the island. All those places were prosperous because they had no competition and plenty of customers. The Port Authority had the right to issue, deny, or revoke all commercial licenses within the Freeport area. And it permitted only enough establishments to meet the needs of the community.

That December in Freeport there were shopping trips, teas, parties, plays, and warm afternoons on the beach. But after a while, though still enjoying myself, I began to feel rather guilty about my being in that high society. And New Year's Eve was the limit. I went with Bruno to the private opening of the new Lucayan Beach Hotel. Standing in the casino on a rug so thick that the nap covered the heels of my shoes, chatting with the governor, Sir Robert de Stapleton, being served by scantily clothed waitresses who winked at me—we knew each other from the Caravel Club—I got the feeling that I was out of place. Bruno had a right to be there because he represented the Catholic Church on the island. But as a hermit, my principal value in that materialist society was to live in a way that demonstrated that wealth and power had nothing to do with happiness. Yet there I was, sort of "putting on the Ritz." I realized why, after lecturing all day, Merton would clam up for hours, even days. He had exhausted his social energy and betrayed his self-ideal.

Consequently on New Year's Day, I persuaded Bruno to help me find a suitable spot for a hermitage—"suitable" meaning isolated, beautiful, and on the beach. So we set out in the Hillman for West End, which I had not seen for over twenty years. Yet the area had changed so that I couldn't find many mementos over which to get maudlin. I recalled the highway we were on, Bay Shore Road, and the old Star Hotel, but not all the new bars and stores and certainly not the rising Catholic Church of St. Michael, begun in 1957. I surely didn't want to live in that neighborhood when they completed it.

Farther west, we passed the new Grand Bahama Hotel with its jetstrip, golflinks, shopping arcade, and marina. Years before, there was nothing but bootleggers' warehouses on that thoroughfare. Near Hope Estates, the road turned eastward again and eventually we came to Boodle Bay, the old homestead. Not a trace of the white cottage my father had built before his departure. Even the environs had changed, for someone had dug dogleg canals into the coastline and marked out the property with sticks bearing red bows. But as Bruno and I got out of the car and strolled down to the shore, I noticed a patch of sea flora, about the size of a tennis court, that turned the otherwise clear, green water into a deep purple. That is where Grandfather and I used to fish in the evenings, near enough to the cottage to hear Mother calling us to dinner. I seemed to feel my grandfather's presence, just as if he had walked up behind me and encircled my shoulders with his arms.

A few miles down the road, we passed Buccaneer's Cove, where an old bootlegger named Paul Mack used to live. In fact, I had heard that he was still around and ran a hamburger stand in Tin City, just out of Freeport. But I didn't like that area either, so we took Government Road—Queen's Highway, as it's called today—east until we came to Pine Ridge, the site of the old Abaco Lumber Company, which, in 1946, belonged to Wallace Groves, the soft-spoken Virginian with three degrees from Georgetown University and the insight and drive to make Freeport his empire. Just off the road, inland, we pulled up before a brick officelike structure bearing a bronze plaque over the lintel of the front door, reading, "Groves Community Church." Bruno smiled and said, "This is the place for you, Gerald. The signs of divine providence couldn't be clearer." As we entered, rats scurried into the holes of the rotting floor, and out of them came the fetid odor of garbage they had brought there from the adjoining public dump.

Back on Government Road, Bruno drove eastward for five miles and, unhesitatingly, as if he knew exactly where he was going, turned into a kind of path. Bruno said it was a logging trail formed by dragging—repeatedly—tall, thin, pine trees over the same areas of coral surface. It was full of shallow declivities, the result of water erosion, and made riding in a car feel like boating on a choppy sea. We followed the trail until it forked off, and then took the route southward. At length we drove under a canopy of sapodilla trees and stopped before a lonely palmetto and a small dune covered with sea wheat.

Bruno winked at me as we got out of the car and started up the dune. Just two steps and there it was: the most beautiful, isolated beach I had ever seen. The words, "O thalita, O thalita!" from the *Anabasis* came to mind and the image of Father Augustine, who had taught me Attic Greek at Gethsemani. I thought of how much he would have liked this place, where he could exercise his corpulent body and soak his ever-festering stump in the saltwater. And I realized how much the sea was a part of me. As a monk at the abbey, I used to think of the seemingly boundless ocean as analogous to the immensity of God. And as a scripture student, I recalled standing on the shore and seeing birds on the horizon apparently rise out of the sea. For that reason, I felt sure, the author of Genesis declared that God had created the birds and the fishes on the same day.

About three miles out to sea lay Peterson's Cay, with its small beach of pink sand and the many perforations in the coral surface, which the terns used as nests. I remembered the island vividly, for, when we were children, Richard Boswell and I often landed there in his sailboat. He took a particular dislike to the birds and loved to throw pieces of coral at them. Once I scolded him and demanded he stop. But he continued and remarked defiantly, "I shall leave no tern unstoned." I thought that was about the best pun I had ever heard and never brought anyone to the island without trying it.

Richard and I had never visited the mainland in the area. The three magnificent casuarina trees farther down the beach, that seemed to give it identity, probably were only seedlings back in the thirties. Bruno pointed out that they were almost equidistant from one another, and suggested that they had been planted by someone with a penchant for symmetry. He had seen them before but did not try to penetrate the overgrowth of cocoplum and seagrape bushes that hid their trunks. But coming upon the first and largest, we agreed to explore and, struggling through the thicket, soon came upon a wall about four feet high, fashioned of unmortared coral stones. Beyond the wall, the only vegetation were two large oleander bushes covered with purple and white flowers and the trunk of the casuarina. When I saw what stood beside it, my heart began to beat as if I had come upon a ghost. There stood the faded-white walls of a building.

Walking around it, I observed that none of the four doors remained; only one of the eleven windows had shutters; almost all of the cedar shakes had fallen off the roof joists; the wooden-plank floor had crumbled and sunk into the crawl space; and in one corner, leaning against the walls and mounted with a cross, stood a pulpit. We had no doubt that the building had been a church and, judging from the date of construction etched into the marl foundation near the front of the steps, had been here since 1902. Since churches are not made to decorate the wilderness, we concluded that a community must have lived here. When we investigated the two other casuarinas, we found standing beside each the ruins of a house, smaller than the church but similar in design. I wondered what had happened to the villagers, but the question foremost in my mind was: How can I get this property?

The next day Bruno and I visited Major Bernard, chief surveyor for the Developing Company. He turned us loose in a room filled with records of deeds and maps of the island. On one of the latter we discovered, between Smith's Point to the west and Freetown to the east, an area designated, appropriately enough, "Lost Beach" (It is now on the charts under the name of "Barbary Beach.") I had hoped it was still owned by the British government, since, in those days, a person could lease "crown land" for ninety-nine years at seven pounds an acre. However, after verifying our find, Bernard produced his company's deed to the property and its price: 100,000 American dollars. Seeing my chagrin, he proposed that I settle at Lost Beach until it became slated for development. He figured that would take about ten years.

Had I been a true hermit, in the manner of St. Antony of Egypt and St. Macarius the Elder, I would have thrown up a tent on Lost Beach and moved in right away, confident that divine providence would wash up some flotsam on the shore as material with which to repair the old church. But I was an American hermit, used to certain amenities in life and quick operations. With only about four hundred dollars to my name, I could not prudently hope to pay for making the church livable—let's say comfortable—without borrowing money from my mother or going to work for the diocese. And I didn't want to do either.

But through Father Bruno, the news of my predicament got reported about Freeport. One morning the Franciscan sisters came by the rectory and left a wheelbarrow filled with tools, construction manuals, a hard hat, and an Igloo water cooler. Although they could not understand how I could live in solitude or why I wanted to, they embraced my cause as a kind of hobby. The nursing sisters bet that even should I revamp the old church, I would stay only two months in that desolate spot. And the teaching sisters took the bet, but at three-to-one odds.

A few days later, at the Caravel Club, a man introduced himself to me as Colonel Rodumsky, president of Grand Bahama Builders and friend of the teaching sisters. I knew then that the game had started. He was small, nattily dressed in a gray flannel suit, with thick, graying-brown hair hanging over his shirt collar in the back; and below his bushy mustache, a sinister smile suggested a temperament bordering on both the whimsical and volatile. I had seen him before. In fact I had seen him introducing himself to a woman—a beautiful woman—who actually trembled as he kissed her hand while bowing and fixing on her his smoldering, brown eyes. His charm was only enhanced by the slight limp in his walk, caused by having had his left foot broken by a guard in a Nazi prison camp, and by the absence of an arm—riddled off by a machine gun used by a Messerschmitt pilot—from the right sleeve of his jacket.

"Roddy," as he asked me to call him, proposed that he and I drive out to Lost Beach to look at the old church. I congratulated myself on finding a person with both the enthusiasm and the *cum quibus* to help me get my project off the ground. In his Buick station wagon we tore down Government Road, unpaved and full of potholes, while a metal detector banged around in the back seat. With his only arm he steered, worked the automatic shift, held a lighted cigarette, and gesticulated as he spoke about buried treasure. When we turned into the undulating logging trail at fifty miles an hour, my head hit the ceiling, and the metal detector slammed against the window. Passing under the canopy of sapodilla trees, we then shot over the small dune near the lonely palmetto and pitched upon the beach, hard and wet from the incoming tide.

Pulling up before the old church, Roddy grabbed the metal detector and hopped out of the car. He beat his way through the thicket, around the building, and into the far recesses of the court. For about fifteen minutes he continued his search, crying out now and then, "I can smell it! I can smell it!" until I reminded him of my reason for accompanying him out there. He smiled and returned to the car, where he exchanged the detector for a hardback sketch book and pencil. Sitting on the ground with his materials in his lap, he made a few drawings and computations. But on the way home he resumed his speculations on buried treasure, and I felt as if I had wasted a morning on an adventurous kook.

But I was wrong. For five consecutive Sundays after, a five-ton Mack truck picked me up at the rectory around six in the morning. It was usually filled with plywood or roofing shingles, a generator, tools, and six Polish carpenters. They were, of course, Catholics but hadn't been in a church since they followed Roddy from the old country. And I did little to recall them to their religious duties since, while the project lasted, I had no time for mass on Sundays either. Moreover, because the Poles were working gratis, I felt obliged to keep up their spirits as they hammered and sawed by supplying them with plenty of beer. By the time Roddy came out in the late afternoons to hunt for his buried treasure, the Poles were too drunk to hammer a nail straight.

Even after I had begun to live in the renovated old church, friends from Freeport continued to drop in every so often to see how I was and to help me dig out a septic tank, clean out an old well, install a hand pump, prepare the ground for a garden. Father Paul, the pastor of the Catholic church in Hunter Village, sent me his old gas-operated refrigerator. Having such a luxury might have been unascetical, but it eliminated my need to go to town for supplies every week. Mr. Groves and his family visited me several times and left behind them an aluminum rowboat, a pair of oars, a glass-bottom bucket, and a lobster gig. Eventually, I agreed with Bruno to say mass once a week at the American Missile-Tracking Station in exchange for the loan of an old Ford sedan. The sisters came out on Friday afternoons for a picnic and purposely brought too much food. All they asked in return was that I whistle a warning should any beachcombers come along while they were having a swim.

My two best friends were Peter and Isabelle Barratt, originally from England and Malta, respectively. Peter had just taken a job as town planner for the Developing Company and, consequently, had not much money or many friends. Isabelle, a qualified architect, was in a worse condition, since she had nothing to do but keep their cheap, inelegant flat in town. I don't recall exactly where or when we all met, but I know she complained to me about her unhappy situation, so I invited her and Peter to Lost Beach.

The following Saturday they arrived at my door, wide-eyed with wonder at being the guests of a hermit who lived in one of the most remote and beautiful spots on the island. I took them for a sail out to Peterson's Cay. I anchored the boat about one hundred yards from shore and handed Peter a casting rod with the hook baited. After several minutes, the debutante angler shouted and began reeling in the line. We all stood up, watching the sport and cheering Peter on. But when I lifted his trophy from the sea, it was nothing but a tiny grunt, hooked through its eye!

Almost every Saturday thereafter, the Barratts and I were together. We made other excursions to Peterson's Cay; or put on masks and snorkels and swam out to the reefs, where, at low tide, we could sit on the exposed rocks and watch the groupers, ten feet below us, glide in and out of their caverns. On rainy days we sat around the large kitchen table I had made out of a telephone-cable spool, eating Isabelle's sandwiches and listening to Lanza tapes. Some days, in the evening, I would follow them into Freeport in my Ford and have dinner with them in their ugly little flat. Eventually, when the drive-in movie theater was finished, we went to mock at its idiotic repertory of films, such as "Frankenstein

Meets the Wolfman" and "Blacula."

Sometimes, in the evenings especially, while all alone at Lost Beach, I would wade out into the ocean to a point from which I could see miles down the coast, where the lights of the Lucayan Beach Hotel shone, and beyond which I knew were the homes of the Rands, the Henehans, the Haywards, the Groves, the Rodumskys, the Barratts. While at Gethsemani, I thought I had gotten friends out of my system. It seemed ironic that, in becoming a hermit, I had discovered that I appreciated them as much as I did when I was a child. And though I was less than the ideal hermit, I didn't care much. My health was good, I had recently published my second article—"The Success of William Inge"—and I had every reason to hope that I would spend the rest of my life at Lost Beach.

25

A Visit to La Grande Chartreuse

Just as the night is darkest before the dawn, so the sun is most spectacular before it sets. After four halcyon years as a quasi-hermit on Grand Bahama, the extension of my indult of exclaustration came to its end and darkened my vision of growing old at Lost Beach. I found myself in the position of being attached neither to Gethsmani Abbey nor to the diocese of the Bahamas. The Roman Catholic Church considered me an anomaly and I received a letter confirming this fact from Abbot Fox.

He began in his familiar paternal manner, praising me for my perseverance in the eremitical vocation—he called it "a daily martyrdom of solitude"—and assured me that he and the Trappist monks were praying for me. After a few more unctuous phrases, he came to the point. He encouraged me to be incardinated into the diocese of the Bahamas and assured me that, despite the recent incorporation of the eremitical life at Gethsemani, it would not be open to me should I return to the abbey, without my spending a year or so in the community to prove my obedience. He ended with his "All for Jesus, through Mary, and always with a smile."

I soon received a letter from the bishop informing me that he had been in communication with Fox and that I was welcome to join his diocese should I agree to go where I was most needed. The implication was that I was not needed at Lost Beach, and I couldn't argue about it. He reminded me that Monsignor Hawes had successfully combined the eremitical life with a little pastoral work and that the mission on Andros Island could use me. In the envelope was a two-way plane ticket to that island.

The next morning I tried to pull myself together by practicing the Prayer of the Blank. I sat quietly on the floor, closed my eyes, and concentrated on the mental image of a light switch until the blood stopped coming into my head and images began to fade. Then it happened. I don't know whether I fell asleep or not, but I suddenly became vividly aware of every detail in the grained wood of the cabinet before me and the silliness of worrying about problems I couldn't solve. Every philosophical axiom I had ever learned seemed to spell itself out before my inner vision, and I decided to check out Andros with an open mind.

At the Andros airstrip, I was met by a young Bahamian in a 1950 Volkswagon. When I climbed in and sat down, swarms of gnats rose out of the upholstery like vapor from a tea kettle. They attacked my eyes, ears, nostrils. And when I clapped my hands trying to crush them in midair, the driver looked at me as if he thought I had lost my mind. And, indeed, though they covered his black, sweating face, he apparently didn't feel them. He just kept saying how "hawppy" he was that I would be settling on the island.

We stopped before an unpainted frame shack with a wooden cross mounted on the roof. Across the muddy road two Bahamian children in ragged shirts and no pants to cover their behinds drew water from a public hand pump into their small buckets. A few yards behind them stood a woman, presumably their mother, nursing a baby and waving hello. She looked so friendly that I envisioned her inviting me into her hovel for a dinner of peas and rice.

The back door was open, so Reggie the driver and I entered what seemed to be the living quarters used by the missioners who came from Nassau each Sunday morning to hear confessions and offer mass there at the village and in the chapel of the American Submarine Base down the coast. The floor sagged under the old gas-operated refrigerator—like mine at Lost Beach—and the kitchen table still bore bread crumbs from the last meal. The gray walls quivered from the hot wind blowing outside. But the effects of the Prayer of the Blank were still with me, so I said nothing and smiled at Reggie.

Leaving the shack, we strolled down the road toward the village. On the way we came to an inlet where, lying several yards offshore, the hull of a small ship rusted tranquilly, having once crashed into a pile of boulders—called "nigger heads"—found many places in Bahamian waters. In the village itself, a group of about a dozen shanties and a grocery store, I noticed clotheslines in the yards strung with slabs of skinned bonefish and barracuda and covered with flies. It was sort of a comfort to find the village so universally disgusting since, as such, I found no difficulty in deciding to leave it forever.

On the plane back to Freeport I thought about staying in Lost Beach despite the bishop and the abbot. But that would have involved excommunication from the Catholic Church, which I considered an unhappy alternative. It would mean forfeiting the status of priest and monk acquired with much effort over the past two decades. In the minds of my friends in Freeport, even the non-Catholic ones, the hermitage would be no more than a cottage, and the hermit would be nothing but a premature retiree or a bum. It would also mean that I had become weak and had given up. And indeed there were moments when I felt so burnt out that I think I should have quit. I recalled T. S. Eliot's words in *Murder in the Cathedral*: "The last temptation is the greatest treason/ To do the right deed for the wrong reason."

But I decided neither to stay in the Bahamas nor to leave the religious life. It seemed to me a most appropriate time to accept a friend's invitation to visit him at Kingstree, South Carolina. I had met Father Ed Gaffney a year before through Elinor Smith, one of the lay-teachers at Mary Star of the Sea. He wanted to do some fishing, so Elinor brought him out to Lost Beach. Even though the waves were about two feet high, we set out one cold January morning for Peterson's Cay. Just as we began casting, a heavy rain began to blow in from the southeast, and I knew we were in trouble. Back in the aluminum rowboat, we headed into the waves, which got so high they spilled over the gunwales. One knocked Ed, who weighed over two hundred and fifty pounds, halfway into the sea. By the time I was able to pull him into the boat, we were swamped. He bailed frantically with his porkpie fisherman's hat but not quickly enough. Seeing we were about to sink, I jumped into the water and quickly turned the boat upside down. It floated well enough, so we let the gas can, oars, rods, and tackle sink or float away and clung to the hull for dear life. Because the tide was going in, we eventually reached the shore.

Wrapped in blankets and drinking the hot coffee Elinor had made for us, Ed confessed how hard he had prayed during those five hours in the cold sea. But I couldn't remember having prayed at all, even when I realized the boat had stopped moving and I knew I had to dive twenty feet below the surface to loosen the anchor hung up on the coral. The only time I mentioned God was when I swore at a passing bluefish that looked too much like a barracuda. That was ironic, I thought, being startled by a craven barracuda while undisturbed by a tempest. But I was frightened later—after the warming, the coffee, the talk. And by the time Ed left Lost Beach late that evening, our shared adventure had forged between us a bond of friendship. He insisted I visit him one day in South Carolina.

The pain in leaving Grand Bahama was mitigated by the Barratts' assurance that they would watch the hermitage during my absence, which they chose to consider temporary. Even though I had no option but to leave most of my tools, books, furniture, boat, and other effects, Peter insisted on buying them. Moreover, since he gave me a check for two hundred dollars—more than twice their worth—he didn't even get a bargain. Also I reflected that the project of staying with Ed on a kind of southern plantation might be an experience worth the forced exodus. Through Ed, I had already received an invitation from the bishop there to stay as a guest of the diocese. My stay, considered as a period of probation, could last as long as a couple of years before commitments had to be made.

Springbank, just outside of Kingstree, South Carolina, conformed to my notion of what—as far as locality is concerned—a plantation should be. It had giant, angel oaks festooned with Spanish moss; a sprawling, white frame mansion partly converted into a chapel; and a polite, black family caring for the grounds, cleaning the house, and doing the cooking. On weekdays little could be heard but foxhounds barking in the woods and the house workers going about their chores. But on weekends it was something else. Priests, sisters, seminarians, Knights of Columbus, even members of Alcoholics Anonymous swelled the limits of that facility. Masses, confessions, lectures, meals, followed one another like acts in a long morality play. Naturally, I was asked to help out, and I did. But the experience only served to prove that such a life was not for me.

As much as I admired Thomas Merton, I could never tolerate that prima-donna self-concern he showed in regard to his food, his jobs, his solitude, his vocation. Yet it became more and more evident that I had the same preoccupation, at least in respect to how and where I wanted to live. In letters from Sylvanus—still in Vancouver—I learned that Gethsemani was no longer the prestigious abbey it once had been: The abbot-general had curtailed many of its lucrative enterprises, monks were leaving and not being replaced by postulants, and old abbot Fox had resigned and lived, like Merton, in a chalet on the abbey grounds. Even with Fox out of the way, I still had no desire to return to Gethsemani as a monk. Moreover, the fact that Fox himself had become a hermit seemed to make the eremitical life less attractive. So I was almost determined to ask the bishop to give me a job in his diocese and to make myself, if not contented, at least useful. But just before carrying out that decision, I learned—again from the seemingly ubiquitous and omniscient Sylvanus—that some Canadian sisters in Mexico were looking for a chaplain-hermit who could speak French. Whether that opportunity derived from divine providence or fate, I figured it was too good to miss.

After several months of corresponding with the sisters in Mexico and a series of Spanish lessons from an Argentinian girl teaching at the local high school, I bought an old Ford Galaxy, almost identical to the one I had in the Bahamas, and took off for the Southwest. That I should do such a capricious thing would be too embarrassing to admit if I did not harbor some hope of—to use the effete term—"finding myself." Yet I was fully prepared to discover that this new adventure would merely reveal some other form of religious life contrary to my taste rather than the compatible one I had found at Lost Beach.

It took me an entire tiresome week to travel from South Carolina to Huapuapa de Leon, Mexico. I recalled the morning sessions in the chapter room back at Gethsemani, during which I could not imagine being so bored. But I had never driven along the monotonous highways of Alabama or through the twisting mountains of Mexico in a car with no radio and an engine that continually pinged from burning low-octane gas. The only excitement occurred near Monterrey, where, as I tried to pass a bus, a car filled with Mexicans came speeding from the opposite direction. When I swerved to safety only ten feet in front of them, one leaned out of a window and shouted, "Bravo!"

It was a dusty town populated by mestizos, the men almost uniformly dressed in white, straw sombreros, and the women in muslin blouses and long sarilike skirts. On the way to Calle Fernando, where the Canadian sisters were staying until their hermitages were built, I passed a bar that had a red lightbulb glowing even in the daytime. Through the windows I could see people dancing to the Beatles' tune "And I Love Her." Farther down the street stood a theater with a marquee designating the current film: "Hawaii." Then I saw a sister standing in front of a hut waving to me, seemingly confident that the only six-foot-two gringo in view was her expected guest.

At the dinner table, Sister Gabrielle served me an aperitif in the form of straight tequila that went down my throat like a blast of fire. There I met the other prospective hermitesses, Mère Ida, the former superior of a convent in Montreal, and Sister Jean-Baptiste, a towering woman with muscular forearms and the smell of Esau. They also tossed down their drinks and, after a short prayer, loaded their plates with cheese, red beans, and tortillas. Despite their crude dwelling and soiled robes, their courtesy and determination aroused in me an unguarded generosity. I proposed that I help them build the hermitages, starting on the following morning. About nine o'clock, they all walked me over to a large, dilapidated guest house belonging to the local bishop.

For about three weeks I accompanied the sisters in their Volkswagon bus to the site of their "laura" (group of hermitages), about five miles up the International Highway. It consisted of about seven acres overlooking the highway below and so high that on some mornings one looked down on white clouds. Two hermitages were already finished and, at the moment, attention was given to the community chapel. It was at that project that I learned how to lay bricks, Mexican bricks, twice as big as those in America, without the holes necessary to make a good bond with mortar, and often severely warped. Each evening after work, we would return to town, have dinner together at the sisters' place, and plan the next day.

I did not think much—if I remember rightly—about the importance or silliness of the sisters' project, but I know that I had a good feeling about working with the sisters and their Mexican employees in that wild country. Sometimes, during a lunch break, I would take a few of the raw vegetables and fruits Mère Ida had brought for us, and go for a solitary walk through the nearby woods. And several times I came upon huts and even tents occupied by Indians, half naked and filthy but extremely gentle and polite. Neither they nor I spoke enough Spanish to communicate, so after my first encounter, I brought along a notebook and pencil so that I could make myself understood by drawing pictures. One old Indian seemed to want me to marry a girl who, I presumed, was his daughter. Were it not for her teeth, black from chewing some kind of weed or root, I could have been tempted, for she was quite good looking and charming as well. Rather than try to explain to him that I was celibate, I made him believe that the sisters were my women.

That December, things were still peaceful but static. I was looking forward to our proposed trip to Mexico City, where we planned to buy a marble altar for the chapel. And I guess I was daydreaming while driving a burro loaded with bricks, when one slipped out of the saddle bag and landed on my foot. Sister Gabrielle, a former nurse, took me to the infirmary in town for an x-ray. It wasn't broken—just badly bruised. Consequently, I could do nothing for a while but stay in my room at the guest house and read or listen to the radio. One morning, as I was soaking my foot, I switched on the radio and heard the words, "Thomas Merton . . . muerto." I waited all day for Sister Jean-Baptiste to come by. When she did, she bought along not only my

Merton in Bangkok with Father Francis Acharya.

dinner but a Mexican newspaper. On the second page was a picture of Merton in a black clerical shirt with the collar unbuttoned. He had died in Bangkok, on December 10, just after having given a lecture on the spiritual life to a congress of monks and nuns. He had stepped out of a shower, soaking wet, and touched the uninsulated part of the cord on an electric fan. I couldn't help mark the irony: killed by one of the banes of his monastic life—a machine.

After a few more weeks, my foot healed enough for me to walk at least to a friend's house in the center of town. As I was coming home one night—about eleven o'clock—two dogs ran out from one of the houses and confronted me in the street. Determined not to be intimidated by anything Mexican, I yelled at them in English. In the dim light I could see them sucking their lips above their teeth. Then without a bark or growl, both rushed at me, possibly sensing that I was somewhat disabled. I concentrated my healthy foot on the one nearest and, as he lowered his head, kicked him so solidly in the neck that he flew through the air, end over end. But the other managed to nip the heel of the sick foot before retreating. Not much of a wound, yet he had drawn blood. As a result I was obliged to take shots for rabies in a clinic that had roach powder sprinkled along the baseboards of the floor. After that, as I told my friends and the sisters, I decided that I had no future in Mexico.

During my uneventful departure from Mexico, I had plenty of time to reflect and, of course, the subject most often on my mind was Merton. I had known of his living full time in the woods of Gethsemani, but I didn't know, until later, that all during those two-and-a-half years of solitude—from 1965 to 1968—he had been badgering Abbot Fox to release him for a trip to the Orient. Merton had often referred to himself as "a sign of contradiction"—accommodating the biblical term to his own meaning—and, indeed, he was the most non-eremitical of all the hermits I had known. Yet as I reflected on my own life, he might have said the same about me, although I really never wanted to travel after I found my place at Lost Beach.

But there were signs of contradiction, or at least opposition, at Gethsemani beside Merton and me. As I mentioned before, Fox, who had disparaged the eremitical life, resigned from his office and retired in a chalet similar to Merton's in the same neck of the woods. I wondered how Fox got along as a hermit. Like Merton, he had a nervous stomach and had taken his special meals in private, showing up in the refectory only for a dessert of canned pears. Moreover, he would miss all those ecclesiastical gatherings—ordinations, congresses, general chapter meetings in France—he had once attended. And was it logical for a man who wanted to be a bishop as much as Fox did—at least that was Merton's and my conjecture—to have chosen a life of solitude? It must have seemed to Fox better than his other option after resignation—to return to the community as a monk. I recalled how being a retired abbot had shamed Dom Vital. He used to point to the abbatial cross around his neck and say, "See this? That means I'm abbot. But a retired abbot. Good for nothing." Fox had become a man of contradiction for a good reason—to avoid the humiliation of descending to what he had been, he opted to become someone he hadn't been before. Unlike Dom Vital, he seemed to have no desire to become a "manure saint."

It seemed a miracle that Merton didn't become a bishop. He certainly had more clout with the American clergy than Fox had. And he must have toyed with the idea and even feared that he might opt for the lofty but limiting state of prelacy rather than the sublime but flexible sphere of the eremitical life. But Merton, as he later wrote, was ever the "marginal man," the uncommitted man, the monastic-solitary-traveling man who was so many things that he was nothing definable. As a result, even before he died, many of his critics predicted that he would leave Gethsemani. I would have asked them, "How do you mean . . . leave?" He might not have ever returned to Gethsemani, but he would never have left it. Despite his many denials that Gethsemani was his home, he made as many affirmations that it was. The abbey was the source both of his identity and his funds. Had he lived, it seemed to me, he would have continued his journeying, living in hermitages, monasteries, hotels sending, now and then, a "miss you" letter to the monks back home.

And as I rode along, somewhere between Laredo and Beaumont, I amused myself speculating on Merton's ideal of being a person—as Fox used to admonish us to be—"unknown, unheralded, and unsung" and his actual flashy self. I thought that if he could continue to write after death, he would simply add another installment to his interminable autobiography—something with a title like *The Posthumous Journal of Thomas Merton*. However, as a disembodied spirit, he would not be able to project in it the image of the witty, sophisticated, irreverent, paradoxical, itinerant hermit who, despite his sufferings from ill health, spiritual acedia, self-imposed overwork, and crotchety superiors, could write or speak on ecumenism, social justice, Zen Buddhism, and solitude with enthusiasm, insight, and especially humor. I figured that many of his critics would remember Merton for his thinking on the morality of war and the modern industrial world, for his championing of Western and Eastern mysticism. But for those of us who knew him well, remembering him principally for those things seemed like remembering Jack Benny mainly for his violin recitals. I wondered if he were laughing and making the spirits laugh in heaven.

When I arrived at Kingstree, Ed Gaffney seemed genuinely glad to see me and to voice his I-told-you-so, for he had predicted the dismal outcome of my Mexican adventure. He also handed me a letter from my mother in St. Louis. She had heard of Merton's death and had arranged for masses to be said at the Kingstree retreat house where she knew I had been staying. "Not that he needed them," she insisted, "for that man is surely a blessed saint in heaven now." She invariably linked the terms *blessed* and *saint* despite my pointing out the redundancy. She also reminisced on the "confidential chat" she had with Merton during one of her visits to Gethsemani. He had told her "confidentially" that Don Ameche had begged him for the screen rights to *The Seven Storey Mountain* in 1949, but that he had refused, believing that only Gary Cooper could do justice to the part. Mother had agreed with him thoroughly, despite the fact that neither physically nor temperamentally did Cooper resemble Merton. Nevertheless, Mother cherished her confidential information and disseminated it throughout her parish just as Merton would have liked.

The memory of Thomas Merton had followed me back to South Carolina, and the influence of his energetic, curious, mischievous spirit seemed to have possessed me. After my foot had completely healed, solitude was the farthest thing from my mind; I needed some good, old Merton hyperactivity. So that January I took a furnished room in Columbia and enrolled in the graduate school as a candidate for a Ph.D. in English literature.

Luckily, I managed to get an assistancy that paid for my tuition, books, and a small stipend. On weekends I said mass, heard confessions, and even translated—as well as I could—for the non-English-speaking draftees from Puerto Rico. And to follow even closer in Merton's footprints—although, of course, not consciously—I became a member of James Dickey's first class at the University of South Carolina and began to write poetry.

But unlike Merton's verses, full of edifying madonnas, saints, monks, and—by all means—hermits, mine actually satirized ecclesiastical entities or they flopped. My best mark was on a poem entitled "Gifts for Priests on Fathers' Day." Each verse was couched as an advertisement that the druggist could stick on his wall or soda fountain and each featured some kind of devotional gimmick. Dickey especially liked the one: "Guitars and drums for the hippie mass/ And a beaded vestment that's a gas." Since I had such a penchant for satire, my advisor suggested that I specialize in eighteenth-century British literature. I studied many authors of that period, and I never read a poem by William Blake without thinking of Merton, who had done his master's thesis on that mystical writer.

For my own Master of Arts degree I wrote "The Role of Alexander Pope in the Roman Catholic Church" and would have, two years later, expanded it into a doctoral dissertation had I not fallen in love with French Symbolist poetry. Consequently, I geared my Ph.D. toward comparative literature and chose for my subject a poet and mystic and Bohemian that Merton would have liked: Germain Nouveau, friend of Charles Verlaine and Arthur Rimbaud. After submitting my dissertation entitled *Germain Nouveau's "Valentines": Introduction, Translation, and Commentary*, in August of 1972, I received the doctorate and, by the previous arrangement of my dean and head of the department of languages and letters at the University of Grenoble III, I left for France to begin a year's lectorship at that institution.

I think it was during my flight to France that I read one of the first and best biographies of Merton. It was *The Man in the Sycamore Tree*, by his friend at Columbia University, Ed Rice. Of course it covered only Merton's life as a student, not as a monk. But in it Rice mentioned a bit of sensational gossip that other Mertonologies of the time didn't—the reason why Merton's uncle in England refused to go on sponsoring him at Cambridge. Rice declined to define that reason but implied that it had to do with a girl. Many of the biographies of Merton that followed were mere eulogies, and neglected that dark secret. Not until long afterward, until the eighties, did authors such as Monica Furlong and Michael Mott probe into Merton's past to reveal that Merton had impregnated an English girl who bore him a child. And while Merton was safe in America, both mother and child were killed in a Nazi air raid over London. With that scandal exposed, it was rather easy to divulge Merton's affair with a student nurse at St. Joseph's Infirmary, just before he became a full-time hermit. I didn't know it even in 1979 when I wrote a profile of Merton—"The Gregarious Hermit"—for *The American Scholar*. Naturally the news had disappointed me. But after the close call I had with a nursing sister at the same hospital, I sympathized with Merton. The passion that swept him into his unlawful sex seemed less ignoble than the fear that kept me chaste.

I arrived in Grenoble an entire month before classes were scheduled to begin. So, rather than explore the city where I was to live for a year, I bought a little Simca Mille and headed for Rome. During my stay, I wandered into the Church of Saints Cosmas and Damian to see the mosaics Merton had so admired. Later, after leaving Italy, I visited his birthplace in Prades, France. By then I had to return to Grenoble to teach, but I promised myself, during the Christmas holidays, to trace Merton's footsteps through England. Although I had not explicity formulated a resolution, I knew I would someday write about him.

In Grenoble I lived in a small furnished apartment on one of the main thoroughfares, Cours Jean Jaures. From there I could walk to the train station, several movie houses, the principal shopping district, the central park, and the Catholic Church of St. Jean. I continued to go to mass but never attempted to offer one. In fact, I wore secular clothes and kept my clerical status to myself. Many of my students frequented a little piano bar called "Le Cheminie" just a few blocks from my apartment, and I often accepted their invitations to join them. Joe, the Algerian manager, and I got to be friends. But he never addressed me except as "Monsieur l'anglais." The situation reminded me of Hemingway's *For Whom the Bell Tolls* in which the Gypsy continually refers to Robert Jordan as "Inglés," although Jordan is American. And there I also met a beautiful English girl studying French at the university. We were together nearly every Saturday evening and Sunday afternoon, if not at the piano bar, then at La Grave or Chamrouse or Geneva on short tours. Of course, I fell in love with her but had sense enough to keep the expressions of our relationship avuncular—an appropriate hug or kiss on the forehead—since I was thirty years older than she. But until she left the university in December, I never felt younger.

Without her, life in Grenoble became rather lackluster. I hoped to see her again in London over the holidays, but when I phoned her home no one was there. So I visited Oakham and Cambridge, Merton shrines as they were, attempting to distract myself from the memory of the girl until the new term started and work would force me to concentrate on other matters.

That spring I had only one course to teach. My students were the elite of the university, candidates for the *agrégation* diploma, and the future American literature professors in France's schools of higher learning. The main subject of the course was Jack Kerouac's *On the Road*. It was ironic that the dean had picked me to teach that work, which reflects events in the 1950s, a period that had simply passed me by. Until I began to research the novel, I had no idea who the beatnicks were. Although many of the students rightly considered *On the Road* trite, I enjoyed it for supplying me with some of the Americana that I had missed.

On my last day in Grenoble, I was alone at an outdoor table in Place Grenette, an area paved with flagstone the size of a tennis court in the center of the city, from which I could see all the surrounding mountains. I suddenly thought of Gethsemani, which lies in the center of the wooded hills of Nelson County, Kentucky, and I wondered who was living in Merton's chalet. Probably a much better hermit than either of us, I guessed. Had Merton been with me that day, he would have, like many of the other patrons enjoying the balmy morning in June, sipped on his citronade and opened his *Figaro*. But had we been there twenty years before, we would have been on our way to the Carthusian Monastery of St. Pierre, otherwise known as La Grande Chartreuse. Now Merton was dead, and I had lost my interest in that institute. Yet I was curious to see what I might have gotten myself into before the opportunity was lost.

I had sold the Simca Mille, so I took one of the autocars stationed nearby. It crossed the Isère River, which ran through the city, went past the ancient Fort de la Bastille, climbed a steep, winding road, and eventually leveled out with its back to a panoramic view of the entire city. In scarcely forty-five minutes of streaking through the canopy of almost black pine trees covering peaks and crags, the autocar turned into a side road called St. Laurent-du-Pont and followed it down into a deep valley. From that vantage point, I could see the church, monastic cells, and outbuildings with the compound below. But what struck me was the landscape directly opposite the road. It seemed to be layered, with one layer rising upon the other. And I wondered if Merton hadn't been there at some time and had chosen the Chartreuse Range as the material representation of *The Seven Storey Mountain*, a title borrowed from Dante's *Purgatorio*, which describes the purgation of the soul from the seven deadly vices: pride, vanity, envy, anger, sloth, avarice, and gluttony.

The ultimate objective of climbing Dante's and Merton's spiritual mountain is to reach paradise. How close Merton came to it before his death, I would not dare to judge. And how near I would be to that beatitude before mine, is equally impossible to say. Yet it did seem that no matter how much Merton had indulged himself in unruly pleasures, even to the fracturing of his vows, he had faith. In fact, he had died just after lecturing on the spiritual life. And it is my experience that a person cannot preach the faith continuously and enthusiastically, as Merton did, without having it himself. I have heard actors, confirmed agnostics, deliver an inspiring sermon—but only once, not habitually. And I have known ministers who preach every Sunday but whose words lack enthusiasm. The only exception are those who use religion to make money. And Merton certainly never did that. But I, on the other hand, was conscious of my lack of faith. Just as I was as a child roaming the beaches of Grand Bahama with my "freethinking" grandfather, I did not believe in God and the Catholic Church; I simply refused—out of sheer terror of the consequences—not to believe. However, there was a time in my life when I could not imagine doubting my faith. Ironically, that was during my youth, when my morals were the weakest. What a pest faith was while I sowed my oats as a student. Faith overcame passion when I was a young monk. Yet when the blood cooled and ambition waned, when faith ceased to inhibit and promised to comfort, it stole off like a thief in the night. In fact, all that kept me holding on to faith was the possibility that, unknown to me, I was still being purged in the dark night of the soul.

After the autocar stopped to discharge its passengers, we followed the driver into a small building reserved for tourists. It was like the bookstore at Gethsemani, where one could buy not only books but rosaries, statues, holy water fonts—even the Chartreuse liquor the monks made from a secret formula. A Carthusian monk, all in white, stood behind one of the display counters, leaning on one arm resting on the countertop, apparently unimpressed by the visitors and certainly unconcerned about his impressing them. I wandered over and noticed on one of the shelves several copies of *The Seven Storey Mountain*. Because I had been thinking of that work or because I had never spoken with a Carthusian, I pointed to them and asked: "I see you have Merton's autobiography. What do you think of it?" Without changing his position, he turned his tired eyes upon me and replied, "It's a good seller."

Epilogue

Keeping the Faith

I returned to St. Louis that summer in a blue seersucker suit and with an indult of laicization in my pocket. Mother was of course "destroyed" (her word) that I had given up the priesthood. She liked to think of me as a modern-day St. Augustine and of herself as his saintly mother, Monica. She had enjoyed considerable prestige among the parishioners because of me, and I was sorry for her diminution of status. During the entire week of my visit, she coercively predicted my change of mind, not convinced as I was that any change not involving a change of character is transitory.

But I might have stayed in St. Louis with her had I found a job teaching. Instead, I went to work at Coastal Carolina College, a campus of the University of South Carolina, where I still am, teaching Latin and literary criticism. Early in the seventies, William Inge, living then in California, committed suicide, despite his rise to fame as a playwright and screenwriter. Not so long ago, I attended the funeral of my mother. And I learned that Marcy had been placed in a mental hospital in London. The last time I saw Peter and Isabelle was during a reunion at the hermitage at Lost Beach. As far as I know, Abbot Fox is still in his hermitage on the grounds of the abbey. Maggie is still married and has six children.

Without a doubt the most significant event in these my latter years has been my marriage to a woman much younger than I, whom I had known at the university in Columbia, and our consequent production of two adorable boys. They more than anything keep me from lamenting my past, for unless I had made those mistakes, they wouldn't have come into existence. Had Merton heard me utter that platitude, he would have countered with another, such as "God writes straight on crooked lines," and proposed himself as an example.

In my community many know that I had spent two decades, either behind abbey walls or on distant islands. Some consider me a romantic adventurer; others, simply the product of a broken home. And although I am no longer a monk or a hermit—or would want to be again—I still go to church on Sundays, as I did as a child, hoping for a short sermon.